GROWING UP FEMALE

Recent Titles in
Contributions in Women's Studies

GROWING UP FEMALE

*Adolescent
Girlhood in
American
Fiction*

BARBARA A. WHITE

Contributions in Women's Studies,
Number 59

Greenwood Press
Westport, Connecticut • London, England

Library of Congress Cataloging in Publication Data

White, Barbara Anne.
  Growing up female.

  (Contributions in women's studies, ISSN 0147–104X ;
no. 59)
  Bibliography: p.
  Includes index.
  1. American fiction—20th century—History and
criticism. 2. Girls in literature. 3. Adolescence in
literature. 4. American fiction—Women authors—History
and criticism. I. Title. II. Series.
PS374.G55W45 1985   813′.5′09352042   85–5480
ISBN 0–313–24826–5 (lib. bdg.)
ISBN 0-313-25065-0 (pap.)

Library of Congress Catalog Card Number: 85–5480
ISBN: 0–313–24826–5
Paperback ISBN: 0-313-25065-0
ISSN: 0147–104X

First published in 1985

Greenwood Press
A division of Congressional Information Service, Inc.
88 Post Road West, Westport, Connecticut 06881

Printed in the United States of America

10 9 8 7 6 5 4 3 2 1

11-15-90

CONTENTS

PREFACE

[I]n a hundred years' time people will read the novels of this century and conclude that everyone (no less) suffered adolescence like a disease, for they will hardly be able to lay hands on a novel which does not describe the condition.

—Doris Lessing, *Martha Quest* (1952)

For the past twenty-five years American literary critics have been making the same observation as Doris Lessing. They point to a disproportionate number of adolescent protagonists in modern fiction, especially American fiction. Ihab Hassan, Leslie Fiedler, and other critics argue that the number of important novels with adolescent protagonists has increased rapidly through the twentieth century forming a definite trend, perhaps even a "cult of adolescence" in fiction.[1] W. Tasker Witham's survey, *The Adolescent in the American Novel, 1920–1960* (1964), is a study of this trend, and Witham's book has been updated by doctoral dissertations which treat novels of adolescence or initiation stories. There are now a number of anthologies available for classroom use.[2]

Who are the adolescent protagonists who appear so prominently in modern American fiction? The most frequently discussed are Sherwood Anderson's George Willard, F. Scott Fitzgerald's Amory Blaine, Ernest Hemingway's Nick Adams, Thomas Wolfe's Eugene Gant, James Farrell's Studs Lonigan, William Faulkner's Ike McCaslin and Charles Mallison, and J. D. Salinger's Holden Caulfield. One might assume that "the adolescent" in the inclusive

titles of the critical works includes girls as well as boys, but in fact
female characters—and authors—are underrepresented, if not
missing altogether, in the articles and surveys.[3] Many critics actually define the adolescent protagonist as male. In works entitled
"Themes of Adolescence" or *The College Novel* "the hero" can
be considered undefined in gender only until it is discovered that
he must establish a relationship with a girl friend or encounter a
temptress or a lorelei.[4] Thrall, Hibbard, and Holman in their handbook of literary terms define an apprenticeship novel as "a novel
which recounts the youth and young *manhood* of a sensitive protagonist who is attempting to learn the nature of the world"; they
give exclusively male examples of the type.[5]

Novels about adolescent boys are more numerous than those
about adolescent girls, and the male authors outnumber the female. However, about one-third of the works on Witham's list of
nearly six hundred novels of adolescence published between 1920
and 1960 have female authors or characters; novels by women with
female protagonists comprise over one-fourth of the total. Several
of the latter works have been widely recognized for their excel-
lence. Witham and the critics who mention fiction by women single
out the following: Elizabeth Madox Roberts' *The Time of Man*
(1926); Katherine Anne Porter's sequence of Miranda stories (1934–
1941); Carson McCullers' *The Heart Is a Lonely Hunter* (1940)
and *The Member of the Wedding* (1946); Jean Stafford's *Boston
Adventure* (1944) and *The Mountain Lion* (1947); Shirley Jackson's
Hangsaman (1951); and Jessamyn West's *Cress Delahanty* (1954).
They might have added two distinguished novels by black women,
Paule Marshall's *Brown Girl, Brownstones* (1959) and Toni Morrison's *The Bluest Eye* (1970).

Although these works are sometimes mentioned in criticism on
the novel of adolescence, they are seldom discussed on their own
terms. The only references to female development are Leslie Fiedler's comment that McCullers' female adolescents are "boy-girls"
and James Johnson's statement that when she discards her dream
of riding race horses, Porter's "Miranda takes a definite step toward assuming her feminine nature, just as Frankie [of McCullers'
The Member of the Wedding] does when she gives up wanting to
be a pilot."[6] Fiedler disapproves of "boy-girls," nor does he show
any interest in McCullers' characters in themselves; he uses

McCullers' novels as evidence of a regrettable "homosexual sensibility" he detects in modern (mostly male) authors. Johnson neglects to explain what "feminine nature" might be that it precludes being a jockey or a pilot. For the most part he follows Fiedler in taking the adolescent male character as standard and considering girls only insofar as they support the male pattern.

Thus Johnson cites Frankie and Miranda as examples of adolescent protagonists who escape their families and undertake journeys, even though Frankie runs away from home for a few hours and Miranda leaves her convent school to get married. In no way are their experiences commensurate with his other examples—Nick Adams, Eugene Gant, and Holden Caulfield. Frankie and Miranda are brought into the discussion to support generalizations already formed from observation of the male protagonist. As Lillian Schlissel puts it in her essay "Contemplating 'The American Eve,' "

The patterns of American fiction which we have so far constructed—and considered universal—patterns dealing with the nature of innocence and with the nature of adolescence and experience—apply in reality to the male in America. We have still to discover the patterns of experience that hold true for women.[7]

It is my purpose to illuminate some of these "patterns of experience that hold true for women" in the fiction of adolescence. In so doing I hope to provide more comprehensive and well-rounded interpretations of some important novels like *The Member of the Wedding* that have suffered particularly from the universalizing of male experience. My concern is not only to redress a lack in the literary criticism just described but also to contribute to the growing body of criticism on fiction of female development; the novel of adolescence is a sub-genre which has not yet received proper attention.[8]

It may be that a study of female adolescence in fiction will interest people who are not literary critics. Witham assumes that the novels in his survey accurately reflect real life problems of adolescents and that his survey will thus be of use to psychologists, social workers, teachers, parents, in fact anyone working with adolescents.[9] I believe such an assumption must be qualified (see my discussion of this issue in Chapter VIII) and am primarily

interested in the images of adolescence which novelists have projected. I discuss real-life adolescence only as it has led to the
development of the form and influenced its growth. Nevertheless,
I tend to agree with Witham that the novel of adolescence has
reflected social reality to a large degree. Some of the similarities
in novels of female adolescence are so striking that if they do not
reflect reality, they certainly point to an odd literary form and a
most peculiar psychology on the part of authors who choose to
write about adolescence.

I have limited this study to novels about female adolescence
written for adults by American women.[10] For reasons that will
become clear in Chapter I the "novel of adolescence," although
it shares some characteristics with developmental forms like the
Bildungsroman and the initiation story, has to be defined in terms
of the age of the protagonist. Accordingly, I have as a general rule
restricted my discussion to fiction with major characters between
twelve and nineteen; they may be introduced at an earlier age and/
or taken beyond their teens, but this period is emphasized in the
novel. A more detailed discussion of the criteria I used in selecting
the novels may be found in Bibliography A.

When I began this study I intended to take a strictly historical
approach. I thought I would consider the origins of the novel of
adolescence and its emergence as a viable form around the generally agreed upon date of 1920. I would then analyze the novels,
tracing various changes through the decades of the twentieth century to the present time. However, it soon became clear that these
changes have been relatively insignificant. Plot, theme, characterization, image, tone—all have remained surprisingly consistent in
the novel of female adolescence from 1920 to the early 1970's and,
indeed it might be argued, to the present day; form has changed
only in accordance with broad developments in the form of the
novel in general.[11] For this reason, and because I wanted to go
beyond a superficial survey and examine some novels of adolescence in depth, I decided to restrict my general survey of women's
novels of adolescence to two chapters. In other chapters I discuss
fiction by three writers whom I found to be representative novelists
of female adolescence: Ruth Suckow, Carson McCullers, and Jean
Stafford. These authors seem particularly appropriate for detailed
discussion because they are respected writers who showed through-

out their careers a special interest in adolescence; all three wrote more than one adolescent novel.

Chapter I is an introduction to the American novel of adolescence; I consider its definition, the origins and development of the form, and its relationship to the creation of adolescence as a concept and stage of life in the late nineteenth and early twentieth centuries. In Chapter II I discuss female adolescent prototypes in nineteenth-century fiction and in Chapter III I examine Edith Wharton's *Summer* (1917) as a transitional novel, standing between this earlier fiction with its Good Girl heroines and the modern novel of adolescence. Chapters IV, V, and VI are devoted respectively to Ruth Suckow's fiction of adolescence (1925–1934), Carson McCullers' *The Member of the Wedding* (1946), and Jean Stafford's *The Mountain Lion* (1947). In Chapter VII I make a general survey of the novel of female adolescence from 1920 to 1972 based on my reading of some two hundred novels. In Chapter VIII I extend the survey to the present, noting the effects of the current women's movement and speculating about the future of the form.

Several people have helped me in the writing of this book. I owe the most to Melody Graulich who provided inspiration, support, and good advice. I am grateful to her, and to Deborah Lambert, Elizabeth Oien, and Annis Pratt, for reading sections of the manuscript at various stages of its growth and making useful suggestions. The University of New Hampshire granted me leave to complete the project; several members of the UNH Library staff assisted in various ways, especially Jane Russell and Barbara Widger who obtained many obscure novels for me.

It is customary for authors to acknowledge the support of various institutions—foundations, universities, libraries, etc.—but the institution that allows women with small children to write books is day care. I want to thank everyone who is working to develop quality day care and, in particular, the staff of Live and Learn Day Care of Lee, New Hampshire. This book is dedicated to my daughter, Elizabeth Ruth Epstein-White, and to the memory of my mother, Mary Elizabeth Busacker White (1919–1979).

GROWING UP FEMALE

I

INTRODUCTION TO
THE AMERICAN NOVEL
OF ADOLESCENCE

Critics usually associate the novel of adolescence with either the *Bildungsroman* or the initiation story. They define it as "a sometimes foreshortened, always modified, bildungsroman" or an initiation novel, a longer form of the initiation story where the protagonist experiences a significant change of knowledge or character.[1] Like the *Bildungsroman*, the novel of adolescence tends to be heavily autobiographical and its hero is frequently gifted or extraordinarily sensitive. As in the initiation story, the protagonist may acquire new knowledge about the world or make a lasting character change. The novel of adolescence often incorporates plot elements similar to those of the *Bildungsroman*. In the traditional *Bildungsroman* the hero rejects the constraints of home, sets out on a journey through the world, obtains guides who represent different world views, including a philosophy of darkness, and meets with many setbacks before choosing the proper philosophy, mate, and vocation.[2] The typical pattern of the novel of adolescence is said to be estrangement from the social environment, conflict with parents, disillusionment in love, departure from home, and encounter with different people and ideas.[3]

But if the novel of adolescence shares some features with the *Bildungsroman* and the initiation story, it differs in terms of the protagonist's age and readiness for experience. In his study of the American college novel John Lyons notes that the undergraduate is younger than the hero of the traditional *Bildungsroman*. The undergraduate protagonist may have similar experiences but is too young and sheltered to come to a real questioning of traditional values or flirt with a philosophy of darkness. "Normally the undergraduate is not only too young to recognize 'The Everlasting No' when he meets it, but the college conspires to insulate him from the doubts experienced by the *Bildungsroman* hero."[4] What Lyons says about the undergraduate applies doubly to the younger adolescent and to the protagonist who happens to be a girl.

While the *Bildungsroman* requires an older hero than the novel of adolescence, the initiation story might include characters of any age. The definition I referred to above, from Mordecai Marcus' "What Is an Initiation Story?", specifies a "young protagonist" and observes that change must lead the character "towards an adult world." Marcus obviously has the adolescent in mind, but there are stories about young children, like Katherine Anne Porter's "The Circus," and stories about middleaged adults, like Ernest Hemingway's "The Short Happy Life of Francis Macomber," that turn upon significant change of knowledge or character. Initiation is not limited to adolescence any more than the novel of adolescence has to involve successful initiation.

If the novel of adolescence is more age-specific than the *Bildungsroman* or the initiation story, it might better be defined very simply according to the age of the protagonist(s). Witham ends up doing so in his survey although he regrets having "to set specific chronological ages for the beginning and end of adolescence, because . . . the ages for intellectual, social, moral, and emotional adolescence may vary. . . . Indeed, it is often said that, in a nonphysical sense, some people never progress beyond adolescence."[5] But whenever critics try to characterize adolescence without reference to fixed ages they run into difficulty. If the adolescent hero is a "youth nearing maturity,"[6] then what is "maturity"? Witham's final definition of adolescence as a stage of life in which individuals "have begun to show physical and social signs of maturing but have not yet assumed full adult responsibility"[7] raises the same objections. What is "adult responsibility"? Is a self-supporting youth who unthinkingly follows convention more responsible than an economically dependent person who has developed an inner self-sufficiency? Is a junior executive by definition more "mature" than a student? It has been said that adolescence is hard to discuss intelligibly in English;[8] certainly it lends itself to begging the question.

I believe, however, that we do have some common sense of what we mean by adolescence. Hemingway's Francis Macomber, who was just mentioned in connection with the initiation story, provides a good example of Witham's postulated adult character who "in a nonphysical sense" has never progressed beyond adolescence. Although Macomber possesses some of the same qualities as adolescent heroes of initiation stories, we would probably hesitate to classify "The Short Happy Life of Francis Macomber" as fiction of adolescence. Our reluctance to do so, I think, stems from the recognition that adolescence has a social, economic, and political reality, as well as a psychological one, and that in this latter sense Macomber is not an adolescent. Since it has a social, economic, and political reality, adolescence also has a history, and some understanding of this history is useful in trying to separate the realities of adolescence from its representations in our national mythology.

A comprehensive history of adolescence, or even a full definition of its contemporary nature, would require another book or two; fortunately all that is necessary for further consideration of the novel of adolescence is a sketch of the ways in which adolescence is a social construct, in particular a modern social construct. The novel of adolescence followed closely upon two developments: the emergence in the late nineteenth and early twentieth centuries of a new stage of life, a period in which people in their teens are institutionally segregated from children and adults, and the creation of the concept of "adolescence" to explain and justify this period. I will first examine the origins of adolescence and then consider how its major characteristics as a stage of life and a concept are incorporated in the novel of adolescence. Because most sources for the history of adolescence emphasize male experience, my initial comments on the rise of adolescence will apply more to its male than its female version. Ultimately I will make some important distinctions between male and female adolescence and point to the reflection of these differences in the novel with female protagonists.

In twentieth-century America adolescence seems an inherent part of the life cycle, a universal stage of development, but it is actually a product of modern civilization. It does not really exist in so-called primitive cultures, the initiation rites we hear so much about being a case in point. Before the rites of passage the candidate is considered a child; afterward he or she is an adult. The only period comparable to our adolescence is the period of separation from society where the candidate receives instruction and preparation for the adult role. During this relatively brief interval the candidate usually lives apart from the rest of the community; the functioning society consists of children and adults.[9] Western cultures used to have the same composition. Although the word "adolescent" comes from the Latin *adolescere*, meaning "to grow up," and thus has a long history, Philippe Ariès tells us that it was originally a purely theoretical term. Adolescence is mentioned in medieval texts on the ages of life as the age when a person's body comes to full growth, but it had no social meaning. "People had no idea of what we call adolescence, and the idea was a long time taking shape."[10] Indeed, it had to wait for the development of the modern concept of childhood.

The thesis of Ariès' pioneering book, *Centuries of Childhood* (1960), is that childhood as we know it did not exist in earlier times. In the middle ages the child was absorbed into the world of adults as soon as possible, usually between ages five and seven; children were considered miniature adults—they dressed like adults, socialized with them, played the same games, and even attended school with adults. Not until the end of the sixteenth and beginning of the seventeenth centuries did childhood come to be seen as different in nature from adulthood, requiring a special culture. According to Ariès, "The concept of the separate nature of childhood, of its difference from the world of adults began with the elementary concept of its weakness, which brought it down to the level of the lowest social strata" (262). He says the persons who contributed most to the development of the new concept of childhood were seventeenth-century priests, moralists, and pedagogues who saw children as "fragile creatures of God who needed to be both safeguarded and reformed" (133).

These men might also be considered the architects of adolescence since they fashioned the institution which would lead to the rise of adolescence, the modern school. Ariès tells us that medieval schools were characterized by random mixing of ages, lack of gradation in curricula, and, because children who went to school were thought to be entering the adult world, great personal liberty. But the seventeenth-century pedagogues introduced changes in the educational institutions and practices they supervised. Gradually students were separated according to age, with adults being pushed out of the schools altogether; the curriculum was organized and gradated according to difficulty of subject matter; and, in what Ariès considers the major point of difference between medieval and modern schools, personal liberty was modified by school discipline.

The new disciplinary system, which included whipping and organized spying, was at first confined to the youngest students, but its use spread in the course of the seventeenth century. It finally affected the whole school population, involving even those scholars near the age of twenty.

Inside the school world, the adolescent was separated from the adult and confused with the child, with whom he shared the humiliation of corporal punishment, the chastisement meted out to villains. Thus, a childhood prolonged into an adolescence from which it was barely distinguished was characterized by deliberate humiliation. (261–62)

Although this discipline was relaxed to some degree in later centuries, Ariès notes that the original concept of subordination remained intact.

The focus of Ariès' book is on childhood rather than adolescence. Beyond placing the establishment of adolescence as a distinctive period of life in the early twentieth century, he has little to add to his remarks relating adolescence and school discipline. But more recent historians, taking a cue from Ariès, have looked specifically at the rise of adolescence. John and Virginia Demos and Joseph Kett agree in tracing it to the turn of the last century, specifically the years between 1890 and 1920. They find in America before that time almost no usage of the word "adolescence" and only a limited degree of concern with youth as a stage of life. There were advice books for young people and occasional complaints about youthful "disorder" and "disobedience" but hardly any institutions marking the passage from childhood to adulthood.[11]

Most historians see the emergence of adolescence as a response to demographic and economic changes in America after the Civil War. In the decades after the war the farm family, where children

worked alongside their parents until they married and started their
own families, began to disappear. The transformation of America
from a rural agrarian society to an urban industrial society had a
pronounced effect on the economic prospects of young people.
Urban youth served a less important economic function than agricultural youth, and in a labor market that was becoming increasingly complex they found themselves relegated to casual labor and
dead-end jobs. In his book *Rites of Passage: Adolescence in America 1790 to the Present* (1977) Kett contrasts the "growing number
of open-ended jobs held by adults" with the "grim condition of
youth."[12] In order to give their children access to the more attractive new jobs, middle-class parents placed them on the track
of formal education. After about 1880, Kett says, the major de-
terminant of a youth's economic future was the "sheer length of
time passed in the setting of formal education" (152).

A prolonged education required different qualities in youth.
Independence and willingness to strike out on one's own, the pre-
conditions for economic success in the early 1800's, seemed later
in the century a prescription for failure. By 1900 young people
were being urged to cultivate self-restraint and self-denial instead
of independence and autonomy. The rigidity and loss of personal
liberty Ariès describes in seventeenth-century European schools
Kett sees developing in nineteenth-century American schools. He
notes that the common school revival led by Horace Mann and
others had European models, particularly the Prussian system with
its graded texts, classification of pupils by attainment and age,
compulsory attendance, and strict discipline. The emphasis on order and obedience had its initial impact on students between seven
and twelve or thirteen but eventually affected older students too.
According to Kett, the immediate environment of people in their
teens became increasingly structured not only within the school
but outside it. He contends that toward the end of the nineteenth
century the authority of adults extended from school life to extracurricular activities so that youth organizations of every type, from
school and church groups to the YMCA, changed character; they
moved toward adult leadership, passive involvement of youth, and
insularity—the latter because adults wanted young people to "practice their adult roles without direct engagement in adult affairs"
(211).

The segregation of people in their teens into institutions exclusively for them made the teen years more conspicuous than they had previously been and thus more open to conceptualization as a distinctive stage of life. Several historians speak of the "discovery" or "invention" of adolescence, by which they mean the invention in late nineteenth-century America of the concept of adolescence. According to Kett, in the years before 1920 a host of educators, psychologists, and what we would now call social workers "gave shape to the concept of adolescence, leading to the massive reclassification of young people as adolescents" (6). The principal inventor was G. Stanley Hall, a psychologist engaged in "child study" at Clark University and author of the monumental work, *Adolescence: Its Psychology, and Its Relations to Physiology, Anthropology, Sociology, Sex, Crime, Religion, and Education* (1904).

The basic assumption of Hall's book is that the human life cycle is divided into stages predetermined by "man's" biological makeup; adolescence constitutes a stage so dramatically different from childhood that it might be considered a period of rebirth. Hall attributes a special importance to adolescence as a stage in the life cycle because he subscribed to the theory of "recapitulation," the idea that each individual passes through the major steps in the development of the race as a whole. According to Hall, adolescence matches the prehistoric period where "man" moved from savagery to civilization, and it thus represents (or "recapitulates") a time of great possibilities for growth. In order for these possibilities to be fully realized adolescence must be a lengthy period, the length of the interval between childhood and adulthood providing the "index of the degree of civilization."[13] But every possibility has a corresponding danger. Hall also describes adolescence as a time of turbulence. Caught at the point of change between primitive past and civilized future, the adolescent experiences a variety of contradictions and alternates between "antithetic impulses"—inertness vs. excitement, self-confidence vs. humility, selfishness vs. altruism, etc. (II, 40).

That this characterization of adolescence sounds familiar is a testament to Hall's continuing influence. His name and his book may be forgotten today, but adolescence is still regarded in exactly the context he established. In 1904 when *Adolescence* was published some of Hall's contemporaries criticized it. They accused him of romanticism and overstatement and deplored the lack of concrete evidence for his ideas. Many scholars refused to see growth in terms of fixed stages and felt that Hall exaggerated the storm and stress phenomena of youth;[14] in the next generation Margaret Mead, in her *Coming of Age in Samoa* (1928), would show that adolescent turmoil was more a function of culture than biology.

But Hall's concept of adolescence proved impossible to shake. Not only did it fit perfectly with the evolutionary orientation of turn-of-the-century thought, but it also provided a neat justification for changes in the experience of youth. If the interval between childhood and adulthood was being prolonged, it was because civilization was advancing to a higher state. If adolescents were being separated from children and adults and carefully overseen by adults, it was because of their own peculiar nature and importance. As Hall put it, the adolescent "must be subjected to special disciplines and be apprenticed to the higher qualities of adulthood, for he is not only a product of nature, but a candidate for a highly developed humanity" (xii).

In his discussion of Hall's work Kett notes that "adolescence was essentially a conception of behavior imposed on youth, rather than an empirical assessment of the way in which young people actually behaved." He claims that the "architects of adolescence," Hall and his followers, "used biology and psychology . . . to justify the promotion among young people of norms of behavior"—specifically, conformity and passivity (243). Perhaps the most striking similarity in the various accounts of adolescence we have considered is the emphasis on subordination of youth. Kett and Ariès agree that the history of childhood and its prolongation into a substantial segment of life called adolescence has been a history of diminishing status. The miniature adult of the middle ages has become the helpless child of today, the "gentleman scholar" a mere schoolboy; the young American whom Alexis de Tocqueville considered a typical product of democracy, a being too independent to be an adolescent,[15] is now in Hall's words "apprenticed" and "subjected to special disciplines."

Adolescence has been from the beginning not only a period of status discontinuity but a prolonged period of low status. Sociologists have identified many similarities in status between adolescents in our society and persons over sixty-five. Both belong to age-segregated groups, which are defined (and stereotyped) by the dominant middle group; both are often poor and lack influence on the decision-making apparatus. Neither group is considered adequately educated or entitled to sex relationships. Both youth and age are continually reminded of their non-productive role in society. Richard Kalish states:

The intermediate age group . . . seems bent upon reducing the control of youth and age, expecting, perhaps, that both be grateful and at least moderately subservient. I would not claim that the working-age group wants a dependent youthful or elderly population, since dependency implies a certain form of mutual responsibility. What is desired is submissiveness, rather than dependency.[16]

Whether the desired goal for the adolescent has been submissiveness, "dependence" (Ariès), or "passivity" (Kett), the actual results have been mixed. Many of the developments Ariès and Kett discuss as preparing the way for adolescence have generated quite opposite behaviors. Thus Ariès notes that the institution of school discipline in the seventeenth century immediately provoked resistance, even in the form of armed revolts and mutinies. In our time prolonged education has sometimes led to further questioning rather than acceptance of discipline; increased adult regulation and leadership has produced a reaction against it; the creation of special institutions for adolescents has eased the development of a separate "youth culture" often at odds with adult society. In other words, the experience of a long period of dependence and low status can lead to rebellion as well as submissiveness. Even Hall warned that adolescents might show an unfortunate "obstinacy" or put up "active resistance" (xii). If adolescents are, as Edgar Friedenberg would have it, "another discriminated minority group," they take on the qualities of minority group members. By the 1950's Friedenberg could actually define adolescence as "conflict—protracted conflict—between the individual and society."[17]

The main points I have made about adolescence in my sketch of its history apply equally to the novel of adolescence. It is a modern phenomenon, it is characterized by conflict, and it reflects the diminished status of youth essential in the creation of adolescence. First, the novel of adolescence is a modern form. Children and adolescents have only recently found a place in fiction. Whereas the new concept of childhood came into existence in the seventeenth century, literary historians find hardly any representation of childhood in literature until the latter part of the eighteenth century.[18] As we have seen, adolescence is a more recent construct, and its portrayal in fiction has emerged fully only in the twentieth century.

Johnson calls the adolescent protagonist "a distinctly twentieth-century manifestation, virtually without precedent in British or American fiction." He mentions several characters who are "nominally adolescent"—for example, Pamela, Tom Jones, David Copperfield, Richard Feverel, Huck Finn, Daisy Miller, Henry Fleming, and Clyde Griffiths; but he contends that these heroes face the "adult problems" of making fortunes, adjusting to marriage, and fighting wars. "The psychological climate of adolescence itself is nowhere treated extensively . . . and none of the novelists involved shows much understanding or interest in the state of adolescence."[19] Johnson's conclusions are open to argument, and if we do not want to consider Huck Finn and Henry Fleming as more than nominally adolescent, we might try to make a case for other characters, such as Hawthorne's Robin Molineux or Melville's Pierre. At any rate, nineteenth-century and early twentieth-century precedents are few. Most critics, even those writing before the appearance of Kett's history, trace the beginnings of the novel of adolescence to his end date for the emergence of adolescence as a recognizable stage of life. Thus Witham says in his survey of the novel of adolescence, "It was not until about 1920 that there began a general trend among American novelists to consider seriously and sympathetically the wide range of problems that may be considered primarily pertinent to adolescents."[20]

The "problems" Witham refers to usually involve a clash with adult society. The novel of adolescence stresses conflict, whether it be antagonism between the youth and society or inner ambivalence about the value of the adult order. The relationship of the individual to society has, of course, been fundamental to the novel, and a certain amount of conflict has thus been an enduring aspect of the form. But in many types of novels conflict is not the major focus and/or it occurs as part of the protagonist's development. In this respect the novel of adolescence can be further distinguished from the *Bildungsroman* and the initiation novel, both of which are primarily concerned with development.

The traditional *Bildungsroman* depends on the concept of *Bildung*, an ideal of personal culture and individual self-development. The hero seeks experience in a conscious attempt to cultivate inner powers. He (or less often, she) must question whatever values prevail in the society and construct his own morality and philosophy of life from the bottom up. The goal is not only the harmonious development of the whole personality but the reconciliation of the transformed self with political and social contradictions in society. When this end has been reached, the *Bildungsroman* concludes on an affirmative note.

It is difficult to apply the German tradition of the *Bildungsroman* even to those nineteenth-century English novels like *David Copperfield*, *Pendennis*, and *The Ordeal of Richard Feverel*, which are usually classified as *Bildungsromane*; the protagonists seem to develop more by accident than design and without the unfolding of inner powers that is supposed to modify their original nature.[21] The novel of adolescence has more in common with these English novels than with the traditional *Bildungsroman*. The modern novelist may question the very assumption upon which the *Bildungsroman* rests—the possibility of developing a coherent and harmonious self within existing social contexts. Plot elements from the *Bildungsroman* may be put to a different use; for instance, the journey, which in the *Bildungsroman* is a vehicle for vertical development, may become in the novel of adolescence an oscillation from side to side. Instead of progressing from A to B, the hero vacillates between A and A' and never gets to B or, perhaps, rejects the idea of B.

Many adolescent protagonists fail even to gain the knowledge or undergo the change of character required in the initiation story with its much looser definition. Not all novels of adolescence include initiation; in fact, the protagonists may actively avoid or refuse it.[22] If the hero is initiated at all, the initiation often occurs suddenly at the end of the novel and is ambiguous in nature. This is not to say that the novel of adolescence never involves some development on the part of the protagonist, or that the *Bildungs-*

roman and the initiation novel do not present conflict. However, the novel of adolescence is less developmental than the other two forms, with the emphasis on the conflict rather than its resolution.

One might expect conflict to be central to the novel of adolescence because it is such a vital part of the concept of adolescence. Hall conceived of conflict as an inevitable accompaniment of biological maturation, and so it has long been viewed. Everyone now "knows" that the harmony of childhood is naturally disrupted in the teen years. As part of the developmental process, adolescents experience internal conflict—Hall's "antithetic impulses"—and rebel against society. They become "juvenile delinquents" or at least fight their parents; rebellious acts like stealing and running away from home, the two given prominence by Hall, seem a "normal" part of adolescent growth.

In the novel of adolescence, however, conflict is more often presented as a function of adolescence as a sociological state. Many adolescent protagonists clash with society over their reluctance to undergo a lengthy period of low status wherein they are separated from children and adults and denied the privileges of either. For instance, stealing and running away from home occur in the majority of novels of adolescence; yet the novelists depict these acts less as the outgrowth of natural urges, in the manner of Hall, than as conscious protests against a long interval of dependence between childhood and adulthood. Adolescents are portrayed as rebels with a cause: they often steal because they lack legitimate control of money and material goods; they run away from home because they hate being dependent and want to be "free" to live their own lives. It is significant that of the major themes critics have identified in the novel of adolescence, only one—obsession with physical changes—has any direct relation to biological maturation. The other themes—a sense of loss, isolation and loneliness, flight and attempted escape, conflict with family, and rejection of current social and moral trends in America[23]—reveal either dissatisfaction with adolescence as a socially created state or direct protest against it. Indeed, the novel of adolescence resembles the social protest novel as much as the developmental modes, the *Bildungsroman* and the initiation novel.

Social protest takes a distinctive form in novels of adolescence by women. The broad conclusions I have drawn about the novel of adolescence apply equally to its male and female versions: both are twentieth-century forms and both are characterized by conflict relating to the low status of adolescence. However, female adolescence has its own particular history and nature which is reflected in the novel. The backgrounds of female childhood and adolescence are harder to determine than the male. Like literary critics, historians have tended to ignore female experience and universalize the experience of boys. The recent histories of childhood and adolescence are histories of boyhood; for instance, Kett's inclusive "Adolescence in America 1790 to the Present" is really white male adolescence. For some suggestive remarks about girlhood we must return briefly to Ariès and to Hall's chapter on female adolescence.

According to Ariès, the emergence of modern childhood in the seventeenth century applied only to boys of the upper and middle classes. In the case of girls and lower class boys the growing distinction between child and adult was not made and the custom of a very brief childhood remained unchanged. Female children were dressed like women as soon as they came out of their swaddling clothes, and "by the age of ten, girls were already little women: a precocity due in part to an upbringing which taught girls to behave very early in life like grown-ups."[24] Ariès quotes a seventeenth-century diary that describes a girl of ten running a large household; when girls reached twelve, thirteen, or fourteen, they usually married.

Schooling was a monopoly of men: girls received virtually no education apart from domestic apprenticeship and were often illiterate. Ariès says, "Without a proper educational system, the girls were confused with the women at an early age, just as the boys had formerly been confused with the men" (58). This state of affairs persisted largely unchanged from the middle ages to the nineteenth century. Formal education for girls, begun only at the outset of the eighteenth century, developed slowly; it was operating with a time lag of about two hundred years. Through much of the nineteenth century, if a girl went to school, she usually left at thirteen or fourteen and was then considered a woman.[25]

That the idea of adolescence for girls was a late development is clearly illustrated in Hall's *Adolescence*. In most respects Hall's book, which was published in 1904, has a very contemporary sound.

Like current textbooks on adolescence, it is divided into discussions
of physical, sexual, emotional, intellectual, and social development; adolescent psychology, as we have seen, is conceived in
terms of dualism and conflict. The tone of the book also strikes a
familiar note. It vacillates between the benevolent (we ought to
try to understand adolescents) and the austere (we should "drill"
and "regiment" them). Just as no contemporary work on adolescence would be complete without its section on juvenile delinquency, Hall's *Adolescence* includes a chapter entitled "Juvenile
Faults, Immoralities, and Crimes," wherein he mentions the existence of gangs.

The chapter on adolescent girls provides a strange contrast to
the modernity of the rest of the book. Hall devotes an eighty-five
page chapter almost entirely to the question of whether girls should
receive formal education. He fears that a high school education
equal to a boy's will endanger a girl's health and thus weaken her
progeny; a college education could be even worse because it might
influence her not to marry at all. Hall shows hardly any interest
in the "emotional, intellectual, and social development" of girls.
Instead, he solemnly presents the reader with pages of statistics
on the marriage and reproduction rates of educated women.

In focusing his attention exclusively on women's reproductive
function, Hall was simply following tradition. Ellen Morgan notes
that historically women have been viewed

as static rather than dynamic, as instances of a femaleness considered
essential rather than existential. Women matured physically, at which
point they were ripe for being loved. . . . Once physically mature, they
were thought to have reached the peaks of their potential and development, which were defined in physical rather than spiritual, intellectual,
or emotional terms.[26]

The available evidence suggests that nineteenth-century Americans considered the period of physical maturation critical for girls.
In his article "Adolescence and Youth in Nineteenth-Century
America," Kett notes that the onset of sexual maturity seemed
crucial because it posed a threat to female virtue.[27] Perhaps just
as importantly, it was seen as a threat to female health. Carroll
Smith-Rosenberg, in her study of nineteenth-century medical lit-

erature, finds puberty described as a traumatic event in the cycle
of femininity. Physicians supposed that the development of a girl's
reproductive organs, which they thought controlled her entire system, would lead at least to a temporary weakness and at worst to
lasting illness and insanity.[28]
    The period after puberty received comparatively little emphasis.
If girls were supposed to undergo at puberty a sudden "wrenching
adolescence," in Kett's words, they "were not really viewed as
having, like boys, a period of youth." In contrast, "boys went
through a relatively painless physical adolescence, but followed it
with a critical period of youth" (108). The experience of a short
but wrenching interval at the time of menses after which a girl is
considered a woman resembles the so-called primitive rite of passage more than modern adolescence. So long as women were conceived of solely in terms of their reproductive role, it was
unnecessary for girls to go through any prolonged period between
childhood and adulthood.
    Paradoxically, however, there arc indications that in the latter
half of the nineteenth century anxiety over women's reproductive
role was producing a more substantial discontinuity between childhood and adolescence. If the Victorians viewed women as "static
essences" capable mainly of physical development, they also considered motherhood a crucial function requiring some skills beyond
the proverbial "maternal instinct." According to Smith-Rosenberg, the ideal mother was expected to be "strong, self-reliant,
protective, an efficient caretaker in relation to her children and
home"—in short, the opposite of the ideal woman, the passive
and dependent essence.[29] In an important article entitled "Tomboyism and Adolescent Conflict: Three Nineteenth Century Case
Studies," Sharon O'Brien contends that post-Civil War advice givers set about reconciling this contradiction. They were alarmed by
the growing incidence of female weakness and invalidism, then
called "hysteria" or "neurasthenia," and looked to childhood to
develop stronger and more competent mothers. Since it seemed
that active girls would more likely acquire the good health needed
for motherhood, many advice givers began to prescribe "free,
active, untrammeled" childhoods, even including "tomboyism."[30]
    At puberty, of course, the girl's indulgence in "masculine" be-
havior was to end. She had to exchange activity for rest so that

her energy would not be drained from her developing uterus and ovaries. As she rested, the girl's "feminine" qualities and domestic interests would quietly unfold. Apparently it did not occur to the Victorian social arbiters that the contrast between childhood freedom and pubertal restriction might create problems of adjustment. O'Brien concludes that

in removing one inconsistency that promoted conflict, these prescriptive writers substituted another. Unknown to themselves they were making stress more likely at an earlier stage in feminine development than marriage or motherhood. . . . In trying to promote a vital continuity between childhood and woman's domestic role . . . they unwittingly introduced a crucial discontinuity between childhood and adolescence which made stress and conflict almost inevitable and subtly undermined their goals. (352–54)

"Unknown to themselves" and "unwittingly" are key words in this account, for it seems that adolescence for girls came about more by accident than design. The institutions of adolescence, the schools, colleges, and clubs, were originally created for boys. So also was the concept, as is clear from Hall's reluctance in *Adolescence* to apply it to girls. In fact, there was no need for a female adolescence. We have seen that the emergence of childhood was marked by a diminution of status for middle and upper class boys. However, there was no need to create a status discrepancy in the case of girls. It is no accident that childhood and its extension into adolescence pertained originally neither to the lower classes nor to women; they had no status to lose and none to prepare for. As Shulamith Firestone states:

Both girls and working-class boys did not have to be set apart . . . for in their adult roles they would be servile to upperclass men; no initiation into freedom was necessary. Girls had no reason to go through [a long childhood and adolescence] . . . when there was nothing for them to grow up *to*: adult women were still in a lower class in relation to men.[31]

By 1904 when Hall's *Adolescence* appeared, his chapter on adolescent girls was an anachronism: girls were already entering en masse the institutions created for boys and Hall's own followers were quickly extending his concept of adolescence to cover girls as well as boys. Yet even after female adolescence had been firmly established, it remained different from male adolescence in the one crucial respect Firestone describes. If a prolonged education for girls on a somewhat equal basis as that for boys created female adolescence, the status of women, relative to men, did not keep pace with their increased education. Women have continued to the present day to be in a lower class in relation to men, and there is still less for girls to grow up *to*.

We have seen that adolescence is a lengthy period of low status wherein the adolescent lacks the economic, political, social, and sexual privileges of an adult. Yet in the case of the boy this state is only temporary. Eventually he will be economically independent, he will (if he is white) belong to the group which controls the processes of government, and he will be allowed to exact the same subservience from children and adolescents as was originally required of him. On the other hand, when the girl becomes an adult, her status will not change significantly. Most likely she will remain economically dependent, and if she does work outside the home she will seldom be paid very highly; she may vote but will have little political power; her sexual rights and control over her body will still be limited; she may exercise the dubious privilege of dominating her children but will be expected to be subservient to her husband and other men. If the young girl becomes one of the minority of women who remains unmarried or achieves professional status, she will find her overall status lowered again by social disapproval. No matter what happens when the young girl grows up, she is still "only a woman," a member of a group socially defined as inferior.

Thus female adolescence is not simply a temporary period of low standing. Unlike male adolescence, it portends a future of continued secondary status. If the preadolescent girl has received an education much like her brother's, she may anticipate something more; but when she reaches puberty she will be pressured to identify herself with traditional female roles. The situation resembles the late nineteenth-century active childhood/passive puberty dichotomy described by O'Brien as making "stress and conflict almost inevitable." As one writer puts it, girls learn to prefer male roles which they are then taught are inappropriate for themselves; "thus is conflict built into the foundations of the female character."[32] This conflict appears prominently in the novel of female adolescence. Although boy characters sometimes hesitate to adopt male roles, their ambivalence seldom becomes more than a minor issue. In novels of female adolescence conflict over gender identity is the major theme.

Before approaching this theme as presented in a variety of twentieth-century novels, it will be useful to explore the literary backgrounds of the novel of female adolescence. We need to know what kind of young heroine was established in the American literary tradition before the emergence of adolescence as a definite "stage" in life. Perhaps the youthful protagonists of nineteenth-century fiction were only "nominally adolescent," but the images of girlhood created by early novelists would influence generations of writers, even into the mid 1900's. What traditions, then, has the novelist of adolescence had to draw upon, and what young girl prototypes has she found in earlier American fiction?

II

THE GIRL PROTAGONIST BEFORE 1920

The literary tradition available for modern women novelists of adolescence seems to be a barren one. In his discussion of American college novels John Lyons contends that the novels with female protagonists are backward compared to those with male heroes because there were no fruitful conventions for the novelist to draw upon.[1] W. Tasker Witham finds the youthful male hero as established in American literary tradition "far more readily adaptable to the newer interests in fiction [that is, the novel of adolescence] than the female. Obviously Tom Sawyer and Penrod Schofield are more closely related to the soul-searching modern protagonists than are Little Eva and Elsie Dinsmore."[2]

It is not surprising that the traditional male youth should resemble the modern adolescent protagonist more than his sister does. As noted in the previous chapter, female adolescence was of later development than male adolescence, and at the beginning of the twentieth century it was still being questioned whether women needed to undergo any prolonged period between childhood and adulthood. Tom Sawyer and Penrod Schofield are at an in-between stage that would now be called adolescence, but nineteenth-century novelists usually present the female protagonist as either child or adult. Little Eva and Elsie Dinsmore are clearly children; the only other famous young heroines, Alcott's Meg, Jo, Beth and Amy, are supposed to be "little women." Not only do our early novelists lack any conception of female adolescence, but they also tend to ignore the years from eleven to sixteen or seventeen. What would now be designated early and middle adolescence is quickly passed over as a period of little importance in itself or of little interest to the reader. One finds a lack of concern for this age period no matter what type of novel is considered. For the sake of convenience, let us follow Lillie Loshe's classification of early American novels into those that are heavily didactic and those "more romantic in spirit, describing sentimental vicissitudes for their own sake."[3] The authors of the more romantic novels seem bent on disposing of the heroine's childhood (which may include our modern "adolescence") as quickly as possible. Thus the first few chapters of *The Female American; or the Adventures of Unca Eliza Winkfield* (1814) describe the protagonist's antecedents, birth, and early childhood; the years from ten to eighteen are summarized in one sentence: "I continued here [in England] till I was eighteen years of age; during which time I made great progress in the Greek and Latin language, and other polite literature; whilst my good aunt took care of the female part of my education with equal success."[4] Having assured us that the heroine has received a proper education, the author is ready to embark on the important part of the book, Unca Eliza Winkfield's "adventures."

In Maria S. Cummins' *Mabel Vaughan* (1857) the protagonist appears in the first chapter as a child of eight. At the beginning of the second chapter her life between eight and eighteen is condensed into a few lines. "During ten years passed in a plain but well-ordered New England homestead, where the highest mental discipline was combined with instruction in the simplest female duties, Mabel acquired strength of principle, soundness of knowledge, cheerfulness of disposition, and useful and industrious habits."[5] With this equipment Mabel is thought to be well-armed for her future trials.

The age at which the novelist considers it appropriate to begin her heroine's adventures varies. Susanna Rowson believed Charlotte Temple ready to be seduced and abandoned at fifteen; the protagonists we have just mentioned were quickly advanced to eighteen. One critic says the ideal age for the sentimental heroine was thought to be seventeen.[6] The important point is that the romantic novelist generally chooses to begin her protagonist's story at the age she believes to mark adulthood. The character's apprenticeship has ended and she is supposed to be a woman. Some writers make it explicit that they consider their protagonists adults. Rose Terry Cooke in *Happy Dodd* (1878) and Constance Fenimore Woolson in *Anne* (1882) inform the reader directly that their young heroines have left childhood because they have fallen in love. "Marian Harland" (Mary Hawes Terhune) claims that the protagonist of *Alone* (1863) is one of the nine girls out of ten who are fully grown at fifteen. Indeed, Terhune was herself only sixteen when she wrote *Alone*.[7]

In moving from the romantic novels to those that are more didactic, we find that the protagonist tends to be a child. The primary concern of these works is perfectly summarized in the quotation above from Maria Cummins' *Mabel Vaughn*. What Cummins condenses into one sentence—the female child's acquisition of "strength of principle," "useful and industrious habits," etc.— is expanded in the didactic novel into volumes. This type of novel appealed strongly to nineteenth-century audiences. Three of the biggest sellers of the century, Susan Warner's *The Wide, Wide World* (1852), Maria S. Cummins' *The Lamplighter* (1854), and Martha Finley's *Elsie Dinsmore* (1868) have heroines about eight years old who are being educated for womanhood.

Leslie Fiedler claims that the emphasis on pre-pubescent heroines can be traced to the expurgation of the seduction theme from American literature early in the nineteenth century. The "sexless child" became heroine after the "nubile Maiden" was considered "too ambiguous and dangerous a subject for polite literature."[8] While there is some truth in Fiedler's contention, there were seduction novels even in the middle part of the century, for instance, Alice Carey's *Hagar* (1852) and Sara Parton's *Rose Clark* (1856). Furthermore, the theme of the proper upbringing of the young girl occurs in very early American novels, such as *Rose; or, American Genius and Education* (1810). Susanna Rowson, in the same year that she published the famous *Charlotte Temple* (1791), wrote *Mentoria*, a collection of didactic tales on the duties of young girls. Most likely, the popularity of the child heroine stemmed in large part from continued interest in female upbringing. Since the character of the "nubile Maiden" was considered to be already formed, the child protagonist was the appropriate means of embodying the advantages of a sound education.

Some novelists try to gain the best of both worlds by using in the same book the didactic plot with the child protagonist and the romantic plot with the young adult. Loshe's distinction between romantic and didactic novels was not meant to be precise—the didactic novel has romantic plot elements and the romantic novel can often be didactic; but the patterns of the two types differ enough so that their combination in one novel produces some strange hybrids. *Rose Clark* (1856) by "Fanny Fern" (Sara Parton) provides a good example. The protagonist, like so many child heroines of the nineteenth century, is introduced as a mistreated orphan. The six-year-old Rose is made to suffer first by the cruel mistress of an orphanage and then by her cruel aunt who forces her to work long hours, half starves her, and locks her up in dark rooms. Although we might not consider this upbringing felicitous, the author reassures us that Rose is receiving valuable lessons in humility and stoicism.

The heroine's "education," however, will soon be terminated. About one-third of the way through the novel, when she reaches eleven, there is a sudden break. The reader turns the page and finds a seventeen-year-old Rose with an illegitimate child. The rest of the book is devoted, after the manner of *Charlotte Temple*, to the trials of the grown-up Rose. Significantly, Parton does not find it necessary to mention her protagonist's experiences between age eleven and age seventeen. That the adoption of the two favorite plot patterns of the sentimental novel should produce this gap highlights the nature of these patterns: one required a child protagonist and the other an adult.

It is not only the age of the youthful heroine in early American novels that makes her less adaptable to the modern novel of adolescence than the male protagonist. When Witham compared Tom Sawyer and Penrod Schofield to Little Eva and Elsie Dinsmore, he obviously had in mind the boys' character traits and behavior as well as their age. Tom and Penrod are lively and mischievous—we remember them in connection with such episodes as the fence painting and the Great Tar Fight. On the other hand, Little Eva and Elsie Dinsmore are more angelic than human. The perfectly good Little Eva, in fact, always dresses in white and seems to float rather than walk; Harriet Beecher Stowe even flirts with blasphemy in comparing her with the child Jesus. Elsie Dinsmore is said to have "a very lovely and well-developed Christian character" and "a very clear and correct view on almost every subject connected with her duty to God and her neighbor." She is truthful, conscientious, diligent, "respectful to superiors and kind to inferiors and equals, gentle, sweet-tempered, patient, and forgiving to a remarkable degree."[9] Martha Finley's attitude toward her heroine is revealed in her unconsciously ironic comment that Elsie is "not yet perfect" (14).

The Eva/Elsie type of heroine has been labelled by Fiedler the Good Good Girl. He contrasts her with the Good Bad Boy (Tom Sawyer and Penrod Schofield) who is good at heart but allowed to misbehave and rebel.[10] The Good Good Girl does not have to be a child, like Eva and Elsie. If Stowe compares Little Eva with Christ, she likens the teenaged Mary Scudder in *The Minister's Wooing* (1859) to the Virgin Mary. Older heroines are also sweet and timid, passive and submissive, pious and pure; their favorite pastimes seem to be fainting and weeping. Some appear, in addition, not a little stupid—the protagonist of Eliza Pope's *Henry and Julietta; or Virtue Rewarded* (1818) gets lost within walking distance of the house she has occupied since birth.

If the Good Good Girl seems an unlikely model for the modern adolescent heroine, the stereotyped plots built around her are just as inappropriate. Returning to our previous distinction between romantic and didactic novels, we find that the romantic novel has been called a "novel of victimization." The heroine passively receives one blow of fate after another. She is, as Henri Petter puts it, "hardly ever in a position to act instead of merely reacting or truly to be herself instead of thinking and existing mainly in terms of flight and sacrifice."[11]

Alexander Cowie gives the following recipe for this type of novel:

The heroine may be menaced by a proud, handsome, moody, Rochester-like man aged about thirty who has traveled and sinned (very vaguely) in the Orient.... If it weren't for Queen Victoria, he would try to seduce her, but as it is he is reduced to proposing marriage. To his astonishment she refuses. This sends him darkly off on more travels. The girl meanwhile ... endure[s] many trials and perform[s] many pious acts. Monotony may be broken ... by the introduction of some physical peril such as a carriage accident, an attack by a mad dog, or a fire. One day the moody man comes back, and finds her sitting in a cemetery. He proposes again and is accepted. Don't be alarmed at this: he is now reformed. . . . For her part, the heroine now . . . realizes that a woman's greatest glory is wifely submission.[12]

Cowie's description aptly characterizes the romantic novel as it was written by such authors as Ann Sophia Stevens, Mary Hawes Terhune, Constance Fenimore Woolson, and, especially, Augusta Evans Wilson in her best-selling *St. Elmo* (1867).

As for the didactic novel, we already have some idea of its nature through our acquaintance with Rose Clark. The child heroine also must suffer. Her mother has died and her father, if still alive, does not love her; she has to undergo a succession of mistreatments by cruel stepmothers, aunts, and guardians. The protagonist's "adventures," however, are usually subordinated to what we have seen is the main theme of these novels—the proper upbringing for young girls. Questions of formal education may be debated: Should the girl be educated at home or at boarding school? Does a school education neglect her physical well-being? What subjects should the girl study, and what books should she read?

The novelists' main concern is the girl's "moral education," her development of Good Good traits. This development turns out to be an education in submission. The modern reader can hardly imagine how characters like Elsie Dinsmore could be any more submissive, but Martha Finley is serious when she tells us that Elsie is "not yet perfect," that is, not yet perfectly submissive. Her problem is that when she is unjustly punished (which seems almost all the time), she has "feelings of anger and indignation" (14). It is not enough for the author that Elsie suppress these feelings; she must learn not to have them at all. Elsie's "triumph" comes when she no longer feels indignant at her father's sadistic treatment of her.

Finley's idea of submission is a bit exaggerated even for the nineteenth century, but in novel after novel young heroines must learn to conquer their pride and become humble, docile, and obedient. Any spirit or resistance against injustice is considered a "sickness" that must be cured by strong doses of religion. In Susan Warner's best-selling *The Wide, Wide World*, Ellen Montgomery makes the error of reproaching her aunt for insulting her dead mother. The narrator comments:

Strong passion—strong pride,—both long unbroken; and Ellen had yet to learn that many a prayer and many a tear, much watchfulness, much help from on high, must be hers before she could be dispossessed of these evil spirits. But she knew her sickness; she had applied to the Physician;— she was in a fair way to be well.[13]

The heroine of another popular novel, Cummins' *The Lamplighter*, at least has some "evil spirits" to exorcise. Gertie Flint hates her cruel foster mother, calls her bad names, and even throws a stone through her window. When Gertie is adopted by a kindly old lamplighter, she gradually learns to govern her temper and exercise self-control and humility. She comes to love the lamplighter in the sky, discovering that only they can be content "who have learned submission; those who, in the severest afflictions, see the hand of a loving Father and, obedient to his will, kiss the chastening rod."[14]

Contemporary novelists of adolescence find little to emulate in these dreary tales of submission. Many writers who are aware of the tradition of the Good Good Girl and her struggle to become Perfectly Submissive consciously react against it. Jean Stafford has the heroine of *The Mountain Lion* (1947) scorn Elsie Dinsmore. Ruth Suckow makes fun of Elsie in her novels and even devotes a satirical essay to *Elsie Dinsmore*. Peggy Goodin in *Clementine* (1946) has her adolescent protagonist yawn over *Little Women*; although Louisa May Alcott's characters are more lively than Elsie, they seem to the modern girl insufferably Good Good, and thus dull. Ruth Suckow, in an article expressing her dismay at that "fearful tomb of 'female virtue' " who is the traditional heroine of fiction, notes that most books about girls were marred by the author's "teachery Sunday school attitude." She complains: "Boys could have their Tom Sawyer and Huckleberry Finn and Peck's Bad Boy, but every heroine, no matter how hoydenish and companionable she might be at the start, was chastened by suffering at the end."[15]

Although there is much truth in Suckow's remark, we cannot conclude that the contemporary young heroine has no prototypes in earlier American fiction. The picture so far seems bleak, but in fact, some novels of the late eighteenth and the nineteenth centuries do have female protagonists who are within the adolescent age range and who exhibit psychological traits and conflicts like those of modern adolescents. One may even detect some uneasiness behind the facade of the Good Good Girl as child. A few heroines seem uncomfortable with their Good Goodness and others are not so Good Good at all.[16]

Our first observation must be that there is *too* much emphasis on submission. One asks why characters like Elsie Dinsmore, Ellen Montgomery, and Gertie Flint must learn over and over again to humble themselves and "kiss the chastening rod." This question has an analogue in one we might pose about the sentimental novel in general: why the overwhelming stress on women's suffering? Both the misery of the adult heroine and the struggle of the child imply dissatisfaction with female subservience. One of the critical issues regarding sentimental fiction is whether it advocates conformity to nineteenth-century gender roles or rebellion against them. Some readers have observed beneath the conventional plots of the sentimental novel an undercurrent of protest against the low status of women; Helen Papashvily calls the sentimental novel a "handbook of feminine revolt."[17] This term is too strong for the works I have been considering; for instance, we are never allowed to see Ellen Montgomery's "strong pride" and "strong passion" in action. But the unrelieved emphasis on the heroine's need to humble herself and learn obedience suggests that she might be proud and rebellious underneath. When the protagonist must apply so often to God, the devil may be lurking nearby.

Another reason for questioning the unrelieved Good Goodness of the heroine has to do with the equivocal nature of the religious theme as presented in the didactic novels. Although religion is supposedly the means and justification for submission, it turns out to be a double-edged tool. Learning to "kiss the chastening rod" of the heavenly father actually gives the girl a means of rebelling against her earthly one. In several novels the religious young heroine is put in the hands of an impious father or guardian. She must willingly obey the guardian's every decree, *except* when it comes into conflict with her religious principles. Thus Ellen finds a way of standing up to her materialist aunt, and Elsie can test her will against her tyrannical father's. In the most memorable scene in *Elsie Dinsmore* the author claims that Elsie regrets having to disobey her father's order to play piano on Sunday; but the modern reader is hard-pressed to believe this sorrow sincere, and the nineteenth-century reader must have thrilled to Elsie's victory, her refusal to give in even when her father tortures her. The fact that Elsie's first allegiance is to God becomes her revenge against her father.

From one point of view religion is just another instrument of oppression—the girl must subordinate herself to one more set of patriarchs, God and his ministers. On the other hand, a heavenly ruler is more remote than an earthly one and, in some cases, can serve as an ally. In a novel of the early twentieth century, Helen Reimensnyder Martin's *Tillie, A Mennonite Maid* (1904), the fourteen-year-old heroine rebels against her father by adopting the Mennonite plain dress against his wishes. In most of the father-daughter struggles that are the essence of this novel, Tillie finds herself on the losing side; but when she argues that God has willed her to become a Mennonite, her father does not dare interfere.[18]

If one looks closely enough, it is possible to find many more signs of discontent, and even revolt, behind the Good Good heroine's submissive exterior. Sometimes the girl becomes involved in actions which can only be taken as symbolic. In her father's garden Elsie Dinsmore finds a "tiny and beautiful humming-bird [which her father had] confined under a glass vase; in its struggles to escape it was fluttering and beating against the walls of its prison" (163). Elsie's letting the bird go seems a pointless incident except as it reflects her own suppressed desire for freedom. In other novels the author introduces a "bad" girl as foil to her heroine.[19] While the bad girl's naughtiness (the novelists have a difficult time portraying "badness") may be intended to set off the virtues of the protagonist, it often seems that the bad girl represents the protagonist's hidden self. One wonders whether Topsy speaks for part of Little Eva when she contends that it is useless to be good when she will never be free and whether bad Nancy of *The Wide, Wide World* acts out Ellen Montgomery's unconscious impulses when she harasses Ellen's aunt.

Most of the characters who have just been discussed are children, and we see in them only intimations of rebellion. However, there are a few older heroines who are portrayed as consciously chafing against Good Good Girl limits. It is tempting to call these heroines "new" types since they differ so radically from their conventional sisters and so prefigure the modern adolescent protagonist. But, in fact, the defiant young heroine is not a creation of late nineteenth or early twentieth-century novelists: she has popped up here and there throughout the history of the American novel. We find one rebellious prototype as early as 1797, in Hannah Foster's novel of seduction, *The Coquette*. The other "new" heroines I will discuss appear in a romantic novel, E.D.E.N. Southworth's *The Hidden Hand* (1849), and a didactic novel, Alcott's *Little Women* (1868).

At first glance Hannah Foster's *The Coquette* seems to be a typical seduction novel of the day. Foster tells the story, after the manner of Richardson, in epistolary form, and has the heroine, Eliza Wharton, seduced by a rake called a "second Lovelace."[20] Eliza is punished in the usual way, death in childbirth, and the female reader is duly warned to avoid her fate. But *The Coquette* differs from the conventional novel of seduction in the nature of the heroine's character. Generally the seducee is such a model of innocence and virtue that it is hard to see how she could possibly "fall"; apparently women are naturally virtuous (Charlotte Temple has the "natural sense of propriety inherent in the female bosom")[21] but naturally weak. Eliza Wharton, however, is never an orthodox Good Good Girl. She "falls" not out of weakness but because she refuses to accept the strictures of her society.

At the beginning of the novel Eliza has just escaped an unwanted marriage with an elderly clergyman who died before her parents could get him to the altar. She is delighted to be launched into "society" again but is soon courted by a young minister named Boyer. Eliza cannot bring herself to marry Boyer right off; she flirts with the attractive rake, Sanford, and is finally rejected by Boyer as a "coquette." In some ways Eliza seems coquettish and vain—she takes great pride in her looks and the male attention she receives, but her delay in consenting to Boyer's proposal is not merely frivolous. Eliza's problem is that she does not want to marry at all. Marriage she calls the "tomb of friendship," a "selfish state" that forces people into a "very limited sphere" in which they center all their concerns in one family and neglect their former associates (61). For this reason Eliza regrets the marriage of her confidante, Lucy. She rebukes the attempts of her friends to marry her off as soon as possible.

"I hope my friends will never again interpose in my concerns of that nature. . . . I am young, gay, volatile. A melancholy event [the death of her elderly fiance] has lately extricated me from those shackles which parental authority had imposed on my mind. Let me, then, enjoy that freedom which I so highly prize." (43–44)

The response of Eliza's mentors is that she has "wrong ideas of freedom and matrimony" (69). In a series of letters that spread only a thin veneer of virtue over the sexual politics of the time, they warn her that she had better accept Boyer; he is a good enough man, and since she is not rich, she cannot expect anything better. But Eliza recognizes that marriage to a minister will be especially confining. She dislikes the thought of being dependent for her subsistence "upon a class of people who will claim the right of scrutinizing every part of my conduct" (68). Besides, Boyer himself seems intolerably priggish. Eliza cannot say so outright, but in speaking of him she indulges in a weapon quite foreign to the conventional heroine, that is, irony. She writes her friend Lucy:

"I have just received a letter from Mr. Boyer in the usual style. He expects the superlative happiness of kissing my hand next week. O, dear! I believe I must begin to fix my phiz. Let me run to the glass, and try if I can make up one that will look *madamish*." (117–118)

Eliza impishly suggests that her mother would make Boyer a better wife than herself.

Eliza intends to marry Boyer eventually—she dimly sees that her practical situation requires it (women must marry and might as well take their best offer); but she tries to postpone the marriage as long as possible. When Boyer rejects her and her reputation is tainted through association with Sanford, she finds herself in a precarious position. Eliza has come to realize that what she really wants—"freedom" and "some variety to the journey of life" (133)— is impossible for women of her day, but she has damaged her chances at women's traditional compensation. Thus she becomes depressed and melancholic, and her health declines. The world seems a "desert" in which she can expect an "awful" future (231).

Only when she sinks into this depressed state does Eliza give in to Sanford. In the typical seduction story the seduction takes place early, and its "fatal effects" form the substance of the novel; in *The Coquette* Eliza is already defeated before she loses her virginity. The fatal effects of her rebellion against women's role lead to her seduction. She wants to die and, in succumbing to Sanford, seems to be deliberately bringing about her own end. Ruth Suckow's contention that the nineteenth-century heroine is always "chastened by suffering" at the close of the novel applies to Eliza. She accepts her punishment as just and is finally made to mouth warnings about the dangers of being a coquette. However, Eliza is a memorable heroine in her initial revolt, her attempt to "enjoy that freedom which I so highly prize."

Another heroine who prizes her freedom is Capitola Black of E.D.E.N. Southworth's *The Hidden Hand*, and Capitola may be unique in that she is not thereby punished or humiliated. Southworth models Capitola after Shakespeare's more spirited comic heroines; in her witty speeches, full of word play, she resembles Rosalind, and, indeed, she is first introduced dressed in traditionally male attire and passing for a boy. Southworth was not the first American novelist to disguise a female protagonist as a boy. In *The Female Review* (1797), for instance, the heroine dresses as a soldier and fights in the American Revolution. But the early authors try to deny the subversive implications inherent in this motif. The protagonist of *The Female Review* adopts male attire only because of "the most endearing attachment to her country"; we are assured that she preserves "all sense of virtue and decorum."[22]

E.D.E.N. Southworth, however, turns Capitola's disguise into a direct comment on the status of women. When she is arrested for masquerading as a boy, the thirteen-year-old Cap explains:

"While all the ragged boys I knew could get little jobs to earn bread, I, because I was a girl, was not allowed to carry a gentleman's parcel or black his boots, or shovel the snow off a shopkeeper's pavement, or put in coal, or do anything that I could do just as well as they. And so because

I was a girl there seemed to be nothing but starvation or beggary before me."[23]

Cap thus "felt bitter against Fate for not making me a boy," donned male clothes, and became "happy and prosperous" (43–44).

When Cap is adopted by the elderly Major Warfield, she changes to female attire but refuses to embrace traditional female roles. Major Warfield, upset that Cap "has never been taught obedience nor been accustomed to subordination" (171), tries to make her submit to his authority. Cap contends that "freedom and peace is even sweeter than wealth and honors" (120) and threatens to return to her old life in the slums if her guardian tries to control her behavior. When Warfield upbraids Cap for riding alone at night, she waits until he does the same thing and then turns the tables on him:

"Old gentleman, tell me instantly and without prevarication, where have you been? Don't you know, you headstrong, reckless, desperate, frantic veteran . . . the jeopardy in which you placed yourself in riding out alone at this hour? Suppose three or four great runaway negresses had sprung out of the bushes and—" (124)

Southworth derives much comedy from the reversal of expected gender roles. She also makes fun of many conventions in novels of the day. In one incident Warfield has a minister scold Cap for her disobedience. Cap modestly accepts the rebuke and then confesses that she has been worse than anyone knows—she has been meeting Albert secretly in the woods. When the minister begins a lecture on the evils of seduction, Cap reveals that Albert is the neighbors' poodle!

As a foil to Cap, Southworth introduces a parody of the Good Good Girl, a sweet, passive victim-type appropriately named Clara Day. In another reversal of the expected situation, Cap, rather than a male character, saves Clara from her kidnappers. Cap's adventures also include capturing the notorious brigand Black Donald and challenging a man to a duel. The latter Southworth accurately calls "the most astounding thing that ever a woman of the nineteenth or any former century attempted" (368). Obviously

Cap comes entirely from the author's imagination. She is a two-dimensional character, like all Southworth's creations, and a counter in an absurd melodramatic plot. That *The Hidden Hand* became a best seller, in spite of Southworth's failure to criticize her heroine's behavior, is an index of the book's distance from reality. Nevertheless, it is surprising that in 1849 a novelist could even imagine a Capitola Black, say nothing of applaud her refusal to submit to authority and her indulgence in behavior reserved for men.

Jo March of Louisa May Alcott's *Little Women* would never think of disobeying her father or making fun of a minister. But Jo, like Capitola, wishes she were a boy. She does not seem "feminine" either in appearance or in behavior. Instead of being small, rounded, pale, and dainty, she is "very tall, thin, and brown" with "long limbs" and "big hands and feet."[24] She is fearless and outspoken and prefers physical activity and serious reading over the more domestic occupations of her sisters. Meg and Amy constantly admonish Jo to be more "ladylike." In the following exchange Meg says:

"You are old enough to leave off boyish tricks, and to behave better, Josephine. It didn't matter so much when you were a little girl; but now you are so tall, and turn up your hair, you should remember that you are a young lady."

"I'm not! And if turning up my hair makes me one, I'll wear it in two tails till I'm twenty," cried Jo, pulling off her net and shaking down a chestnut mane. "I hate to think I've got to grow up, and be Miss March, and wear long gowns, and look as prim as a China aster. It's bad enough to be a girl, anyway, when I like boys' games and work and manners! I can't get over my disappointment in not being a boy; and it's worse than ever now, for I'm dying to go and fight with Papa, and I can only stay home and knit, like a poky old woman." (5)

Jo's preference for activities restricted to boys is clearly the cause of her reluctance to grow up. Although it "didn't matter so much" for Jo to be a "tomboy" as a child, womanhood suggests being "prim" and "poky" and staying home to knit. Meg may consider the fifteen-year-old Jo already a "young lady," but Jo herself, at least in the beginning of the book, speaks as an adolescent. She does not like to think of herself as a child, but she still conceives of growing up as a hateful task of the future—"Don't try to make me grow up before my time," she says (124). Her basic conflict is one we will encounter in the modern adolescent heroine. Jo needs to achieve adult status in order to fulfill her goals—she wants to be a famous writer, to "do something splendid . . . something heroic or wonderful that won't be forgotten after I'm dead" (117); but female adulthood also entails a number of restrictions on the "heroic" things she will be allowed to do. Already she is prevented from acting too "rough" or following her father to war.

Jo fears becoming either a prim, ladylike Miss March or a confined and limited Mrs. _____. Like Eliza Wharton, she dislikes the idea of marriage. At the end of Part I, when Meg receives a proposal, Jo assumes her sister will be "strong-minded" and refuse her suitor. She is shocked and dismayed to find Meg "enthroned upon his knee, and wearing an expression of the most abject submission" (170–71). Jo vows that she herself will be an "old maid" (81). However, in Part II of the novel, originally entitled *Good Wives*, Alcott has Beth die, à la Little Eva, and marries off Meg, Amy, and finally Jo.

Alcott first intended to allow Jo to remain single but was persuaded by readers to have her marry in a "happy ending."[25] Indeed, in Part II Alcott seems at a loss as to what to do with the rebel she created in Part I. *Little Women* is full of contradictions; it bristles with anger while at the same time prescribing charity, patience, dutifulness, industry, good housekeeping habits, etc. But Alcott shows the strongest ambivalence concerning Jo's fate. She has Jo refuse Laurie, asserting that she will not give up her liberty for any man, and then makes her unaccountably change her mind and decide against being an "old maid." It takes Alcott almost fifty pages of vacillation to get Jo and Professor Bhaer engaged.

The question of whether Jo will fulfill her ambitions or learn submission is treated with the same ambivalence. When Jo goes to New York and starts publishing stories, it looks as though she may succeed in becoming a famous writer, but she is soon called home to preside over Beth's sickbed. The dying Beth makes her promise to devote her life to her parents: "You'll be happier in doing that than writing splendid books or seeing all the world"

(321). While Alcott agrees that it is a grand accomplishment for "poor Jo" to renounce her old ambition for this "new and better one," she cannot quite turn her into an Elsie Dinsmore.

Now if she had been the heroine of a moral story book, she ought at this period of her life to have become quite saintly, renounced the world, and gone about doing good in a mortified bonnet, with tracts in her pocket. But you see Jo wasn't a heroine; she was only a struggling human girl. . . . Jo had got so far, she was learning to do her duty, and to feel unhappy, if she did not; but to do it cheerfully—ah, that was another thing. (333)

One might reasonably argue, as Ruth Suckow does, that Alcott's "teachery Sunday School attitude" has caused her to chasten Jo in the end. However, Alcott fails to subdue entirely the Jo she presented in Part I, and she seems unwilling to relinquish the idea that she has created a new type of protagonist, a "struggling human girl" rather than a "heroine of a moral story book."

As we have seen, the rebellious young heroine is not really a new American type, having existed since 1797. Nor does she suddenly take over the field in the mid nineteenth century. *Little Women* and *Elsie Dinsmore* appeared in the same year, and both were tremendously influential. Many later adolescent protagonists, such as Sylvia Marshall of Dorothy Canfield Fisher's *The Bent Twig* (1915), owe as much to Elsie as to Jo. However, in the last quarter of the nineteenth century and in the early years of the twentieth, we begin to find a greater number of characters like Eliza Wharton, Capitola Black, and Jo March.

Adolescent protagonists of the novel of seduction, or "fallen woman" novel, tend to resemble Eliza more than Charlotte Temple. In *The Rise of Jennie Cushing* (1914) Mary S. Watts portrays Jennie's "fall" as an actual "rise"; Jennie insists on her independence, refuses to marry her lover, and in an interesting contrast to Jo March and her school for boys, devotes her life to bringing up female orphans. Ántonia Shimerda of Willa Cather's *My Ántonia* (1918) takes pride in her child born out of wedlock, and her friend Lena Lingard deliberately rejects marriage. Lena has affairs, but she says, "I don't want a husband. Men are all right for friends, but as soon as you marry them they turn into cranky old fathers. . . . I prefer to be . . . accountable to nobody."[26]

Capitola Black is reincarnated in the self-willed heroines of Gertrude Atherton, who are also made the center of wildly melodramatic plots. Although Atherton's young protagonists occupy themselves with finding a "superior" man worthy of subordinating themselves to, they are witty, outspoken, and active before superman makes his appearance. They also engage in highly unconventional activities. Magdalena and Helena of *The Californians* (1898) end up getting arrested, like Capitola, for dressing as boys. Magdalena nearly murders her rival in love, and Patience Sparhawk of *Patience Sparhawk and Her Times* (1900) tries to kill her indifferent mother. We can also see some of Capitola's "unfeminine" characteristics in protagonists of the so-called regionalist fiction that was prominent at the same time Atherton was creating her more spectacular plots.

Sarah Orne Jewett and Mary Wilkins-Freeman are famous for their strong, independent New England "spinsters," but they also wrote about adolescents with the same qualities. Polly Finch of Jewett's "Farmer Finch" and Louisa Britton of Wilkins-Freeman's "Louisa" resemble each other. Polly, a girl in her late teens, is the daughter of an unsuccessful farmer threatened with bankruptcy. Although she has been trained to teach, Polly "would rather be a boy and farm."[27] In spite of the ridicule of the neighbors, who think it shameful for her to do a "man's work," she takes over the farm and singlehandedly makes it an economic success. Polly earns further disapproval by rejecting her former suitor and remaining single.

Wilkins-Freeman's Louisa does farm work also, in order to support her poverty-stricken mother and grandfather. Louisa's mother scolds her for ruining her complexion and, when she discovers that Louisa is raking hay with the men, faints from the shock. Mother Britton tries to pressure her unwilling daughter into marrying a wealthy suitor. But, when it looks as though she must marry in order to save her family from starvation, Louisa instead walks seven miles to borrow food from an uncle; then she performs the feat of carrying a huge ham, a bag of meal, a bag of flour, and a basket of eggs the seven miles back. The narrator says, "It was like a pilgrimage, and the Mecca at the end of the burning, desert-like road was her own maiden independence."[28]

While they present their youthful heroines as physically and emotionally strong and as jealous of their independence, Jewett and Wilkins-Freeman hesitate to break altogether with the conventions of sentimental fiction. If their protagonists come in conflict with society and are not entirely Good Good, they must still avoid being too aggresssive or rebellious. Thus, Jewett cautions the reader that Polly Finch never becomes "unwomanly and rough" (81), and in her novel *The Country Doctor* (1884) she has young Nan Prince, who is fighting for the right to a medical career, use the old religious ploy: God has given her the talent to be a doctor and it is her duty to use it.

The protagonist of Wilkins-Freeman's highly ambivalent industrial novel, *The Portion of Labor* (1901), is a mass of contradictions. The pretty, sweet, gentle, always Good Ellen Brewster delivers as her high school valedictory a revolutionary speech against capitalism and turns down a chance to attend Vassar for a job in the local shoe factory. After Wilkins-Freeman has Ellen reject a marriage proposal from the factory owner and lead the workers out on strike, she is overcome by the incongruities of writing a sentimental and an industrial novel at the same time; she makes Ellen see her "mistake," lead a group of workers back through the picket lines, and marry the capitalist.

Although the regionalist writers are supposed to be pioneers in "realism," their tales often follow the same patterns as the earlier romantic novel. Writers such as Mary Hallock Foote, Grace King, Kate Chopin, Sherwood Bonner McDowell, and Mary Noailles Murfree emphasize their characters' love life. Will the young heroine marry the right man? If, as sometimes happens, the girl gives him up to follow her own inclinations (Jewett's Nan chooses medicine and the protagonist of Chopin's "Wiser Than a God" renounces her lover to become a professional musician), she is seldom made to question the gender roles that require such a sacrifice.

The regionalists depart from the sentimental tradition primarily in the personal characteristics with which they endow their heroines. If Wilkins-Freeman's Louisa could traverse fourteen miles, Mary Noailles Murfree tests her female characters in twenty-mile walks through storms. In "Jack and the Mountain Pink" Sherwood McDowell has a mountain girl exhibit both agility and shrewdness in helping a moonshiner escape the law. These heroines do not cry or faint but, like Capitola Black, show courage, wit, and physical strength.

Jo March also has her fictional descendants in the late nineteenth and early twentieth centuries. They have been overshadowed by the success of Eleanor H. Porter's saccharine Pollyanna, an heir of Elsie Dinsmore; however, Elnora of Gene Stratton Porter's *A Girl of the Limberlost* (1909) is as anxious as Jo to earn money and be independent, and Rebecca Randall of Kate Douglass Wiggin's *Rebecca of Sunnybrook Farm* (1903) resembles Jo in several ways. Her name, Rebecca Rowena, suggest Wiggin's desire to make her a combination of "light" and "dark" heroines; she is a Good Bad Girl. Like Jo, Rebecca prefers boys' activities and wishes she were a boy. "Boys always do the nice splendid things, and girls can only do the nasty dull ones that get left over. They can't climb so high, or go so far, or stay out so late, or run so fast, or anything."[29] She hates to sew and tries to escape doing housework. Again like Jo, Rebecca feels dismayed at the prospect of womanhood. Although she looks forward to finishing school and earning money, she hates being called "grown-up" at fourteen. She claims she has three years left before she must act like a "young lady" (237).

In accord with the tradition of the didactic novel of girls' upbringing, *Rebecca of Sunnybrook Farm* is in part a history of the protagonist's education in submission. Rebecca must learn to, as she puts it, "catch bricks . . . catch 'em without throwing 'em back, too" (105). But Wiggin treats this theme with as much ambivalence as Alcott does. Rebecca's stern aunt is rebuked for trying to make her niece a "cringing worm" (108), and Rebecca never learns to "catch bricks" happily, without "some inward repining and rebellion" (306). When she graduates from high school and is about to embark on a teaching career, she is summoned home to nurse her ailing mother. Wiggin tells us that initially "no consciousness of self interposed between her and her filial service," but, as the weeks passed, "there was a mutinous leap of the heart, . . . a beating of wings against the door of the cage, a longing for the freedom of the big world outside" (307–08). Rebecca is finally saved from household drudgery, in the manner of Jo March, by a large inheritance from her aunt.

Rebecca of Sunnybrook Farm, published thirty-five years after *Little Women*, is thus very similar, in theme and in the author's ambivalent attitude, to the earlier book. Some didactic novels of the new century, however, make a definite break from tradition. Their distinguishing characteristic is that the young heroine must *not* submit; her education consists of learning to recognize, and then fight, the social institutions which oppress women and poor people. In Mary Johnston's *Hagar* (1913) the protagonist's name and dark complexion place her immediately as a rebel and outcast. Hagar Ashendyne spends her childhood and adolescence with her father's patriarchal Southern family. Her father is off travelling in Europe; her mother, Maria, is ordered about by the Ashendynes and, seemingly in protest against her fate, has become an invalid.[30]

As a child, Hagar overhears several conversations between her mother and grandmother on the status of women. In one instance the grandmother chides Maria for her restlessness and melancholy, saying:

"God regulated society as it is regulated, and placed women where they are placed. No one claims . . . that women as women do not see a great deal of hardship. The Bible gives us to understand that it is their punishment. Then I say take your punishment with meekness."[31]

This is the final "lesson" learned by heroines of many earlier didactic novels, but Johnston has Maria retort: "There was always . . . something frightful to me in the old notion of whipping-boys for kings and princes. How very bad to be the whipping-boy, and how infinitely worse to be the king or prince whose whipping-boy you were" (17).

Maria considers herself too weak to break through her "trap" (17) and soon dies; however, she has influenced Hagar to resist the education in meekness the Ashendynes have in mind for her. Hagar is told that it is "unladylike" to ask questions (7), but she persists in wondering why women are expected to obey men, why they seldom have money of their own, why they are not supposed to read certain books. Although she is punished for reading *The Scarlet Letter* and *The Origin of Species* and finally forbidden to read at all, she secretly disobeys and dreams of supporting herself by writing or teaching. When she is eighteen, Hagar defies her grandfather and leaves for New York. Here she meets some feminist settlement workers, discovers the living conditions of the poor, and reads about socialism and women's rights; she soon becomes an influential writer and suffragist. Hagar resists several marriage proposals from dominating men and marries only when she meets a man who believes in equal rights and approves her decision to continue writing and working for the women's movement.

The protagonist of Zona Gale's *A Daughter of the Morning* (1917) has a similar career. Her rather absurd name, Cossima Wakely, is apparently intended to suggest Cosmic Awakening. Cossima, like Hagar, is first awakened by the unfortunate situation of her mother. Her mother works too hard and has a "rotten life";[32] she is only slightly better off than the woman next door, who is severely beaten by her alcoholic husband. After Cossy has reluctantly become engaged because she has "got to marry somebody" (23), she suddenly realizes that she will end up like her mother and the neighbor. "Neither of 'em was having a real life. Look what love had brought them to. . . . *And* there was me, starting in the same way, with *Luke*. . . . I'd just fixed it so's that all my life would be the same thing as their lives" (31).

Cossy would probably have married Luke but for a chance meeting with John Ember, a labor leader. He advises that home is the worst place for a girl and encourages her to leave for the city and find her own work. In New York Cossy takes a factory job and becomes a union organizer and feminist. Although her career is interrupted for a time by a college education and an introduction to high society, she rejects society life in order to help working women in a strike. Cossy also gives up her wealthy but conventional suitor in favor of Ember. They decide to work out a marriage without fixed sex roles and devote themselves to the labor movement.

Hagar and *A Daughter of the Morning* provide new models in their heroines who refuse to accept their mothers' fate, leave home for good, and become explicitly feminist. However, the socialist-feminist novel fits clearly into the didactic tradition. The protagonists are, as much as Elsie Dinsmore, mouthpieces for their authors' views on the proper course for women to take. Sometimes the novel is not far removed from a tract; Charlotte Perkins Gilman's *What Diantha Did* (1910) is a fictional working out of the theories she presented earlier in her *Women and Economics* (1898). If the protagonists seem no more real than the passive victims of earlier novels, their experiences fall into patterns just as stereotyped. Instead of Discovery of True Religion, Learning of Obedience and Submission, etc., we find Challenging of Paternal Authority, Escape from Home, Meeting of Feminist Guides, and Resistance to Temptations (such as marrying a sexist or living the life of the rich). The young protagonist is a mannequin with sawdust insides: it is only her outer dress that is considered important.

A lack of emphasis on the heroine's inner thoughts and feelings is characteristic of all the novels discussed so far. Leslie Fiedler states:

The sentimental novel of analysis, once firmly in the hands of genteel females, ceased to be analytic at all. . . . It was clear from the start that the abiding value of Richardson's work lay in his knowledge of the intricacies of the female mind (or, as it was called then, the 'heart'), and in his invention of a technique for rendering in all their complexity and evanescence moments of choice or equivocation within that 'heart.' Neither inwardness nor character, however, interested the scribbling ladies at all. . . . The lady Richardsonians were . . . the enemies of psychology and . . . of candor.[33]

Contrary to what Fiedler implies, gentility was neither invented nor maintained by women. However, female novelists who wanted to be successful did have to consider the tastes of the male editors and publishers who controlled the literary market. Some women may have been interested in inwardness and character, but they could not afford to portray it because "psychology" and "candor" were frowned upon. Nathaniel Hawthorne, who coined the term "scribbling women" in a famous letter to his publisher, is a case in point. In another letter he claims Julia Ward Howe ought to be "soundly whipt" for "making public what she ought to keep to herself—viz. her passions, emotions, and womanly weaknesses." Hawthorne comments: "What a strange propensity it is in these scribbling women to make a show of their hearts, as well as their heads, upon your counter, for anybody to pry into that chooses!"[34]
    A narrative comment by Alcott in *Little Women* reveals clearly

the conventional prejudice against the "novel of analysis." Jo has begun to earn money by writing sensational fiction.

> She thought she was prospering finely, but . . . she was beginning to desecrate some of the womanliest attributes of a woman's character. She was living in bad society; and, imaginary though it was, its influence affected her.
>
> She was beginning to feel rather than see this, for much describing of other people's passions and feelings set her to studying and speculating about her own—a morbid amusement in which healthy young minds do not voluntarily indulge. (267–68)

Alcott does not tell us exactly what "womanly attributes" Jo desecrates, but the point comes through that the study of passions and feelings is not seemly and is especially not for women.

So long as the genteel tradition prevailed in American letters there was little emphasis on "inwardness." Thus, when at the end of the nineteenth century novelists began to discover adolescence, they hardly knew what to do with it. Sarah Orne Jewett interrupts the narrative of *Betty Leicester* (1889) to point out that her fifteen-year-old protagonist has reached a "funny age." "You seem to just perch there between being a little girl and a young lady, and first you think you are one and then you think you are the other."[35] Jewett lets this observation hang and quickly returns to the heroine's adventures. In *The Bent Twig* (1915) Dorothy Canfield Fisher defines adolescence as a stage distinct from childhood or adulthood and asserts that her heroine must undergo the "fever and chills" common to this period.[36] But the novel focuses on nineteenth-century questions of education: will Sylvia's moral training prevail over her instinctive love of luxury?

Grace King, in her New Orleans stories, seems fascinated by female adolescence; she likes to concentrate on the moment of the debut. In *Monsieur Motte* (1889) she spends pages fussing over her debutantes' dress, for "a wrinkle in a bodice, a flaw in a glove, a curl this way or that, is enough to settle a destiny."[37] At last the girls proceed nervously down the stairs "into not the parlors, that was not what frightened them, but the future, the illimitable future, that for which all their previous life had been a preface. One stoop more, it would be the present, and their childhood would be over"

(189). Here King falters—after the dramatic build-up she portrays not the girls' reactions to their debut but the gossip of their elders about them.

Jewett, Fisher, and King all present their adolescents from the outside. They inform the reader that their heroines have reached a special age or they paint portraits of young girls stepping out of childhood; but they stop short of examining their characters' inner selves. The protagonist is either, in the tradition of the didactic novel, made the occasion for the author's views on female up-bringing (Jewett, Fisher) or, in the tradition of the romantic novel, put through the motions of a sentimental love story (King). The didactic or romantic modes of the nineteenth century are not necessarily inferior to modern ones; the point is simply that, since adolescent consciousness had not been discovered, adolescence was not yet the novelist's real subject.

W. Tasker Witham chooses the year 1920 to date the emergence of true novels of adolescence because he thinks it conveniently marks the end of the genteel tradition.[38] According to Witham and Johnson, the novel of adolescence was made possible only by the growth of a new interest in psychology and a new literary tradition emphasizing the frank portrayal of inner consciousness. Freudian theory especially, with its emphasis both on childhood and adolescence and on the inner workings of the "psyche," lent itself to the novel of adolescence.[39] 1920 is, of course, an arbitrary date; in her *Three Lives* (1909) Gertrude Stein had already experimented with techniques for revealing her young Melanctha's inner life. However, after World War I we find many more novelists who present adolescence as a special period of life and concentrate on portraying the thoughts and feelings of the young protagonist.

While the traditional female youth, in the person of the Good Good Girl, might not be easily adaptable to the novel of adolescence, we have noted the existence of less conventional heroines who may be said to be the prototypes of the modern adolescent protagonist. Many of the rebellious traits of Eliza Wharton, Capitola Black, and Jo March are passed on to the post–1920 heroine. The major difference is that the modern novelist shows interest in the adolescent consciousness. The inner conflicts suggested in Eliza's reluctance to marry and Jo's pulling off her hair net are presented more openly and in greater complexity.

In addition, the twentieth-century writer makes more extensive use of the adolescent character's own point of view. We no longer have a Sunday school teacher-narrator looking down at the young heroine and commenting on her moral development; most of the time the novelist suppresses even the background applause Southworth gave her Capitola or the condescending smile Alcott accorded "poor Jo." It follows from the new emphasis on "inwardness" that the modern novel of adolescence should also seem more true to life than the earlier fiction we have considered. Such experiences as walking twenty miles to effect a rescue, capturing a robber, or becoming a famous writer are transferred from the plot to the daydreams of the protagonist.

The modern girl protagonist as she appears in Edith Wharton's *Summer* (1917), the subject of the next chapter, has little in common with Elsie Dinsmore but shares many characteristics with the more rebellious heroines. Like Eliza the coquette, she allows herself to be seduced out of defiance rather than weakness; like Capitola Black, she resists her guardian's authority; like Jo March, she prefers freedom to marriage. However, Wharton's heroine is significantly less Good than Eliza, Capitola, or Jo, and in the respects we have just considered, the fictional world of *Summer* seems far removed from the earlier novels. Edith Wharton thoroughly understands and makes use of nineteenth-century plot conventions, but her real interest is the adolescent consciousness. In *Summer* she explores the inner thoughts and feelings of a tempestuous character who seems less than her predecessors the "heroine of a moral story book" and more truly a "struggling human girl."

III

ON THE THRESHOLD: EDITH WHARTON'S *SUMMER*

"How I hate everything!"[1] With this prophetic exclamation the modern adolescent heroine, or at least her most immediate precursor, announces herself. Charity Royall of Edith Wharton's *Summer* (1917) is never called an "adolescent." Charity is a "girl"— she is seventeen, the ideal age, we recall, for the nineteenth-century sentimental heroine. In fact, if we consider only what happens to Charity, her "adventures" as they would have been called in an earlier time, *Summer* seems another *Charlotte Temple* or *The Coquette.* A sheltered and inexperienced girl from rural Massachusetts is seduced by a sophisticated city fellow. Seduction, as always, has its fatal effects: she gets pregnant and her lover leaves her for someone of his own class. Like Charlotte Temple and Eliza Wharton, Charity is duly punished, not by death in childbirth—it is, after all, 1917—but by enforced marriage to her hated guardian, Lawyer Royall, and entombment in the village of North Dormer.

At the same time that it adheres to the conventions of the seduction novel *Summer* manages to follow the pattern of the "romantic" sentimental novel, as defined in the last chapter. Alexander Cowie's recipe for that type of novel is worth repeating:

The heroine may be menaced by a proud, handsome, moody, Rochester-like man aged about thirty, who has traveled and sinned (very vaguely) in the Orient. . . . If it weren't for Queen Victoria, he would try to seduce her, but as it is he is reduced to proposing marriage. To his astonishment she refuses. This sends him darkly off on more travels. The girl meanwhile

. . . endure[s] many trials and perform[s] many pious acts. Monotony may be broken . . . by the introduction of some physical peril such as a carriage accident, an attack by a mad dog, or a fire. One day the moody man comes back, and finds her sitting in a cemetery. He proposes again and is accepted. Don't be alarmed at this: he is now reformed. . . . For her part, the heroine now . . . realizes that a woman's greatest glory is wifely submission.[2]

Summer resembles this description even in many of its particulars. Lawyer Royall is proud, moody, dark, taciturn, isolated—clearly a Rochester type. Although he cannot afford the Orient, he is prone to mysterious absences; during his travels to nearby towns he has committed certain "sins," never detailed, involving alcohol and prostitutes. Since Queen Victoria is dead, Royall can make a rather half-hearted attempt to seduce Charity, but when she rejects him he quickly proposes. Charity's refusal surprises him (after all, he had saved her as a child from her dissolute relatives on the Mountain) and sends him off on his debauches, while she endures her trials of seduction. At the end of the novel Royall finds Charity on the Mountain near her mother's grave, proposes, and is accepted. He has reformed. He is gentle and thoughtful even to the extent of avoiding the marital bed on his wedding night; "all the dark spirits had gone out of him" (284). If Charity fails to consider wifely submission her greatest glory, she at least accepts it as her fate.

This description of *Summer* as an example of traditional sentimental fiction, accurate though it is, obviously does violence to the whole of the novel. The experience of reading *Summer* differs completely from the experience of reading *Charlotte Temple* or *Rose Clark* or *St. Elmo*; the reader senses immediately that Charity is something new. Wharton's plot may follow the conventional patterns, but the texture of the novel and the characterization of the heroine are dramatically opposed to nineteenth-century models. If Alcott's Jo March went wrong as a novelist by "much describing of other people's passions and feelings,"[3] this is exactly what Wharton does. In her autobiography she says of writing *Summer*, "I do not remember ever visualizing with more intensity the inner scene, or the creatures peopling it."[4] The "inner scene" predominates, and the entire novel is suffused with emotion.

Charity Royall seldom thinks; she simply feels, and her feelings are always described in extremes. When angry she feels "tremors of rage" (48) or "a fierce impulse of resistance" (64). Sadness makes her "whole soul a tossing misery" (77) or brings "great waves of anguish" (231). Her more positive emotions are just as intense, producing a "glow that burned at her heart" (131). Charity is overcome by feelings she seems powerless to resist. Thus she frequently seems acted upon: "a fierce revulsion of feeling swept over her" (40); "a fever of unrest consumed her" (99); "the long flame [was] burning her from head to foot" (106).

This view of Charity as an essentially helpless being swept over, consumed, and burned by outbursts of passion is intensified by Wharton's use of sea imagery. Charity's feelings often come in "waves," as in the "great waves of anguish" noted above, and she fluctuates between extremes of joy and misery. Her soul always seems to be "tossing," as in "tossing misery" above, or "tossing on seas of woe" (102). Several times in the novel Charity loses the sense of solid ground under her feet. The surrounding hills begin to look like the ocean, like "blue heights eddying away to the sky like the waves of a receding tide" (79). In another instance, "aching with emotion, she stepped as if the ground were a sunlit wave and she the spray on its crest" (96). Charity feels as though she is floating and comes to see the abandoned house where she meets her lover as a seashell.

Wharton does not merely describe the intensity and fluidity of Charity's emotions; she creates their counterpart in the natural setting of the novel. Wharton once referred to *Summer* as her "Hot Ethan."[5] The characterization is apt, for the dominant image of her other treatment of rural New England, *Ethan Frome* (1911), is cold. Ethan's tragedy has frozen his feelings: "He seemed a part of the mute melancholy landscape, an incarnation of its frozen woe, with all that was warm and sentient in him fast bound below the surface." The narrator senses that Ethan's isolation contains the "profound accumulated cold" of many New England winters.[6] But in *Summer* the change in season has brought a thaw. When Charity meets Lucius Harney, the man who will become her lover, "all the old frozen woes seemed to melt in her" (52).

Summer begins on a June afternoon with the sun shining brightly, and the sun continues to shine through the major portion of the novel. Whenever Charity can escape the chill of the library where she works, she seeks the warmth of nature. She lies "above a sunlit hollow, her face pressed to the earth and the warm currents of the grass running through her." She hears the "bubbling of sap and slipping of sheaths and bursting of calyxes" and smells the "moist earth-smell that was like the breath of some huge sun-warmed animal." Charity is in harmony with the scene, "passive and sun-warmed as the slope on which she lay" (53–54). As Charity falls in love with Lucius, she becomes increasingly emotional and "part of the sunlight and the morning" (77–78). Her projection of her feelings on to Lucius makes him seem like the sun—his fair hair shines, his voice warms her, his smile sheds "brightness over everything" (60). In contrast, Lawyer Royall is described solely in terms of cold and the moon.

As the summer progresses, the sun gets hotter. On the fourth of July when Lucius takes an exuberant Charity to the celebration at nearby Nettleton, it is sweltering. While everyone else perspires miserably, "to Charity the heat was a stimulant: it enveloped the whole world in the same glow that burned at her heart" (131). The climax comes appropriately at the evening fireworks where the night explodes into light, and simultaneously Charity and Lucius kiss for the first time; the next day they begin their affair. Thereafter, the hot becomes the fiery and Charity's feelings are consistently portrayed in terms of fire—"her short hours with him flamed out like forest fires" (182). Charity will allow nothing, neither Royall's warnings nor her own sense of the gulf between her and her lover, to interfere with her illusion of eternal happiness with Lucius. As Wharton puts it, "her eyes were so full of light that everything about her was a blur" (176). Finally reality intrudes in terms of a "suffocating" heat which descends on Charity in "smothering waves" (198). From this point, when she realizes she is pregnant, to the end of the novel, the heat recedes and an "autumnal dampness" takes over (209). It is always cold, gray, ashen, black, dark, empty, rainy, etc. Charity becomes numb and wooden, with the hot summer sun only a memory. At the end Mr. and Mrs. Royall drive home from their wedding "in the cold autumn moonlight" (291).

Wharton was right in calling her novel "hot," and one can scarcely imagine what Louisa May Alcott or Susan Warner, or even a more rebellious nineteenth-century novelist like E.D.E.N. Southworth, would have thought of it. Even in 1917 Boston was not pleased. Reviewers felt uneasy and faithful readers "shocked," while Wharton received "shy and frightened" letters from old friends.[7] No doubt the seduction theme gave offense; in her autobiography Wharton recalls with amusement the advice she so often received to avoid writing about "unlawful attachment" and "illicit passion."[8] Yet the unlawfulness of Charity's attachment, plus the fact that she is not punished by death or some other catastrophe, pale beside all her tossing and burning—the intensity with which she is allowed to feel.

Paradoxically, in the earlier novel of seduction a fallen woman could still be a Good Good Girl. Charlotte Temple is so decorous the reader suspects immaculate conception. Even after Charlotte's fall her creator assures us of "the superiority of Charlotte's sense and virtue"; she would never have "swerved from rectitude had it not been for bad precepts and worse example."[9] But Charity Royall is barred from Good Goodness by the strength of her passions and her seeming inability to keep them in check. To the nineteenth-century sentimental novelist strong feelings were made to be controlled and, as the heroine's education advanced, suppressed altogether.

Charity might be considered a Good Bad Girl in Leslie Fiedler's terms—a Huck Finn or Tom Sawyer type who misbehaves but is good at heart, who, as in Huck's case, becomes the center of true rather than conventional morality. But even though Charity represents vitality as opposed to the deadness of North Dormer, she is not allowed to be a moral touchstone. Wharton seems determined from the very beginning of the novel to present her as Bad Bad. Charity makes her first appearance hesitating on the threshold of Lawyer Royall's house. She steps inside to look in the mirror and wish she had blue eyes; she steps outside on her way to her job at the library, exclaiming "How I hate everything!" The symbolic lingering on the threshold, the concern with personal appearance, and the sweeping statement all seem typically and innocuously adolescent. But when Charity reaches the library Wharton makes it clear that she is neither typical nor innocuous.

To Charity the library is a "prison-house" (14). She has read hardly any of the books, though Lucius tells her there are some good ones, and considers it too much trouble to dust them or remove the worms. For a month or two, after visiting a nearby town and sensing a larger world, Charity "dipped feverishly and disconnectedly into the dusty volumes of the Hatchard Memorial Library; then the impression of Nettleton began to fade, and she found it easier to take North Dormer as the norm of the universe than to go on reading" (10). She uses a disintegrated copy of Maria Cummins' sentimental novel *The Lamplighter* (1854) to hold the lace she is making.[10]

Wharton could hardly have chosen a more sacred convention for Charity to violate. The heroine's love of reading is so fundamental, so absolutely taken for granted in the nineteenth-century novel (and in most twentieth-century fiction as well) that it is hardly a fact to be noticed. Reading is what the passive Ellens and Ednas and Elsies (and their British prototypes, the Jane Eyres) *do*. It is their substitute for experience and their means of self-improvement. Happiness means finding oneself alone in some gentleman's library; being appointed librarian would be unimaginable bliss. If Charity might be forgiven her loss of virginity and failure to try to control her emotions, her disregard of books—both dislike of reading and negligence as caretaker—put her beyond the pale.

It is important that Wharton introduces Charity in her role as librarian, making this scene precede her communion with nature in Chapter II. When Charity lies in the sun rubbing her face in the grass, she seems a completely different, and more sympathetic, character. No wonder that she "hated to be bothered about books" (21). Wharton presents Charity as a natural being. She resembles an animal, a hawk, a night-bird; her head is a flower; she is a plant experiencing "the reaching out to the Light of all her contracted tendrils" (180). Of course Charity is only Bad in terms of a tradition of Good heroines. To the author and the modern reader she is, like nature, amoral. However, Wharton has to begin by breaking the traditional identification of the reader with the heroine. Thus she concludes Chapter I as follows:

The hours of the Hatchard Memorial librarian were from three to five; and Charity Royall's sense of duty usually kept her at her desk until nearly half-past four.

But she had never perceived that any practical advantage thereby ac-

crued either to North Dormer or to herself; and she had no scruple in
decreeing, when it suited her, that the library should close an hour earlier.
A few minutes after Mr. Harney's departure she formed this decision,
put away her lace, fastened the shutters, and turned the key in the door
of the temple of knowledge.(20)

This passage, with its rather heavy irony, is the furthest in the
novel from Charity's consciousness and may account for the dis-
comfort of some readers with the narrative point of view; they feel
the author's presence looking down and miss the internal narrator
of *Ethan Frome*.[11] Whether or not Wharton intrudes too much,
she clearly felt the need to establish distance. For the remainder
of the novel we see almost entirely through Charity's eyes but are
to realize that Charity's point of view is limited. This fact is crucial
in any interpretation of her experience.

To Charity the events of her summer mean the gradual loss of
her dreams. She had always considered herself set apart from the
other North Dormer girls and marked for a better fate. She could
pity Julia Hawes, who "fell," had an abortion, and became a
prostitute. " 'Poor Julia!' Charity sighed from the height of her
purity and her security. . . . The pity of it was that girls like Julia
did not know how to choose, and to keep bad fellows at a distance.
. . . " (125–26, Wharton's ellipsis). Charity comes to realize that
she is not above the other girls; her love for Lucius Harney is not
enough to keep him. "She understood now the case of girls like
herself to whom this kind of thing happened. They gave all they
had, but their all was not enough: it could not buy more than a
few moments. . . . " (198, Wharton's ellipsis). Even before she gets
pregnant Charity has to face the emptiness of her dream of walking
down the aisle as Lucius' bride.

When Charity finds herself pregnant, she turns to her other
dream—the Mountain. North Dormer scorns the band of outlaws
on the Mountain, insisting that Charity is lucky to have been rescued by Royall. But Charity does not agree; to her the Mountain
represents untrammelled freedom. When Lucius describes the
Mountain kingdom as "a handful of people who don't give a damn
for anybody," Charity is "thrilled"; his words seem "the clue to
her own revolts and defiances" (65). Throughout her life in North

Dormer she keeps in mind the possibility of joining her outlaw relatives. Thus, when all else fails, she embraces the Mountain as her final refuge: "the only answer to her questioning, the inevitable escape from all that hemmed her in and beset her" (236).

The reality of the Mountain is something different. Symbolically, it rains, and Charity finds nothing but poverty, hunger, and filth. Her mother has just died, and in a nightmarish scene Charity tries to smooth the rags on her mother's hideously swollen body while the mountain people quarrel drunkenly over her belongings; they indeed "don't give a damn for anybody." Charity's mother lies like a "dead dog in a ditch," and her other relatives are described similarly as animals or dimwitted children (250). She can no longer blame her mother for having given her up to Lawyer Royall. With the collapse of her dream of the Mountain Charity sees few options left. She can become Julia Hawes or marry Royall, the man she has hated and defied, and reconcile herself to North Dormer. "In the established order of things as she knew them she saw no place for her individual adventure. . . . " (235, Wharton's ellipsis).

With "as she knew them she saw" Wharton again emphasizes Charity's perspective, but there is considerable narrative support for this point of view. We have already noted the change in imagery at the end of the novel—the dramatic switch from brightness and warmth to darkness and cold. In *Edith Wharton's Argument with America* Elizabeth Ammons claims that "the final union between Charity and Royall is not merely depressing; it is sick." Since Royall has acted as Charity's father for most of her life, the marriage is incestuous. Ammons argues persuasively that Wharton considered incest the model for American marriage and "the incestuous nature of patriarchal marriage is the largest, the enveloping, subject of *Summer*." However well-intentioned Royall may be, he is still paternalistic and the union he practically forces on Charity can only be an "unhealthy extension" of their previous relationship as father and daughter. Marriage to her guardian "dooms Charity Royall to perpetual daughterhood—a fate that Wharton surrounds with images of spiritual paralysis and death."[12]

That Charity is "doomed to perpetual daughterhood" is supported by the fact that Royall brings her down from the Mountain at the end of the novel a "tired child" (274), repeating his original act of fetching her from the Mountain when she was five years old. In the time between, Charity might pursue an "individual adventure," as she puts it. But there is no permanent place for this adventure, no place for the independent, sensuous woman Charity would like to be. Symbolically, Charity conducts her affair with Lucius neither in the town of North Dormer nor on the Mountain, but in an abandoned house in the hills between. This house stands open to the sun and sky and is decorated with wild flowers. Its natural beauty contrasts with both the squalor of the Mountain house, a dark shed with broken windows, and the "cold neatness" (24) of Lawyer Royall's; Royall's seems "the very symbol of household order" (85) compared with the Mountain but is dark and suffocating to Charity, as "the roof and walls seemed to be closing in on her" (119). Unfortunately for Charity the hill house, as we noted earlier, is only a seashell—delicate and temporary.

Charity is allowed a brief flowering in middle ground, but she must settle in one of the permanent places, either Mountain or town. If the Mountain, with its childlike inhabitants living in anarchy, may be thought to represent perpetual childhood, the town, where law and order reign and everything is old, represents adulthood. Interestingly, G. Stanley Hall, the architect of adolescence, pictures adolescence as a state midway between savagery and civilization.[13] Within this scheme Charity can be said to make a successful journey from childhood (Mountain) through adolescence (hills) to adulthood (town). Yet it would seem that she ends up a child-wife in North Dormer, rather than a child-prostitute on the Mountain, having simply been passed from her outlaw real father to her lawyer foster father. Ironically, Lawyer Royall's last words in the novel are "You're a good girl, Charity" (290). The Bad Bad Girl has finally been reduced to Goodness and, what is more, is still a girl. From this point of view Charity has grown down rather than up.[14]

On the other hand, we have already observed Wharton establish her heroine's vision as limited. While the narration in part supports Charity's sense of loss, it also affords another view of her experience. In the way we have come to see in the twentieth century as typically adolescent, Charity has a series of dreams and illusions. The loss of some of these dreams can hardly be considered damaging. For instance, before she pictured herself walking down the aisle with Lucius, Charity imagined marrying the clergyman, Mr. Miles, whom she admired for his straight nose and impressive speech. She was shocked to discover that he already had a wife, "but the arrival of Lucius Harney had long since banished Mr. Miles from Charity's dreams, and as he walked up the path at Harney's side she saw him as he really was: a fat middle-aged man with a baldness showing under his clerical hat, and spectacles on his Grecian nose" (92).

Although the loss of Lucius is more serious, it is questionable whether he would be a more appropriate mate than Mr. Miles. Charity always makes the most charitable interpretation of Lucius' behavior, and regarding him, "her eyes were so full of light that everything about her was a blur" (176). Even so, she senses early on that their relationship cannot be permanent. The gulf between them, which Charity can never forget, is not only social, having to do with their respective classes and Lucius' life apart in cities, but also intellectual: they can hardly have a conversation beyond the personal because of "her ignorance and her inability to follow his least allusion" (61). If Lucius does not really want to marry Charity, she has qualms about marrying him. "Instead of remaining separate and absolute, she would be compared with other people, and unknown things would be expected of her" (213). This thought occurs to Charity before she learns she is pregnant; a forced marriage, she thinks, would be even worse, would make her and Lucius hate each other. Thus, Charity feels "stripped . . . of her last illusion" (234).

If we cannot imagine Charity happily married to Lucius Harney, what better options does she have? Let us consider the Charity of the beginning of the novel, the rebellious girl who hates everything, before her choices have been limited by pregnancy. She might do any of the following: 1) pursue her education; 2) get a job and become self-supporting; 3) live on the Mountain; 4) marry Royall; 5) marry someone else. Education seems out of the question since Charity hates to read and has already rejected the possibility of going to school. A job is equally unrealistic because "she had never learned any trade that would have given her independence in a strange place, and she knew no one in the big towns of the valley, where she might have hoped to find employment" (159); prostitution is the only available "job." Living on the Mountain with

her outlaw relatives Charity herself discovers as the worst of her
alternatives. Marriage appears the best choice, but to whom? Most
of the men are, like Mr. Miles, already married; there are only a
"few youths" left in the village, all of whom Charity scorns. Eligible
bachelors from other towns do not flock to North Dormer, and
the only one who does appear is beyond her. On the other hand,
Royall is available and wants to marry Charity; if the marriage
seems incestuous, there are at least no legal impediments since he
is not her real father.

When we view Royall solely through Charity's eyes, it is hard
to find him her best choice. Ammons, for instance, calls Royall
an "old man," who is "weak" and "pitiable."[15] Yet there is no
indication that he is really any of these things outside Charity's
mind. In fact, Royall is middle-aged and to the other characters
in the novel, strong and admirable. Lucius considers him "above"
the other townspeople and treats him with deference. The town
chooses him to deliver the Old Home Day address, which is much
respected by the audience; his speech evokes an outburst of cheers
and Mr. Miles's comment, "That was a *man* talking—" (195).
Although Royall is "weak" in the same way as other characters—
that is, prey to sexual urges—he is also capable of more self-control
and sensitive behavior than the others. Thus, in consideration of
Charity's feelings, he can avoid telling Lucius of her origins, offer
to make Lucius marry her, and sleep in a chair on his wedding
night: all actions which reveal a certain delicacy.

If Charity is mistaken about her own superiority, eternal bliss
with Lucius, and freedom on the Mountain, she also has illusions
about Royall, and part of her growth is to see him more clearly.
The typical heroine of the sentimental novel wants the Rochester-
type man as soon as she meets him; her problem is to attract him
and then change him so he suits her better. In *St. Elmo* (1867) the
hero must not only convert to Christianity and repent his sins but
also become a minister before the heroine will have him; the original Rochester, of course, has to be purged of his pride and have
his house burned down and be blinded to boot. The pattern in
Summer is internalized: when at the end of the novel Charity thinks
that "all the dark spirits had gone out of him," Royall himself has
not changed. Charity has merely divested him of the dark spirits
she originally conferred upon him.

Charity's attitude toward Royall changes gradually during the course of the novel. In the beginning she thinks she hates and despises him. Although she knows he will not repeat his attempt to seduce her, she insists on a woman in the house in order to humiliate him. At times she does have some positive feelings toward him; she considers him "superior" and vaguely notices the respect paid to him by others, sometimes even admiring him herself (27). But basically, as she realizes midway in the novel, she has not thought about him as a person:

Except on the occasion of his one offense he had been to her merely the person who is always there, the unquestioned central fact of life. . . . Even then she had regarded him only in relation to herself, and had never speculated as to his own feelings, beyond instinctively concluding that he would not trouble her again in the same way. But now she began to wonder what he was really like.(110–11)

Charity soon loses this insight and reverts to hating Royall. Not until the Old Home Day speech does she pay attention to him and notice how impressive he looks and how musical he sounds. During the speech, Charity realizes later, she "caught a glimpse of another being, a being so different from the dull-witted enemy with whom she had supposed herself to be living that even through the burning mist of her own dreams he had stood out with startling distinctness" (275). Then, however, "the mist of her dreams [i.e. of Lucius] had hidden him again" (276). This "glimpse of another being" comes again to Charity after her marriage. When she realizes that Royall married her knowing she was pregnant and, simultaneously, that he doesn't intend to get in bed with her, she feels "a stir of something deeper than she had ever felt in thinking of him . . . " (284). At this point the dark spirits leave him and Charity is able to address to him "shyly and quickly" the last words of the novel: "I guess you're good too" (291).

What made Charity misperceive Royall in the beginning? Significantly, her most intense feelings of hatred arise in connection with sex, most obviously when Royall invades her bedroom but also on the occasion of the fourth of July festival when he appears with prostitutes and calls her a whore. This episode causes Charity's fledgling attempt to think of him as a person to be "swallowed up in loathing." Her reaction is described entirely in such extremes: Royall made a "disgraceful spectacle" of himself; the "horrible moment" when he entered her bedroom was not just a "mad aberration" but a "vulgar incident in a debauched and degraded life" (158). Not until Old Home Day, that is *after* sex with Lucius, does Charity begin to see Royall in a more balanced way.

There are indications that before her initiation she reacts to Royall as the embodiment of a sexuality that disgusts and attracts her at the same time. However much she thinks she hates or pities or feels indifferent to Royall, he looms large in Charity's consciousness: he is a "magnificent monument of a man" (27) and "much too big" for North Dormer (22). When he proposes to her, he appears "so towering and powerful that he seemed to fill the narrow room" (117). The Rochester-type man is commonly larger than life, and these images of Royall bring to mind Jungian interpretations of nineteenth-century fiction in which the Rochester type is an animus figure representing a sexuality toward which the heroine is profoundly ambivalent.[16]

When Royall tries to seduce Charity, she is repulsed but also "moved." Then, "her heart gave a startled plunge, but she continued to hold him back contemptuously" (29); the "but," instead of "and," suggests that her heart plunges for some reason besides fear. An unacknowledged attraction to Royall would also explain some odd actions on Charity's part: her apparent willingness at the Fourth of July celebration to abandon Lucius and take Royall away from the prostitutes and her refusal to leave Royall to go to school (her stated reason that Royall would be too "lonely" seems a projection since she claims to feel no affection or gratitude toward him).

Charity's fear of sex is not immediately obvious in the novel because she is established so clearly as a sensual being in her response to nature and in the heat imagery which surrounds her. Nothing could have stronger sexual overtones than the passage we have noted where Charity lies in the warm grass listening to the "bubbling of sap and slipping of sheaths and bursting of calyxes" (54). Yet Charity's ecstatic moment is interrupted by a man in the garden; she cries out, "Oh, don't," as a man's muddy boot tramples some frail white flowers. Male presence is an intrusion into Char-

ity's "green world," much as the coming of the hunter disturbs
Sylvie's peace in Sarah Orne Jewett's short story "A White
Heron."[17] Charity avoids sex with men, not only with Royall but
the North Dormer boys (she "had always kept to herself, con-
temptuously aloof from village love-making"—61) and even Lucius
Harney.

Most readers have noticed that Charity is attracted to Lucius
early in the novel. Cynthia Griffin Wolff, for instance, calls Charity's view of Lucius "inescapably phallic."[18] Wolff points out that
she admires his long slim fingers and one evening stands outside
his room watching him unbutton his shirt and reveal "the vigorous
lines of his young throat, and the root of muscles where they joined
the chest" (103). Yet this "phallic" glimpse *scares* Charity: she
looks at Lucius "with a kind of terror, as if he had been a stranger."
She decides not to reveal her presence, even at the risk of losing
him, because she "suddenly understood what would happen if she
went in. It was the thing that *did* happen between young men and
girls, and that North Dormer ignored in public and snickered over
on the sly" (105). Charity resists the "thing" that she cannot bring
herself to name as long as she possibly can, even though she knows
she can't avoid it forever—when she discovers that North Dormer
thinks she is already sexually involved, she recalls the muddy boot
crushing the white flowers (118). Finally Lucius insists, and "her
dream of *comradeship* was over" (160; my italics).

As is the case with many of Charity's dreams, the loss of the
dream of comradeship without sexual activity has some positive
results. In the novel of seduction illicit sex inevitably leads to
pregnancy, but in a sense Wharton turns the seduction novel on
its head; if the pattern is the same, the meaning differs. "Seduction" means growth for Charity as well as diminution. One cannot
imagine Charlotte Temple enjoying sex with Montraville, but
Charity Royall gets some pleasure before her comeuppance. Once
initiated she burns happily. Although "she had always thought of
love [i.e. sex] as something confused and furtive," it turns out
"bright and open as the summer air" (180).

Charity's initiation also affects her attitude toward Royall. He
is no longer a sexual spectre looming larger than life, and he may
be able to take Lucius' place. In discussing Rochester and Jane
Eyre in *The Madwoman in the Attic*, Sandra Gilbert and Susan

Gubar suggest that Rochester's sexual knowledge prevents an equal relationship. "The prince is inevitably Cinderella's superior, Charlotte Brontë saw, not because his rank is higher than hers, but because it is *he* who will initiate *her* into the mysteries of the flesh."[19] Wharton cannot imagine Charity and Royall as equals, but at least Charity's knowledge makes her more equal and provides some hope for the future of their marriage.

According to Cynthia Griffin Wolff, Charity's understanding of her sexual nature constitutes an "essential step in the journey toward maturity."[20] Wolff interprets the novel as a *Bildungsroman* in which the heroine grows successfully to adulthood.

Charity concludes the novel as she has begun it, at the threshold of the Royall home; but she can enter now out of choice, with the knowledge of maturity to guide her. In order to come back 'for good,' one must go away for a while. That is the dictum of adolescent growth.[21]

In her optimistic reading of *Summer* Wolff emphasizes the metaphor of the seasons. Just as adolescence constitutes one stage of life, summer is only one period in a complete year. Passage to autumn is natural and inevitable; if autumn brings cold and dark, it also holds the promise of renewal in spring. Marilyn French, who also finds the end of the novel positive, puts it this way: "Summer is over. But she has her baby growing within her; she has her intense immersion in natural beauty, her proud stubborn spirit, her dawning awareness that there is good in Royall. Spring will return."[22]

The Wolff/French interpretation of *Summer* is a long way from Elizabeth Ammons' view, which we considered earlier—that Wharton portrays the marriage as "depressing" and "sick" and fills the end of the novel with "images of spiritual paralysis and death." However, it is not surprising to find totally opposite readings because Wharton presents a double perspective on her heroine's experience. Yes, there is good in Royall but he is also paternalistic. Yes, the relationship seems incestuous but it also has positive potential. If marriage to Royall is Charity's best option, we applaud her learning to take it; yet what kind of world allows women such limited choices in the first place?

Charity grows in the course of the novel: as we have seen, she comes to terms with her sexuality; she learns to perceive more accurately, clearing away "the mist of her dreams"; she begins to see other people, such as the North Dormer girls and Royall, as people and empathize with them. In shedding her earlier narcissism, Charity becomes more truly Good than her nineteenth-century predecessors who simply got more pious. But at the same time that she grows Charity is also being reduced. She is trapped in North Dormer; she once went "winging through the forest" and then suffers a "broken wing" (280). The diminished Charity ends up a tired child, a Good Girl in the old sense of submission and dependence. This Charity has "the feeling that if she ceased to keep close to him [Royall], and do what he told her to do, the world would slip away from beneath her feet" (277). The charity case has won the royal prince—but will do what he tells her. Or, alternatively, the charity case is reduced to obedience—but at least she gets a prince instead of a frog.

It is instructive to compare the end of *Summer* with the end of Augusta Evans Wilson's *St. Elmo*, one of the best-selling nineteenth-century novels referred to earlier. *St. Elmo* also concludes with a wedding. The heroine, Edna Earl, gets the prince she has wanted all through the novel—a chastened St. Elmo who has reformed and become a minister. Edna's wedding day should be a joyful occasion; she considers marriage to St. Elmo "the crowning glory and richest blessing of her life." However, at the close of the ceremony, she "lost all consciousness" and, upon recovery, "laid her head down on the altar-railing, and sobbed like a child."[23] The ambivalence in this scene is clearly unconscious on the part of the author: we are to believe in the "happy ending," just as we are to believe that Jo March is better off giving up writing and marrying Professor Bhaer. In her study of nineteenth-century women's fiction Nina Baym says the novelists viewed marriage as a positive conclusion to the story of a young girl who has to win her own way in the world.

This young girl is fittingly called a heroine because her role is precisely analogous to the unrecognized or undervalued youths of fairy tales who perform dazzling exploits and win a place for themselves in the land of happy endings. She also fits the pattern of the comic hero, whose displacement indicates social corruption and whose triumph ensures the reconstruction of a beneficent social order. In Jungian perspective, her story exemplifies the difficult but successful negotiation of the undifferentiated child through the trials of adolescence into the individuation of sound adulthood. The happy marriages with which most . . . of this fiction concludes are symbols of successful accomplishment of the required task. . . . [24]

Yet in *St. Elmo* and in numerous other cases the heroine seems animated by her struggle and not her reward; she grows and shrinks, ending up a child rather than an adult. In the nineteenth century, when the novelist was not supposed to explore her heroine's deeper feelings, she had to rely, consciously or unconsciously, on some correlative. A heroine could not say, or even know, she wanted freedom—she let a bird out of a cage; she could not express any doubts about marriage as her "crowning glory"—she fainted at the altar. In the twentieth century, as the heroine's inner life is opened up, the underside of the essentially optimistic nineteenth-century plot is plainly exposed. Edith Wharton elevates this "underplot"—the shrinkage of the girl, the unchanging corruption of the social order—to parallel importance with the main plot, the positive growth as described by Baym. In novels of adolescence after *Summer*, the underplot will come to overshadow the basic nineteenth-century story altogether.

Summer is a transitional novel in other ways. If Wharton uses nineteenth-century plot conventions, transforming them in the process, she adopts a narrative stance midway between Louisa May Alcott, with her hand on the little women's shoulders, and the modern novelist of adolescence whose presence is markedly unobtrusive. As we have observed, Wharton creates distance from Charity Royall and occasionally provides ironic commentary on her character and situation; however, the focus is on Charity's consciousness and we see mainly from her point of view. The "teachery Sunday school attitude" Ruth Suckow disliked has subsided. There is reason to ponder Suckow's other complaint about the models available to her, that the traditional heroine is a "fearful tomb of 'female virtue' " who is always "chastened by suffering at the end."[25] Although Charity's copy of *The Lamplighter* is falling apart and the contents seem irrelevant to a modern girl, she does end up like Gertie Flint, having "learned submission."[26] But in no way is Charity a tomb of female virtue; she represents a departure from the Good Good Girl tradition. As we will see, in the modern novel of adolescence, even in the works of Suckow herself, the Good Bad or Bad Bad heroine often gets chastened in the end. Ruth Suckow's own fiction of adolescence differs from Wharton's *Summer* less in the nature and fate of its typical heroine than in the treatment of her inner world. Wharton stresses the intensity of her protagonist's feelings—the hot passions that are cooled when they come into conflict with society's expectations of women. In Suckow the major conflict occurs within the heroine and is given form through her relationship with her family. Charity Royall is separated from her parents at age five; like most of her nineteenth-century predecessors, she is essentially an orphan. But Suckow's heroines always have families, usually with both parents intact, and the figures of mother and father dominate their attempts to move from child to adult.

As I noted in Chapter II, the "new psychology" of the 1920's contributed to the development of the novel of adolescence. The discovery of the unconscious promoted an emphasis on inner life, and Freudian insights about childhood and adolescence affected the portrayal of family relationships. In *Freudianism and the Literary Mind*, Frederick Hoffman notes that "such terms as the oedipus complex and the electra complex became watch words for writers whose province had always been the field of domestic relationships. . . . The novelists gave their family portraits undeniably Freudian qualities."[27] Ruth Suckow was one of these writers. Although as a feminist she often differed with the psychoanalysts and modified their conclusions, she pioneered in introducing Freudian theory to the novel of adolescence.

NICE GIRLS AND THEIR FOLKS: THE ADOLESCENT AND THE FAMILY IN RUTH SUCKOW'S FICTION

IV

Ruth Suckow was America's first important novelist of adolescence. In literary histories she is classified as a midwestern "regionalist" who contributed realistic portraits of her native Iowa. However, her true subject was the middle-class family, in particular the relationship of children and parents within the family. Adolescent characters appear in all eight of Suckow's novels and in many of her short stories and novelettes. Female adolescents predominate in the novels we will be most concerned with in this chapter: *The Odyssey of a Nice Girl* (1925); *The Bonney Family* (1928); *Cora* (1929); and *The Folks* (1934). With the possible exception of *The Folks*, none of these novels is remembered today, but at the height of her career in the 1920's and 30's Suckow was considered a leading novelist. Her work received favorable reviews and high praise from such writers as H. L. Mencken, Sinclair Lewis, and Robert Frost. By the time of her death in 1960, Suckow had been consigned to the limbo of regionalism, and her fiction is only now being rediscovered.[1]

The protagonist of Suckow's first novel of adolescence, *The Odyssey of a Nice Girl*, has much in common with Edith Wharton's Charity Royall. Marjorie Schoessel is waiting for something to happen to her, for her "real life" to begin.[2] Like Charity, she holds herself above the other girls in town, set apart for "some vague splendour" (13). She dreams of marrying the president or an English lord. These projected marriages are sexless; like Charity, Marjorie resists any sexual advances from the local boys. If Charity's only clear ambition is to escape her "prison house" in the sleepy town of North Dormer, Massachusetts, Marjorie's is to leave her small-town Iowa birthplace with its ironic name of Buena Vista. Marjorie also finds her home a "prison" (315), and she gradually focuses her dreams on going away to school. But while Charity Royall is an orphan, Marjorie has a family that stands in her way. Her parents urge her brother to attend college but have no such plan in mind for her. Marjorie thinks, "They didn't want her to go away from them. They were proud of her—but they thought that what she wanted to do didn't really matter" (141).

Buena Vista proves almost as difficult to escape as North Dormer. It takes Marjorie a year after her high school graduation to convince her parents to let her go to Boston. College is out, but Boston is "where all the very nicest girls in Buena Vista had gone, to study music, or expression, or physical culture" (150). After studying "expression," Marjorie wants to get a job in London but accedes to her parents' expectation that she return home to live. She finally makes another break, to work as a typist in Chicago, but is soon summoned home to care for her ailing mother. She feels resentful: "They would not have asked the boys to give up their work and come home because mamma was ill" (286).

The conflict between family ties and development of self is a major theme in all Suckow's novels. The strength of this theme probably accounts in large part for H. L. Mencken's patronage of Suckow. Mencken no doubt recognized that the patriarchal family she portrays is not limited to her native Iowa but is the general type of the farm/village/town bourgeois family he so despised.[3] This family is controlled by the father: he makes the family plans without consultation and exacts from his wife and children hard work, thrift, industry, piety, and obedience; he has little tolerance for opposition, which he calls "weakness" or "emotionalism." The mother is timid and resigned, having submerged her identity in marriage; sometimes her personality, "smothered and silent for many years," makes a faint "blossoming" after the children grow up.[4]

The role of the children and adolescents in this scheme is to obey their parents, especially the father, and perform their "duty" to the family. Boys must find financial security in a job (girls in their husband's job) and raise their financial status higher than their parents' without moving too far away geographically, mentally, and morally from "the folks." The generations which come of age before the 1920's seldom oppose the familial plan: boys willingly become their fathers; girls either marry quickly or contract a mysterious illness like Eliza Wharton's in *The Coquette*. The later generations put up some resistance. Marjorie Schoessel, Cora Schweitert, all the adolescents in *The Bonney Family*, Carl and Margaret Ferguson of *The Folks*—all make some effort to "get away" from the family and "do something."[5]

But the attempts of Suckow's adolescents to grow beyond their Buena Vistas often fail. Carl Ferguson, like Marjorie, wants to leave home for the East where he thinks he could at last begin to "be himself."[6] Carl never pursues his dream. He will not cut his ties to the family; he cannot "stand the severed pain of growing beyond the roots of his early affections" (210). Carl, however, breaks away to the extent of attending college away from home, moving to a larger Iowa town, taking over the position of superintendent of schools, and becoming head of his own family. Carl cannot bring himself to disappoint the folks' expectations of him, but, because he is male, their expectations allow him a wider range. Girls are lucky if they are permitted to attend a hometown college or spend a year or two as country schoolteacher before getting married. Sometimes when a girl wants only to make an early marriage and be transferred from one family situation to another, she cannot escape the physical bounds of her parental home. Tradition demands that girls sacrifice themselves for the family.

Two of the short stories in *Iowa Interiors* (1926) concern women who have used up their youth caring for their invalid mothers. Suckow's novelette "The Best of the Lot" is about a country girl who foregoes a teaching job and a chance to marry in order to care for her parents. After their death she is left alone and poverty-stricken with the sole occupation of keeping up the family graves. Georgie Kramer of *The Kramer Girls* (1930), a young woman of unusual intellect and stamina, has to relinguish her goal of becoming a doctor in order to nurse her paralytic mother. Even in the novels where girls have escaped home for a time, they are often, like Marjorie Schoessel, recalled to care for an ailing parent.

Suckow suggests that the restriction of young women is repeated in a seemingly endless progression. It is "handed down" from generation to generation. In "The Best of the Lot" she notes, in referring to widows with large families, that

each one had providentially one daughter left to her for her sole benefit. It was so nice for the mothers, everyone said sympathetically. 'Such a comfort to her that she has Mary.' These women had led the average lives, with the average mixture of pleasure and joy in their sorrows; but still it was felt that, as women and mothers, a 'comfort' was due each of them.[7]

Apparently these women believe they are entitled to some "comfort" because they themselves had been held back in their youths.

Suckow refers frequently to the desire of matrons to "claim" adolescent girls to women's estate. Georgie Kramer seethes with anger when her sister Rose returns home for a visit and the women of the town try to discourage her from returning to her job in Chicago. They

seemed to Georgie to take a kind of ancient delight in having got Rose down among them again, in proving that all her work and training went for nothing, that she was just a woman like the rest of them and her place was in the home.[8]

It is wrong to conclude, as some critics do, that because her female characters do not leave home readily, Suckow believes "women's place is in the home."[9] Instead, Suckow tries to show that, no matter how strong a girl's urge for self-development, family tradition conspires to keep her at home.

Rose Kramer turns out to need little encouragement to leave Chicago and marry an Iowa boy, for she has a routine job rather than a satisfying career. If Suckow's heroines manage to overcome tradition and set out on their own, they encounter discrimination against women in the outside world. When Marjorie Schoessel takes the typing job in Chicago, she is initially happy to be in a big city "earning her own living—free" (282). But she can hardly ignore the boredom of the job, the low pay, the necessity to pretend to worship her boss, the "helpless, hurt look" she sees in the eyes of the other office women. Suckow remarks, with some asperity, "If she stayed years and years, thinking of nothing else, making this one little job her life, she would have achieved a humble, small, feminine place for herself" (284). Ironically, Marjorie is no more "free" than she was at home. The job "opened no vistas, but closed them instead, and penned her into its own tiny, hard, methodical world" (284).

Suckow compares the prospects of a boy and a girl who try to earn their own way in her accounts of Gerald Rayburn in "The Man of the Family" and Daisy Switzer in "A Start in Life." The adolescent protagonists of these short stories begin in the same position. Their fathers have recently died, and they are obliged to go to work. Both feel important in their new role but reluctant to give up school and play. Gerald's first day as a drug store clerk brings him, in his view, ample compensation. When he returns home from work, he washes his hands in the kitchen, drinks coffee, and gets the larger share of the family supper—all privileges once claimed by his father. At the end of the story Gerald turns away his mother's prospective suitor. "He was man of the house now. Art Fox could stay at home where he belonged."[10] Gerald's mother meekly accepts her son's authority, but his indignant sister protests that Gerald "thinks he's so smart now just because he's starting in to work. . . . You'd just think he *owned* us to hear the way he talks" (166). As new "man of the family," Gerald has gained power and privilege.

In contrast to Gerald's, Daisy's first day of work brings misery. Her gender requires that she be transferred from one family to another; she is to live with a young farm couple as hired help. At first Daisy feels proud and enthusiastic about her new position, but she soon learns her "place." "She sensed something different in the atmosphere than she had ever known before—some queer difference between the position of herself and of the two babies."[11] Although with her younger sisters and brothers Daisy had been "the boss," she must now do the bidding of the two young children; her status is even lower than theirs. Moreover, the farm couple treat her as an outsider and make no attempt to include her in their activities because they consider her a "homely" girl. While Gerald's new responsibility brings him privilege and self-esteem, Daisy's leads to reduced status and humiliation.

The attempt of Suckow's adolescent girls to grow up is fraught with difficulty. Parents are supported by all the force of social tradition in their effort to keep their daughters dependents within the home. If the girls can summon courage to part from their families, they often find themselves even more powerless to direct their own destinies; Daisy and Marjorie find that leaving home and earning money may lead not to "freedom" but to worse bondage. In all Suckow's fiction, however, the external barriers to escape from Buena Vista are less important than the internal barriers. Wharton's Charity Royall has nowhere to go from North Dormer, but she is singleminded in her desire to escape. Suckow's heroines are divided in their desires: even as they seek independence and new experience, they are attracted to the safety of home. While Charity "hates everything" about North Dormer, Marjorie has to contend with the "treacherous clinging love of home" which she senses may "spoil her shining future of Europe and travel and art and beauty" (266).

In her treatment of Iowa's Buena Vistas, Ruth Suckow is less heavily satirical than the typical "revolt from the village" writer patronized by H. L. Mencken, and her matter-of-fact realistic treatment of her material provides some advantages. It is not always clear why, if the farm/village/town of the twenties was truly so ghastly to its young inhabitants, and their main barrier was filial duty, more of them did not break away. Why do we have so few Lulu Betts and George Willards and so many youthful Babbitts? One of Suckow's strengths is her honest portrayal of the attractions of the bourgeois family. The awesome power which the family exercises over the adolescent is shown as internalized not only in the form of guilt, as with Sherwood Anderson's George Willard, but also in the form of attraction to the very things the young person would reject.

At the same time that Marjorie Schoessel hates her parents' house as "so familiar, so little and confining—as if she could break the walls in her hands," she also "loves" it (315). Suckow, who often invests domestic items with symbolic significance, makes the furnishings of Marjorie's room symbolize the attractions of home. When Marjorie is twelve or thirteen, her furniture gives her status with her girl friends. The girls do not look to nature for a sense of belonging as Charity Royall does; they turn to material possessions, striving to own the "prettiest" things. Because Marjorie's father runs a furniture store, she has the nicest room and can compete for leadership of her crowd. Marjorie is so entranced with her possessions she sometimes makes a ceremony of touching each piece of furniture in her room. When her parents give her a new furniture set for high school graduation, Marjorie wants to "stroke" it, even "eat" it—"she scarcely knew what" (128). But this gift has strings attached—the Schoessels intend it to keep her at home. The furniture is so expensive that Marjorie feels she cannot ask her parents to send her away to school for the coming year.

It was her new bedroom furniture that was responsible for the compromise. It stood there, mute unanswerable witness to all that papa and mamma had done for her, all the things they had given her. . . . Once she ran up to her room for the express purpose of standing and declaring to her own self that she *hated* the furniture, wished she didn't have it . . . but when she was actually standing there, her clenched hands relaxed, and the eyes which she saw in the glass looked hurt and softened. She could not harden her heart to reproach and defy her Circassian walnut. (142–43)

The depth of Marjorie's ambivalence is revealed in this description: she is not simply one person who both loves and hates the furniture but one self which looks at it with mixed emotions and another self which is actually reflected in the furniture (in the mirror of her dresser set).

When Marjorie finally reaches Boston to study at the speech academy, her inability to make a real break from Buena Vista is again symbolized by her thoughts of her room at home. Marjorie tries to adopt the opinions of her new friend Emily who scorns everything "bourgeois" and takes her to feminist and anarchist meetings. But Marjorie fears that if she really accepts these new doctrines, and if she accompanies Emily to London to start a career, "she would have to live in some dreadful place with dirty sheets" (242). She contrasts this "dreadful place" with her own room with its crisp curtains and white bedspreads "whiter than things had ever seemed to be [in Boston]—a special kind of whiteness that meant home" (224). Taken on the literal level, Marjorie's thoughts are ridiculously naive, but on a symbolic level they are meaningful. Marjorie's white linen and drapery and her expensive furniture stand for social status, material comfort, "purity," order, security—all the things that her family and the town of Buena Vista represent and that would be threatened by her venturing into the world.

If Boston was not quite white, Chicago is dark and dirty; there Marjorie has to settle for "a small dingy room with a broken-down wicker lounge" (283). Thus, when she is summoned home to nurse her mother she feels relieved as well as resentful. The other girls who are called home to take care of a sick parent react the same way; they resent the sacrifice on principle—why are their brothers exempt?—but are happy to be with their families and willing to trade an inferior position in the outside world for a position of some importance in the home.

During this period Suckow's adolescents abandon their dreams of a "shining future" and return to their childhoods. Marjorie broods over her childhood. She thinks, concerning herself and her friend Jessie, "Their childhood seemed real, but their grownup selves queerly distorted" (307). Marjorie is not merely nostalgic but feels as though she is actually "still a child" (288). Sarah Bonney of *The Bonney Family*, also recalled from Chicago during her mother's illness, feels warm and sheltered at home, and her childhood is "always mingling with the present and getting in the way of it" (237). Sarah tells herself, "How queer it was that childhood should seem all the time only a preparation—a prologue—and then, afterwards, the only part of life that was wholly real!" (285).

For Marjorie and Sarah childhood seems more "real" because it was a time when, dependent though they were, they still perceived themselves as "subjects," to use Simone de Beauvoir's term. De Beauvoir states:

Throughout her childhood the little girl suffered bullying and curtailment of activity; but none the less she felt herself to be an autonomous individual. In her relations with family and friends, in her schoolwork and her games, she seemed at the time a transcendent being: her future passivity was only a dream.[12]

Once Suckow's young protagonists leave home and find that being a grown woman requires some "queer distortion of self" they tend to seek the childhood they earlier tried to escape. From puberty on, they vacillate between childhood and adulthood.

Suckow uses various methods to depict this vacillation. On the level of plot she has her adolescent heroines forever shuttling back and forth between Bostons and Buena Vistas: they leave home, return, leave again. She relies on symbolic devices like Marjorie's furniture to expose the "treacherous clinging love of home" that conflicts with the girls' more openly expressed rejection of family and small-town values. But to portray a more deep-seated ambivalence within her adolescent characters, one she saw embodied in their emotional relationship with their parents, Suckow turned to the "new psychology" of her day.

One reader, commenting in the 1930's on Suckow's work, was delighted to find that

some books actually show that family relationships can be normal. To those of us who have come to believe that every son is suffering from an Oedipus complex and every daughter from an Electra complex . . . to such of us, books like Ruth Suckow's *Country People* (1924), *The Bonney Family* (1928), and *The Folks* (1934) . . . come as agreeable surprises.[13]

Yet we have already encountered one rather odd relationship between a boy and his mother: Gerald Rayburn in "The Man of the Family" takes his father's place to the extent of breaking up an incipient romance of his mother's. Carl Ferguson of *The Folks* also resents any attention his mother gives other men, and his sister Margaret competes for her father's favor. Cora Schwietert of *Cora* considers her parents' bedroom "a little stronghold from which their children were excluded" and feels "shut out and angry and lost."[14]

Family relationships in Suckow's fiction are quiet and understated but never "normal" in the sense of being free from Freudian echoes. We do not know how early in her career Suckow was influenced by Freud. Her view of child-parent relationships, even her perception of the centrality of childhood and adolescence and the importance of motives and impulses beneath the surface, may have been shaped with Freudian theory in mind. On the other hand, she may have formed her basic ideas from childhood memories and independent observation in her youth.[15] But by 1927 at the very latest Suckow was familiar with psychoanalytic thought.

In that year she published an essay on *Elsie Dinsmore* claiming that Elsie suffers from both an "inferiority complex" and an "Electra complex." These terms also begin to appear in Suckow's fiction, along with "sublimation," "frustration," and "neurosis."[16] Sometimes she refers to Freud directly; for instance, she has Carl Ferguson recognize in a moment of introspection that "part of him was closed in that early life [his childhood]. . . . He had always tried to sneer at what he roughly called 'those Freudian ideas'. . . . But now he felt some thrust of bitter truth" (210–11).

The bitter truth Carl senses is that he suffers from an "Oedipus complex." Freud used the term to designate a phase in a boy's growth where he develops an erotic attachment to his mother and regards his father as a rival whom he would like to supplant. At this point the "castration complex" intervenes. The boy, who has earlier noticed that girls lack penises and feared losing his, now fears his father will punish him by castration. Since the boy scorns the "castrated" girl and does not want to be like her, he represses his desire for his mother. According to psychoanalytic theory, the Oedipal conflict takes place in a boy's childhood, somewhere between four and six years of age, and then recurs during adolescence.[17]

If the Oedipus complex is not "smashed to pieces" by the threat of castration, the boy carries a residue to adulthood.[18] This is the situation Suckow presents in her portrayal of Carl Ferguson. Carl's childhood attachment to his mother contains an erotic element: "He leaned fondly against her. He was always demonstrative with her when they chanced to be alone together" (9). Carl feels uneasy with his father; in adolescence he considers trying to improve their distant relationship "but it seemed as if all kinds of things stood between them. They could both talk to mother, but they couldn't talk much to each other, not when they were alone" (133). Carl meets several girls to whom he is sexually attracted but feels guilty about his feelings and decides the girls are "bad." He eventually marries the cold and puritanical Lillian who does not threaten his relationship with his mother. When the adult Carl hugs his mother, "there was a kind of hunger and straining in his embrace that both moved and disturbed his mother." In attempt to deny the force of "those Freudian ideas," Carl then hugs Lillian too. "Lillian tried nervously to draw away, but Carl wouldn't let her, forcing her to believe that what he had given his mother he gave her—and himself to believe it too" (174–75). In the prescriptive language of Freud Carl has "failed" to "resolve" his Oedipal conflict. However, Suckow reverses the values assigned by psychoanalysts in their discussion of the Oedipus complex. She portrays Carl Ferguson much more sympathetically than Warren Bonney, who overcomes his complex in adolescence and becomes insensitive and boorish as a result. Warren is introduced as a shy fourteen year old whose only close relationship is with his mother. To her he pours out his fears and humiliations, his self-consciousness about his awkward body and his hurt at being unpopular in school. Miserable as Warren feels, he consoles himself with the thought that he is at least superior to women. He considers girls "unreasonable and soft and weak"; they are intellectually inferior and "oughtn't to be in school with the men" (73). Warren has special contempt for "homely women," who are "simply futile, not on the map at all" (82). Interestingly, Warren does not include his mother in his classification: "He set his mother apart and never really thought of her as a woman" (82).

Warren finally resolves his Oedipus complex at summer camp after his first year of college. When he manages to kiss a pretty girl, he feels "suddenly masterful and exultant." He is "exultant over her submission. All at once he seemed to break those old straining bonds and to stand free and triumphant" (135). This "sense of change, of transfiguration" is lasting. When he returns home, Warren fits in with his classmates and becomes a popular campus leader. His relationship with his mother has changed—he now takes to "teasingly" bossing her around (153). At first, Warren feels "almost ashamed" of his new position (142), but later in the novel we are given a glimpse of him as a conventional self-satisfied college professor who tyrannizes over his "faded" and "worn out" wife (256). In her account of Warren's development Suckow emphasizes the power he gains. He becomes "masterful" and "triumphant" at a girl's "submission"; he can then boss his mother and later his wife. Warren overcomes his Oedipus complex when he accepts power over women.

Suckow uses Freudian ideas much in the manner of contemporary feminist theorists—as metaphors rather than literal truths. Her characterization of Warren's Oedipal conflict has much in common, for instance, with Shulamith Firestone's restatement of Freud. According to Firestone, the adolescent boy is persuaded to break his attachment to his mother and identify with his father by

the offer of the world when he grows up. He is asked to make a transition from the state of the powerless, women and children, to the state of the potentially powerful, son (ego extension) of his father. . . . It is no wonder that such a transition leaves an emotional residue, a 'complex.' The male child, in order to save his own hide, has had to abandon and betray his mother and join ranks with her oppressor. He feels guilty. His emotions toward women in general are affected.[19]

Warren succeeds better than Carl in making the transition, and he feels guilty; omitting his mother from the category "women" was clearly an attempt to allay the guilt of identifying with men as superior to women. However, Warren, unlike Carl, who cannot quite "abandon" his mother, moves from feeling guilty to "almost ashamed" to self-satisfied.

Suckow treats the Oedipus complex (and the "Electra complex," as we shall see) not as universal and biologically determined growth phases but as logical results of the patriarchal family structure she portrays. Thus Carl Ferguson and Warren Bonney naturally prefer their mothers because their mothers nurture them and their fathers pay them little attention. Carl perceives his mother's love as unconditional and his father's as based on what he accomplishes; he feels "hurt" that "dad wasn't completely confident of him, as mother was" (131). If the "Oedipus complex" seems inevitable under the circumstances, so does the "castration complex." Both Carl and Warren have ample opportunity to observe their father's greater power within the family and his wider access to the outside world. Furthermore, they learn that they are favored over their sisters just because they are boys: more is expected of them and more is offered. Fear of "castration" (loss of power) becomes a strong inducement to overcoming attachment to mother.

Girls' "castration complex" is a different story. According to Freud, it arises prior to the Electra complex and may or may not be resolved by it. The young girl starts out close to her mother but soon discovers that she lacks a penis and thinks she has been castrated; as a result she feels inferior and hostile toward her mother. As Freud puts it, "The situation as a whole is not very clear [!], but it can be seen that in the end the girl's mother, who sent her into the world so insufficiently equipped, is almost always held responsible for her lack of a penis."[20] It is more difficult for girls to conquer the castration complex than for boys to master the Oedipus complex. The best the girl can do is develop an Electra complex where she replaces her desire for a penis with a desire for a child. In hope of getting a child from her father, she takes him as love-object and becomes jealous of her mother. If in later life the girl has a baby (male, of course) she may be able to view it as a penis substitute and transfer her suppressed ambitions to the baby boy.[21]

Ruth Suckow's adolescent heroines are all, when first introduced, closely attached to their mothers, and they all exhibit "penis envy." But Suckow treats "penis envy," in the way of most female psychoanalysts, as a metaphor: what the girls envy is not the male organ but the status society accords the male person.[22] Most adolescent girls in Suckow's fiction have brothers of whom they are jealous. As we have seen, they are bitterly aware that their brothers will go away to college, their brothers will find decent paying jobs, their brothers will not have to interrupt their lives to nurse a parent. Marjorie Schoessel particularly resents her brother's greater freedom of movement; he can leave the house without reporting to his parents, whereas Marjorie, as a girl and especially a "nice girl," is closely watched. Sarah and Wilma Bonney and Margaret Ferguson brood over their parents' seeming preference for their brothers; they believe their mothers especially "side with" the boys and consider them more significant than the girls.

Some of Suckow's minor characters thereby reject their mothers as objects of their love and enter into the Electra complex stage. There is Wilma Bonney, for example, who "adored her father, and had always held him as an ally against her mother" (244). The only major character Suckow portrays with a full-fledged Electra complex is Margaret Ferguson of *The Folks*. As a child Margaret adores her mother but nurses a secret grievance against her. She thinks her mother favors her brother Carl because he is a boy and her sister Dorothy because she is blonde. The dark Margaret per-

ceives Dorothy to be "in secret feminine league with her mother"
(12) and eventually turns to her father for approval.

In adolescence Margaret indulges in what Freud calls the "family
romance"—she rejects her real parents and imagines she has been
adopted. She tries to

imagine the kind of parents it seemed to her she must really have had
instead of just the folks. . . . She wanted a father who adored her, like
those artist fathers in books—the mother had conveniently died at the
birth of the child, who was so exactly like her that the father would turn
pale. (306)

It is hard to conceive of a fantasy which more clearly follows the
pattern of the Electra complex: Margaret has done away with the
mother and gained sole love of the father.

In reality, Margaret's father is a conventional middle-class businessman, and she never succeeds in winning his love and acceptance. Her expulsion from school (for helping a classmate elope)
leads to what she interprets as actual rejection by her father.

The things that dad had said to her . . . were cut deep into Margaret's
memory in a bleeding pain. She felt that she could never have a father
again. But she was frightened of being in the world without one. She
imagined herself leaning her head against a big strong chest . . . a deep
voice telling her indulgently that he would look after her. (306)

At this point in the novel Suckow abandons Margaret to trace the
fates of other family members. When she returns to Margaret's
story, she makes Margaret twenty-five and just leaving home for
New York. It is instructive to follow Margaret in her twenties and
thirties because her life is portrayed as dependent upon her adolescent emotions toward the family.

In Greenwich Village Margaret lives a bohemian existence; she
is rechristened "Margot" by her new friends and considers herself
reborn. She has broken from her family, supports herself, enters
freely into sexual affairs, and generally seems to lead an independent life. Margaret scorns traditional female roles, including
wifehood. "Regular marriage meant being like the folks, presenting a united front to the world, neither one doing as he or she

wanted to do" (307). Marriage is for women like her mother and sister—" 'womanly' women, who were nothing on their own, made out of a rib of man, or pretending that they were so made to keep the man happily conceited" (406). But Margaret is hardly a feminist. She refuses to identify with the "career women" she meets for fear of being "unloved" by men. In fact, Margaret never has the slightest involvement in any job or career she has, in any ideas, arts, sciences, or social movements. It is not that she lacks ability, but her energy has been diverted into one channel; her sole interest is in competing with other women for men's love.

After several amatory triumphs over blonde women (repetitions of her adolescent situation, with herself coming out on top over her mother and sister), Margaret falls for an older man named Bruce. In her eyes Bruce outstrips her previous lovers because he is middle-aged, a businessman rather than a bohemian, and married: in other words, he more closely resembles Margaret's father. Bruce also fits the description of the father Margaret has always wanted. "Strong" and "indulgent," he fondly "scolds" her and "looks after" her, often calling her his "little girl" (401, 403). As Margaret's ideal man it is necessary that Bruce already be married, for now she can imagine his wife as the Eve type, her traditional rival. Margaret identifies with Lilith and concludes that "Through his love for her, she had triumphed finally over Eve immemorial— as somehow she had always felt that it was her destiny to do. . . . Bruce was the kind of man who, until now, had always belonged to the enemy" (421–22). Margaret feels cured of the old wounds of her childhood (422).

But Margaret's triumph is short-lived. If she first believes she can "rule" Bruce (399), she soon realizes that he holds the power in the relationship. She finds herself unable to leave him even though he insists that she take second place to his wife and family. As one critic notes, "Ironically, Margot is doomed to accept the ancient feminine role she has scorned, but without the solacing honor of wifehood."[23] Margaret Ferguson's story abounds in ironies. Although she is the only one of Suckow's adolescent heroines to make a permanent break from the family, she ends up the least independent; her well-being, her very existence as Margot, depends on male love and approval. And, while the intensity of

Margaret's rebellion has led readers to label her "pathological" and "devoid of normal instincts,"[24] her development actually follows what Freud considered the "normal" female route.

In her portrayal of Margaret Ferguson, Suckow adopts the Electra complex model without much variation: indeed, to modern readers her use of the Electra and Oedipus complexes may often seem simplistic. The important change she makes is her interpretation of the meaning of the "complexes." What to Freud seemed the "proper," "normal," "positive"[25] way of development for boys and girls she presents in a negative light.

Margaret Ferguson, with her classic "Electra complex," is actually an exception in Suckow's fiction; she is the only major character to conform to the pattern. In her treatment of other adolescent heroines, Suckow departs from the Freudian model altogether. The other girls never do reject their mothers. Although they envy their brothers and resent the low status of women, they do not, either in childhood or at puberty, transfer their affections to their fathers in preparation for relationships with other men. Marjorie Schoessel, Sarah Bonney, and Cora Schwietert all retain the close childhood tie to the mother, though they are often ambivalent in their attachment. Suckow's portrayal of their adolescence anticipates the emphasis of many female psychoanalytic writers on the difficulty of separation from the mother. As Nancy Chodorow puts it: "Girls cannot and do not 'reject' their mother and women in favor of their father and men." In relation to their mothers most adolescent girls

experience themselves as overly attached, unindividuated, and without boundaries. . . . Adolescent girls in our society tend to remain attached to their mothers. . . . because their mother is their primary caretaker. Her father has never presented himself to a girl with the same force as her mother. He . . . therefore cannot, finally, counteract his daughter's primary identification with and attachment to her mother.[26]

Marjorie Schoessel's father remains a background figure in her life: "He had always been there, going quietly about his work, supplying what was needed, back of all that she and mamma had ever done . . . " (324). It is Marjorie's intense love for her mother that interferes in her struggle for autonomy. Going to London, she realizes, would mean that she could not see her mother when she wished (159); her friend Emily "could talk of being independent and doing what *she* thought and not what other people thought. But Emily had only a stepmother—she did not have mamma" (247). Marjorie can hardly protest when her mother informs her that nice girls do not live unprotected in big cities. "Marjorie set her lips rebelliously. But mamma was so dear with her soft dark hair and slender girlish shoulders in the checked lavender house dress. Marjorie leaned over and daintily kissed mamma's little chin" (229).

At the same time that she chafes at the restrictions placed on a "nice girl," Marjorie loves and models herself after her mother's own "nice girl" aspects, not only her mother's "little chin" but also her "little and slender figure . . . , her dainty ways, her fond delicate hands" (287). From early adolescence Marjorie allies herself with her mother's delicacy against the "uncouthness" of men (32). There are certain major aspects of her mother's role Marjorie would like to discard: she would rather not marry, she hates housework. But when she "rebelliously" escapes her household duties, she feels "troubled at the thought of deserting mamma" (43).

Marjorie's attitude toward her mother carries over into her relations with her female friends. When she attends a high school dance with her friend Jessie, she meets a boy who asks to take her home. Her first reaction is that "Jessie did not count beside this," but on leaving Jessie, "shame gnawed at her eagerness" (96). Although Marjorie has learned that it is male favor which "counts," she cannot readily choose it over Jessie. On the one hand, she would like to avoid the limitations placed on her mother and set herself apart from Jessie; on the other hand, she feels that in "deserting" her mother or girl friend she is symbolically betraying the female sex and thus part of her own identity.

Sarah Bonney has the same ambivalent attitude as Marjorie, though it takes a slightly different form. Sarah, who is more strong-minded and unconventional than Marjorie, would more willingly ally herself with women, but she feels that she herself is being deserted. While Sarah enjoys a "special intimacy" with her mother, she is hurt by her mother's obvious preference for her brother Warren. Sarah's feelings about her mother, like Marjorie's, are mirrored in her friendships. She is "disgusted" when the girls giggle and act silly around boys. When her friends cancel a swimming trip to go out with boys, Sarah feels a "terrible hurt turning and rankling in her breast." The girls "could not have forgotten all the things they had planned to do together.... How mean girls were when the boys came round—they didn't care what they did. Sarah hated it. She couldn't see why they were that way" (59–60).

Sarah would like to date, but she refuses to act like the other girls to win male approval. She "wanted the boys to like her, but she expected them to like her just as she was" (177). Sarah also wants to be closer to her father yet feels "awkward" in making the attempt (233); only with her mother does she feel "sane and secure" (211). Suckow does not comment directly on Sarah's motives for failing to transfer her affection to her father and other men; she suggests, however, that Sarah fears losing her self-respect. Every time Sarah thinks about the advantages in approaching her father or "pleasing the boys," she worries about humiliating herself. "She wouldn't make a fool of herself. She would be what she was. She would respect herself, anyway" (187).

Cora Schwietert distances herself from her father at the very beginning of *Cora*. Cora's father, a warmhearted German tailor, makes little effort to support the family. Cora resents the fact that her mother works hard while her father occupies himself with music and storytelling. Her mother's patience angers Cora, but "ardently, passionately, she took her mother's side" (6). She considers her father an "enemy" (114). Although Cora takes her mother as the principal, indeed exclusive, object of her love, she does not model herself after her mother to the extent Marjorie and Sarah do. Cora's goal, from early adolescence, is "to be independent— her own boss—able at last to hold up her head." To attain this end she believes she must avoid being, like her mother and her friend Evelyn, "a fool about men" (87).

To Cora, girls who are "looking for a man to take care of them" are unwittingly forging their own chains.

When they were married, they found themselves cramped up in someone else's existence and having to order their own lives by what someone else was able to do. That was mama's life—wasn't it? Doing double work, and at the same [sic] actually dependent upon papa, upon what he, not she, was able to make—having to fit in all her efforts to that. (53)

Cora takes a business course and obtains a secretarial job whereby she can support herself and her mother. She comes closer to her goal of being "her own boss" than any other female character in Suckow's fiction, but she is still unhappy. It exasperates her that Mama Schwietert has always renounced her own power, and by extension, Cora's. This is the significance of the scene where Cora is excluded from her parents' bedroom and feels like a lost child. In her "passionate championship of her mother's cause," Cora has never been able to wring from her one word against her father. Although she has "done everything for her mother," her mother's first loyalty is to "Papa" (115).

Thus, while Cora has worked herself up to the position of ruler of the household, Mama Schwietert's clinging to her husband seems to Cora to mock this achievement. Cora's individual success is not enough because, like Marjorie and Sarah, she cannot disassociate herself from women in general. She wants to gain autonomy not merely for herself but also for her mother; she strives to raise her mother's status to what it "should" have been. Although Cora does not model herself after Mama Schwietert, she identifies so strongly with her mother that she often seems to merge with her. She seems to be trying to relive her mother's life for her. This explains the discrepancy which bothered one reader—that, while Cora "has all the force and independence needed for the role of rebel," she does not go the way of Margaret Ferguson but expends her strength of character on the family.[27]

Unlike Margaret, Cora, Marjorie, and Sarah find it impossible to "desert" their mothers and seek justification through men. While they cannot accept their mothers' low status, they can identify with and even try to become a more powerful mother. This mother Freud called the imaginary "phallic mother," whom the girl originally assumed to possess a penis;[28] Chodorow refers to the "preoedipal, active, caring mother" with whom girls identify in certain non-Western matrifocal societies. Chodorow says that "a daughter's identification with her mother in this kind of setting is with a strong woman with clear control over important spheres of life, whose sense of self-esteem can reflect this."[29] But in Suckow's

patriarchal family the mothers are "sick." Cora takes care of her
mother, becomes her financial support and "champion and de-
fender" (227), on an everyday basis. Marjorie and Sarah are called
home to nurse their mothers.

We have already noted that Marjorie and Sarah seem content
during this period, sometimes feeling like children again. They
might be seen as "regressing" to a childhood state where they are
weak and dependent, but they are not only children being moth-
ered but adults doing the mothering. They are happy because they
view their parents as dependent on them. Marjorie revels in being
"necessary" and even "head of the household" (287), while Sarah
"takes the household in charge," reducing her father to the status
of a helpless child (239). Marjorie and Sarah seem to be seeking
what Cora has tried more openly to achieve—power in the family,
the position of the lost "active mother." On this level their return
to childhood is not merely a retreat from failure outside the home,
but an offensive, an attempt to reorder time and recover lost options.

In her portrayal of adolescent boys, Suckow emphasizes the
status they gain in relinquishing their attachment to their mother.
She shows boys surmounting their Oedipus complexes and growing
to manhood because they are given a boon to do so: the resolution
of the Oedipus complex is synonymous with the coming into power.
For Suckow's heroines there is no comparable reward, no sufficient
compensation for turning away from mother to overcome the "castration complex." A daughter may want to avoid "identification
with a devalued, passive mother," in Chodorow's words; but, as
she continues, "rejection of her oedipal maternal identification . . .
remains an unconscious rejection and devaluation of herself."[30]
With the exception of Margaret Ferguson, Suckow's adolescent
girls resist devaluing themselves. They are unwilling to renounce
their claim to equal status with men and give up the direction of
their lives to others. They refuse to transform their own desire for
power to a desire to gain the approval and affection of the men
who exercise power over them.

When placed in its social context, Freud's observation that girls
have difficulty mastering their castration complexes seems a bit
ingenuous. It is no wonder that his comments on female development from 1905 to 1931 become increasingly more prescriptive.
In his 1931 essay "Female Sexuality," Freud says the "task" of

the girl in growing up is to exchange her mother as a love object for the father. He fears that some girls "may remain *arrested* at the original mother-attachment and never *properly* achieve the changeover to men" [my emphasis].[31] Freud's successors continue his prescriptive tendency. Helene Deutsch claims that the adolescent girl's attachment to her mother represents a great "danger"— the mother is an "obstacle to the girl's desire to grow up."[32]

If we ask *why* the girl is required to overcome her attachment to her mother and institute her father as love object (and why Freud and Deutsch are so insistent about it), we can see that the girl must make the switch in order to be reconciled to her role in a patriarchal culture. To translate Freud *à la* Ruth Suckow, girls are supposed to renounce their identification with women in order to be subjugated to men. Suckow presents this "task" as indeed "difficult." Margaret does it, but to Marjorie, Sarah, and Cora the inducements (love and approval from the male, justification through him) are not strong enough. Suckow's adolescent girl has in her mother a living model of what adult womanhood entails, and it seems to her much like the state of womanhood as defined by Deutsch—a mixture of passivity, narcissism, and masochism.[33] If the girl is sympathetic with her mother and indignant over her mother's situation, she resists growing up and clings to her dream of a "preoedipal, active" mother.

Attachment to the mother thus becomes symbolic of the adolescent heroine's protest against growing up to a powerless state. At the same time, however, this attachment can imply perpetual daughterhood. In one sense Marjorie, Sarah, and Cora are eager to grow up. They do not really want to remain children because childhood involves dependence and restriction; we have noted that even as they are attracted to the shelter of home and mother, they struggle against it toward Cora's goal of being "independent—her own boss." Yet adulthood means womanhood which means renouncing that goal and becoming secondary to men. Suckow's heroines would like to be adults but not women. The physical changes of puberty and increased social pressure to be "feminine" make it impossible for them to ignore this basic conflict. Their way of dealing with it is to vacillate between the poles of the dilemma and delay resolution as long as possible.

Interestingly, Marjorie, Sarah, and Cora receive some help from
a source that they find otherwise restrictive: they are "nice girls"—
more like the Good Good girls of the nineteenth century than
Margaret Ferguson or Wharton's Charity Royall. Because they
seem to be growing to womanhood in an acceptable, good-girl
fashion, they can delay without social intervention. Thus Marjorie,
Sarah, and Cora are not "tomboys." They take an interest in their
looks and clothes; they are distant but not hostile with their fathers
and do not reject boys. Inwardly, however, they are not making
the "proper" transference to orientation toward men. Sarah will
accept boys so long as they like her as she is—she will not "make
a fool of herself"; Cora "collects" boyfriends without becoming
emotionally involved; Marjorie becomes popular by acquiring a
desirable "steady," but she actually dislikes him and remains inwardly detached.

Suckow's adolescent heroines seem to be marking time. They
will grow up outwardly "feminine" and see whether womanhood
really entails the restrictions they perceive. When they discover
that it does (Marjorie's Chicago job, for example), they try to
return to childhood and correct the original "error"—change the
family structure and empower themselves. But this is obviously
only a symbolic solution to the problem; in reality their alternative
seems to be to grow up maimed. The conflict could not be resolved
in a positive way, Suckow suggests, without a change in the status
of women.

Suckow is generally pessimistic about the futures of her heroines.
Sarah Bonney's prospects seem brightest because they are least
defined. Sarah finally interprets her retreat to childhood as a "happy
dream" and decides to return to Chicago and "do something"
(296); we do not know just what she will do and how she will solve
the problem of her female identity. Margaret Ferguson ends up
dependent upon her married lover, dreading the approach of middle age and the loss of her good looks; ironically, she is worse off
than her mother. Marjorie Schoessel's "odyssey" also turns out to
be ironic. At the end of the novel Suckow, who has followed
Marjorie's point of view throughout, attaches an epilogue in which
her mother describes Marjorie's sudden marriage to an impover-
ished farmer. This switch in point of view has been criticized; one
reader complains that it "gives a chopped-off effect, almost as if

the protagonist had died."[34] But this seems to be the point Suckow wants to make—Marjorie has in a sense "died," having lost her early ambitions and faded into oblivion.

Suckow follows Cora Schwietert into her thirties and leaves her in a depressed state. Cora envies two of her friends, whose implicit lesbian relationship she perceives as free from "the pain and heat and the bewilderment of the things that beset men and women" (313). However, Cora does not consider this alternative for herself and remains lonely and embittered. Her only close relationship is with her mother. Having rejected all other female identities available to her, Cora ends confined to her daughter role.

In taking leave of Cora, Suckow suggests again, as she did in portraying the desire of matrons to restrict adolescent girls to their own lot, that the fate of women repeats itself from generation to generation. Cora has a daughter, the result of a brief try at marriage, and this child will face the same conflicts as her mother and her mother's mother. When admonished that the baby should be a "comfort" to her, Cora thinks: "As if it could be any comfort to have brought another girl baby into the world to find everything leagued against her—find that, no matter what she did or what she wanted, she was between the devil and the deep sea!" (265). In Suckow's view, so long as womanhood implies inferiority and limitation, girls will continue to vacillate between childhood and adulthood until they are forced to make a choice between two evils. Whether Suckow's female adolescents leave home or remain with their families, whether they retain their sympathetic identification with their mothers or orient themselves toward men, they can never be whole persons.

The dismal futures Suckow provides her heroines seem ironic in light of her complaint about their nineteenth-century predecessors being forever "chastened by suffering at the end." While Suckow avoids the "teachery Sunday school attitude" that punished the rebel by killing her or making her wallow in submissiveness, she cannot imagine a heroine who ends unchastened. Even the double perspective we found in *Summer* is missing from Suckow's fiction of adolescence. No Suckow heroines experience positive growth in the way of Charity Royall. In fact, the older they become the more diminished they seem.

Wharton's metaphor of the seasons suggests an inevitable cycle of growth: as summer gives way to fall with the promise of spring, Charity leaves her past behind. At the end of the novel she can hardly remember the events of summer:

A few days of autumn cold had wiped out all trace of the rich fields and languid groves through which she had passed on the Fourth of July; and with the fading of the landscape those fervid hours had faded too. She could no longer believe that she was the being who had lived them; she was someone to whom something irreparable and overwhelming had happened, but the traces of the steps leading up to it had almost vanished.[35]

To Marjorie and Sarah, in contrast, their childhood selves seem more vivid and "real" than their grown-up selves. Typically, when Marjorie comes across a box of souvenirs of her past, she cannot decide whether to burn it or keep it.

Oscillation, as opposed to forward movement, becomes typical of the novel of female adolescence after *Summer*. The modern adolescent heroine resembles Marjorie, Sarah, and Cora in shuttling back and forth between childhood and adulthood, struggling for adult status and resisting becoming a woman. The only striking new development as we move to the 1940's and Carson McCullers' *The Member of the Wedding* (1946) is the introduction of younger adolescent heroines. This development reflects social change. If in the period between 1900 and 1930 adolescence was "invented" and established as a universal American experience, in the period between 1930 and the present it was extended to cover a broader range; as Joseph Kett notes, adolescent institutions and subculture have affected a progressively younger age group.[36]

McCullers' Frankie Addams, who is twelve, and Jean Stafford's Molly Fawcett, who is taken from nine to thirteen, undergo the same basic conflict that Suckow's adolescents experience at a later age. Whether Frankie's and Molly's comparative youth requires them to make an earlier and clearer choice, or whether their creators' sensibility is darker than Suckow's, their conflict destroys them. In *The Member of the Wedding* Frankie Addams loses her self more definitely than Marjorie Schoessel, who fades away in Suckow's suggestive epilogue. Then, in Jean Stafford's *The Mountain Lion*, we encounter a new alternative, that the adolescent heroine will simply refuse to grow up.

V

LOSS OF SELF IN CARSON MCCULLERS' *THE MEMBER OF THE WEDDING*

"The greatest danger, that of losing one's own self, may pass off as if it were nothing; every other loss, that of an arm, a leg, five dollars, a wife [sic], etc., is sure to be noticed."—Kierkegaard, quoted by J. T. Malone in McCullers' *Clock without Hands.*

Carson McCullers' *The Member of the Wedding* (1946) takes place in a small Southern town where the protagonist, Frankie Addams, lives with her father. During the hot August of the novel Frankie spends her time in the Addams kitchen with the black cook, Berenice, and her six-year-old cousin, John Henry. She becomes enchanted with her brother's approaching wedding, decides to join the wedding and the honeymoon, and is disillusioned when her plan fails.

Although Frankie is only "twelve and five-sixths years old,"[1] there is much about her which will immediately seem familiar. She makes her appearance dressed as a boy, though she also douses herself with Sweet Serenade perfume; she hesitates on the threshold of the kitchen, being "an unjoined person who hung around in doorways" (599). In the first few pages of the novel we learn that Frankie fears the future and resists even the knowledge of sex, which she calls "nasty lies about married people" (610). Her hometown might just as well be North Dormer or Buena Vista, for Frankie wants out: "I've been ready to leave this town so long. . . . I wish I had a hundred dollars and could just light out and never see this town again" (604).

In light of Frankie's resemblance to her predecessors in the novel of adolescence, it is surprising that a well-read critic like Edmund Wilson could not determine what the novel is about. Wilson, in a review which infuriated McCullers, declared that "the whole story seems utterly pointless."[2] McCullers had the same problem when she tried to market her dramatic version of *Member*: "Few [producers] seemed to know what the play was really about."[3] Subsequent readers have turned to her other works in attempt to explain *Member*. Since one of McCullers' continuing themes is spiritual isolation, most critics interpret Frankie's fear of the future as the universal fear of separate identity and her attempt to join her brother's wedding as representative of all people's struggle to overcome their final separateness from other humans. Thus Frankie becomes a "symbol of spiritual loneliness."[4]

Alternatively, Frankie is thought to symbolize the grotesqueness of the human condition. If Carson McCullers writes about isolation, she also includes in her novels a large number of "freaks": deaf-mutes, alcoholics, idiots, hunchbacked dwarves, etc. Frankie, having seen such beings as the Giant, the Pin Head, and the Alligator Boy at the fair, worries that she herself may become a freak; she calculates that if she continues growing at her present rate she will be over nine feet tall. Some readers have taken Frankie's fear literally and regarded *Member* as another examination by McCullers of the "freakish and perverse." Frankie becomes a "little monster" illustrating the general wretchedness of humanity.[5]

Neither the "freak" nor the "spiritual isolation" approach turns out to be helpful in interpreting *The Member of the Wedding*. It is difficult to understand just what is "freakish" about Frankie; if she occasionally lies and steals and dresses up in garish costumes, so does Huckleberry Finn, nobody's idea of a freak. Frankie makes a more promising symbol of spiritual isolation, but isolation is only one theme of *Member* and does not in itself allow us to account for the rich detail of the novel. The eagerness of critics to make her symbolic suggests some anxiety over the subject of female adolescence. To some extent we can see this anxiety operating in critical reaction to Wharton's *Summer* and Suckow's fiction. *Summer* was thought to be about New England life or Lawyer Royall, anything but a girl growing up; Suckow's novels were labelled too domestic and too "intrinsically feminine."[6] But *Summer* and Suckow could easily be ignored—*Summer* relegated to the position of a "minor" novel in Wharton's oeuvre and Suckow dismissed altogether. *The Member of the Wedding*, as the long-awaited novel of a young "genius," invited more extensive critical response. Interestingly, the major part of this response has been barely concealed disappointment at the subject of McCullers' novel, a feeling that it deals with only "a narrow corner of human existence."[7] Although, as I noted in my preface, male initiation is considered a significant subject for novelists to treat, female initiation is not perceived as equally "universal." Thus most critics have tried to make *Member* about something other than female adolescence, such as isolation or freakdom; they have avoided any discussion of the gender of the protagonist.

Not surprisingly, it was Leslie Fiedler who introduced the question of gender when he characterized Frankie as one of McCullers' "boy-girls," her "transvestite Huckleberry Finns."[8] Once we have seen how McCullers portrays Frankie's adolescence, I will return to criticism of *The Member of the Wedding* and show how Fiedler also set a precedent in sexist interpretation of McCullers' "boy-girls," whereby her literary reputation is disparaged; for now the point is that Frankie's gender has at least been admitted as relevant. Taking his cue from Fiedler, Chester Eisinger says:

> The adolescent girl, in Mrs. McCullers' fiction, has the problem not only of sex awareness but of sex determination. It is not the responsibility of womanhood that she reluctantly must take up but the decision to be a woman at all that she must make. She is, then sexless, hovering between the two sexes.[9]

This decision which confronts her, "the decision to be a woman at all," accounts in large part for Frankie's fear and forms a major thematic concern of *The Member of the Wedding*. Eisinger's term "sexless" has no meaning, since Frankie's "sex determination" was made at birth; however, she is "hovering between the two sexes" in the sense that she is a girl who does not want to relinquish the privileges of boys. Like Ruth Suckow's heroines, Frankie exists in a divided state: while she hesitates to stay in childhood, she cannot fulfill her desire to be "grown-up" without accepting her identity as female, and she already suspects that her gender will be confining. Frankie thus vacillates between striving for adult status and resisting it.

Frankie's reluctance to remain a child is shown in her outrage at being given a doll by her brother Jarvis and his fiancee. She also resents being addressed as a child and peppers her own language with such grown-up phrases as "sick unto death" and "irony of fate." The most obvious sign of Frankie's projected change of identity from child to adult is her revision of her name from "Frankie" to "F. Jasmine." While "Frankie" is a child's name, "F. Jasmine" sounds older. Frankie chooses "Jasmine" partly because the initial "Ja" matches the "Ja" of Jarvis and Janice, but "Jasmine," associated with sweet fragrance and pale yellow flowers, has obvious, romantic, "feminine" connotations. Growing up necessitates shedding a "masculine" name, clothing, and activities for "feminine" ones.

In many ways Frankie wants to make this change. When she becomes F. Jasmine she vows to give up being "rough and greedy" (696). Most important, she attempts to change her appearance. Apart from her name, Frankie's most obvious "tomboy" badges are her crewcut and her typical costume of shorts, undervest, and cowboy hat. As F. Jasmine she wears a pink organdie dress, heavy lipstick, and Sweet Serenade perfume. She cannot alter her hair style immediately but she knows what women "should" look like; "I ought to have long bright yellow hair," Frankie thinks (617).

Frankie's avatar, Mick Kelly of McCullers' *The Heart Is a Lonely Hunter* (1940), undergoes the same transformation. At first Mick resists her older sisters when they try to make her stop wearing "those silly boys' clothes." In a passage reminiscent of Jo March's pulling off her hair net, she exclaims:

"I wear shorts because I don't want to wear your old hand-me-downs. I don't want to be like either of you and I don't want to look like either of you. And I won't. That's why I wear shorts. I'd rather be a boy any day. . . ."[10]

But eventually Mick practices dressing up in her older sisters' evening gowns. She decides she is too old to wear shorts and switches permanently to skirts.

Both Mick's and Frankie's attempts to imitate the dress of adult women are confused and naive. The pleats and hem of Mick's skirt have come out, and to other characters in the novel she still looks as much like a boy as a girl. For her brother's wedding Frankie buys a cheap orange satin evening dress and silver slippers, revealing that she does not yet understand society's division of women into "nice" (pink organdie) and "not nice" (orange satin). Furthermore, as Berenice points out, a woman's evening dress and the brown crust on Frankie's elbows do not mix. Even the new "feminine" name "F. Jasmine" is ambiguous because it is generally a male practice to use an initial and a middle name. One might conclude that Frankie is unconsciously subverting her outward attempt to become more womanly.

But even if Frankie approaches the "feminine" art of self-decoration with ambivalence, it is significant that she cares about her appearance. Frankie dislikes what she considers her "dark ugly mug"; as we noted earlier, she worries that she is too tall and will be a nine-foot freak (618). Her preoccupation with freaks has been linked to her fear of isolation; however, to Frankie the true horror of freakdom is the horror of being an *ugly woman*, of not being able to live up to the name "Jasmine." Frankie's questions to Berenice "Do you think I will grow into a Freak?" and "Do you think I will be pretty?" are joined together (620), and her association of looks and male approval becomes clear when she tells Berenice she doubts that freaks ever get married.

Since marriage has traditionally been woman's fate, it is logical that in contemplating growing up Frankie should turn to thoughts of love, sex, and marriage. The younger Frankie had scorned love and left it out of her homemade shows; preferring movies about criminals, cowboys, and war, she caused a disturbance when the local theatre showed *Camille*. But now she recalls the time when she committed a "queer sin" with the neighbor boy Barney MacKean and the time when she surprised one of the Addams' boarders in bed with his wife "having a fit" (643). She thinks about love and becomes fascinated with her brother's wedding. If the wedding provides an opportunity for Frankie to escape her loneliness and become a "member" of something, it is also the marriage of a man and a woman, and in her obsession with a wedding, Frankie anticipates her own destiny. Instead of stopping her ears as she used to when Berenice talked of love and marriage, Frankie now encourages Berenice and listens to her carefully.

Whatever difficulties Frankie has in making the "decision to be a woman" cannot be attributed to her lack of a mother because Berenice performs a motherly function in initiating Frankie into her expected role. Berenice correctly interprets Frankie's concern with the wedding as concern with her own future as a woman. Thus Berenice suggests that Frankie acquire a "nice little white boy beau" (696). Berenice's advice to Frankie is a classic compression of traditional "womanly wisdom." She says: "Now you belong to change from being so rough and greedy and big. You ought to fix yourself up nice in your dresses. And speak sweetly and act sly" (696). In three sentences Berenice has summarized the major traits girls are taught to cultivate in preparation for their relationships with men: "object" orientation ("fix yourself up nice"), passivity and submission ("speak sweetly"), and calculation and trickery ("act sly"). No real mother could do a more thorough job of socialization.

Critics have been unanimous in viewing Berenice as a positive influence on Frankie. They consider her wise and spiritual, a mouthpiece for McCullers and the "Socrates of the novel."[11] However, McCullers presents Berenice as a completely man-oriented woman. For her to talk about her life means to talk about her four previous husbands and current beau. Berenice communicates to Frankie pride in the number of men one can attract. When John Henry asks her how many beaus she "caught," she replies: "Lamb, how many hairs is in these plaits? You talking to Berenice Sadie Brown" (697). Berenice feels proud that men "treat" her, that she doesn't have to "pay her own way." Besides, the company of men is preferable to that of women; she proclaims, "I'm not the kind of person to go around with crowds of womens" (699).

It is surprising how much Berenice resembles a mother who has been the object of much vituperation from critics, Amanda Wingfield of Tennessee Williams' *The Glass Menagerie* (1944). In this play by McCullers' close friend, Amanda tries to transform her shy daughter into a Southern belle. Berenice is in most ways a more attractive character than Amanda; yet her cataloging of her past in terms of beaus is much like Amanda's in terms of "gentlemen callers," and her advice to her reluctant young charge is exactly the same as Amanda's to her daughter.

Much of the humor in *The Member of the Wedding* involves the young and unworldly Frankie and John Henry, but we are not allowed to forget that Berenice also is limited in her perceptions. For instance, Frankie asks Berenice why she married at the youthful age of thirteen (Frankie is almost thirteen herself). Berenice responds, "Because I wanted to. I were thirteen years old and I haven't growed a inch since." Frankie, who we know worries about her height, asks, "Does marrying really stop your growth?" "It certainy do," replies Berenice, unaware of the implications of her statement (628). In this case, the author has distanced herself from Berenice, creating an irony involving her.

Furthermore, the Berenice who in the middle of the novel rejects Frankie's advice that she marry her latest beau, T. T. Williams, ends up by taking it. Frankie tells Berenice to "quit worrying about beaus and be content with T. T. I bet you are forty years old. It is time for you to settle down" (698). Berenice asserts that she will not marry T. T. because he doesn't "make her shiver." She rebukes Frankie, saying, "I got many a long year ahead of me before I resign myself to a corner" (698). But finally Berenice decides that she "might as well" marry T. T. (785). In other words, her experience in the novel is not at a level above Frankie's but parallels it. Berenice, like Frankie, hates sleeping alone, and she submits, resigning herself to a corner, just as Frankie finally gives up her dreams and accepts the role marked out for her.

Even with Berenice's tutelage and her own desire to be treated as an adult, Frankie fears growing up. It is not simply that she might fail to meet the standards of womanhood (be the proper height, be pretty, etc.)—Frankie feels especially afraid when she "thinks about the world." She reads the war news in the paper and wants

to be a boy and go to war as a Marine. She thought about flying aeroplanes and winning gold medals for bravery. But she could not join the war, and this made her sometimes feel restless and blue.... To think about the world for very long made her afraid. She was not afraid of Germans or bombs or Japanese. She was afraid because in the war they would not include her, and because the world seemed somehow separate from herself. (623–24)

She envies the soldiers she sees in town for their mobility, the opportunity they have to travel and see the world—in other words, to gain experience. Frankie feels left out. When she wonders "who she was, and what she was going to be in the world," she gets a "queer tightness in her chest" (624).

No doubt many a boy has had the same thirst for adventure and felt frustrated by his youth. But it is not just a question of youth for Frankie, any more than it is for Richard Wright's Bigger Thomas. When he sees a plane overhead, Bigger tells his friend Gus, "I could fly one of them things if I had a chance." "If you wasn't black and if you had some money and if they'd let you go to that aviation school," replies Gus. The youthful Bigger feels the same tightness as Frankie, "like somebody's poking a red-hot iron down my throat. . . . It's just like living in jail. Half the time I feel like I'm on the outside of the world peeping in."[12]

One might conclude that Wright's novel is a "parable of the essential loneliness of man,"[13] but, so far as I know, no one has ventured this interpretation of *Native Son*. Bigger's problem, like Frankie's, is not isolation but exclusion. It is true that Frankie resolves her "sexual ambiguity," as one critic puts it, and takes a "definite step toward assuming her feminine nature" when she finally gives up wanting to be a pilot.[14] The question is why "feminine nature" (or dark skin) precludes being a pilot. Whenever Frankie senses that becoming a woman entails renunciation, she feels the tightness in her chest and rebels.

McCullers endows Mick Kelly with the same desires as Frankie. Mick would also like to fight the Fascists—she imagines dressing as a boy and being accepted in the army. Like Frankie, Mick wants to see the world; she spends her time at the library pouring over *National Geographic* magazines. But Mick's first love is music, and above all things she wants to be a composer. It seems initially that she has to give up her goal for purely economic reasons: her parents cannot afford a piano or music lessons, and she must work to help support the family. However, just as Bigger's friend Gus puts race first and money second in listing the obstacles to Bigger's becoming a pilot, McCullers reveals that the primary check to Mick's dream is her gender.

Mick has a friend, Harry Minowitz, whose function in the novel is to serve both as the agent of her sexual initiation and as a contrast to her. Mick and Harry, as a poor girl and a poor boy, resemble Ruth Suckow's Daisy and Gerald with their very different prospects for the future. Although Harry must work to support his widowed mother, he can find a high-paying part-time job; thus he can finish studying mechanics at the local high school. Mick comments:

"A boy has a better advantage like that than a girl. I mean a boy can usually get some part-time job that don't take him out of school and leaves him time for other things. But the're [sic] not jobs like that for girls. When a girl wants a job she has to quit school and work full-time." (386)

After Harry and Mick have sex, Harry leaves town, either because he feels guilty or because he wants to avoid being "tied down." We are not informed of Harry's ultimate fate, but he can support himself as a skilled mechanic and has at least escaped the small town to which Mick feels bound. Mick's tiring full-time job at Woolworth's puts an end to her dreams of a musical career. She is cut off from her "inner room," the "good private place where she could go and be by herself and study . . . music" (195), and feels trapped and cheated.

This sense of being trapped is developed in greater detail in *The Member of the Wedding* where the very setting of the novel is designed to reflect Frankie's feelings of being limited and restricted. The Addams kitchen, where Frankie spends most of her time, seems to her "sad and ugly" and is most often described by McCullers as "gray" (602). The walls are covered with John Henry's "queer" drawings which no one can decipher. The kitchen is a place where "nothing happens" and, often, nothing even moves (632). Time passes slowly there (McCullers reinforces this impression by noting frequently that "it was only six" or "only half-past six"), and Frankie, Berenice, and John Henry "say the same things over and over" until the words seem to rhyme (599). In attempt to classify *Member* as a Gothic novel one critic contends that the Addams kitchen parallels the "old dank dungeon" of the classic Gothic romance.[15] Certainly to Frankie it seems a kind of prison.

Frankie cannot find relief beyond the kitchen, for the outside atmosphere is just as stifling. The connotations of hot and cold in Wharton's *Summer* are reversed in *The Member of the Wedding*. In *Member*, as in her other novels, McCullers uses heat to suggest boredom and restriction and cold to suggest liberation. Frankie dreams of snow and ice; Jarvis and Janice blend with her ideals because he was stationed in Alaska and she comes from a town called Winter Hill. But the reality of Frankie's environment is deadening heat. The town turns "black and shrunken under the glare of the sun," and the sidewalks seem to be on fire. The atmosphere is motionless as well as hot. "The world seemed to die each afternoon and nothing moved any longer. At last the summer was like a green sick dream, or like a silent crazy jungle under glass"(599). McCullers' references to heat and stasis create an effect of constriction, almost suffocation, that parallels Frankie's feeling of tightness in her chest. Even the sunlight crosses her back yard "like the bars of a bright, strange jail" (693).

Frankie tries to communicate her feeling of being trapped to Berenice, who expresses it eloquently:

"We all of us somehow caught. We born this way or that way and we don't know why. But we caught anyhow. I born Berenice. You born Frankie. John Henry born John Henry. And maybe we wants to widen and bust free. But no matter what we do we still caught." (740)

Almost everyone who has written about *Member* notes that Berenice is describing people being "caught" in their own individual identities and being ultimately isolated. It is usually forgotten, however, that Berenice goes on to define a special way of being caught. She says she is caught worse

"because I'm black. . . . Because I am colored. Everybody is caught one way or another, but they done drawn completely extra bounds around all colored people. They done squeezed us off in one corner by ourself. So we caught that firstway I was telling you, as all human beings is caught. And we caught as colored people also. Sometimes a boy like Honey [Berenice's foster brother] feel like he just can't breathe no more. He feel like he got to break something or break himself. Sometimes it just about more than he can stand. He just feels desperate like." (740)

Frankie's responses to Berenice are significant. To the first statement she says she "doesn't know" but to the second that she knows how Honey feels. "Sometimes I feel like I want to break something, too. I feel like I wish I could just tear down the whole town" (740). In other words, Frankie believes she is caught in a special way other than the first one Berenice explained. Berenice, having accepted the female role, does not mention the "extra bounds" drawn around women, but Frankie feels them keenly.

Honey Brown, who "just can't breathe no more," is Frankie's double in the novel. Frankie feels a kinship with him because she senses that he is in the same divided state that she is. On the one hand, Honey works hard studying music and French; on the other, he "suddenly run[s] hog-wild all over Sugarville and tear[s] around for several days, until his friends bring him home more dead than living" (751). Although he can talk "like a white schoolteacher" (642), he often adopts his expected role with a vengeance, speaking in a "colored jumble" that even his family cannot understand (751). Honey spends only part of his energy trying to overcome or protesting the limitations placed on him; the rest of the time he accepts society's label of "inferior" and punishes himself.

Frankie exhibits this same psychology. She frequently "hates herself," and her attempts at rebellion against the female role are mainly symbolic. As Simone de Beauvoir puts it, the young girl "is too much divided against herself to join battle with the world; she limits herself to a flight from reality or a symbolic struggle against it."[16] De Beauvoir mentions four common forms of "symbolic struggle": odd eating habits, kleptomania, self-mutilation, and running away from home. While Frankie never carries these behaviors to extremes, she indulges in all four types. She eats "greedily," pilfers from the five-and-ten, hacks at her foot with a knife, and tries to run away. It is characteristic of these acts that, like Honey's rampages, they are ineffective—the young girl is "struggling in her cage rather than trying to get out of it."[17] At the end of the novel we find Honey in an actual prison and Frankie in a jail of her own (784).

Frankie's principal "flight from reality" is her creation of a fantasy world. The adult Honey laughs at her solution to racism, that he go to Cuba and pass as a Cuban. But Frankie still deals with her feeling of being trapped by escaping to the haven of her dreams where she can fly airplanes and see the whole world. Her favorite pastime with Berenice and John Henry is their game of criticizing God and putting themselves in the position of creator. Frankie agrees with the basic modifications Berenice would make. The world would be "just and reasonable": there would be no separate colored people, no killed Jews, and no hunger. Frankie makes a major addition, however. "She planned it so that people could instantly change back and forth from boys to girls, whichever way they felt like and wanted" (714). This plan provides a neat symbolic solution to Frankie's conflicts.

To many commentators on McCullers' work, however, Frankie's
dream is an "abnormal" one, a product of the author's "homosexual sensibility."[18] We saw earlier that Leslie Fiedler initiated
discussion of gender in McCullers' fiction when he referred to
Frankie and Mick as "boy-girl" characters. This point might have
led to recognition of McCullers' portrayal of the conflict between
a woman's humanity and her destiny as a woman; but Fiedler went
on, in a disapproving tone, to call the "tomboy image" "lesbian"
and argue that McCullers is "projecting in her neo-tomboys, ambiguous and epicene, the homosexual's . . . uneasiness before heterosexual passion."[19] Fiedler ends up in the absurd position of
contending that Frankie and Berenice are having a "homosexual
romance."[20]

Some critics have tried to preserve Fiedler's basic argument by
giving Frankie a more appropriate lover. They see her relationship
at the end of the novel with her newfound friend, Mary Littlejohn,
as "latently homosexual"; Mary's name fits conveniently with this
theory—she is a "little John," a "surrogate male lover."[21] Other
critics influenced by Fiedler take Frankie's refusal to recognize
"the facts of life" as evidence of different sexual "abnormalities."
Perhaps she wants to join her brother's wedding so that she can
commit incest; perhaps she is really "asexual" (to Ihab Hassan,
McCullers' "men-women freaks" are "all bi-sexual, which is to say
a-sexual").[22] The critics who have followed Fiedler's lead leave as
many questions unanswered as he does. We never learn what a
"homosexual sensibility" might be and how it is "abnormal," what
the "tomboy image" has to do with lesbianism, how "bisexual"
and "a-sexual" are the same. Because so many terms remain undefined, discussion of sex and gender in McCullers' fiction has
been hopelessly confused.

At issue seems to be McCullers' endorsement of androgyny in
her fiction. Frankie and Mick are only two among many androgynous characters, including Singer and Biff Brannon in *The Heart
Is a Lonely Hunter*, Captain Penderton in *Reflections in a Golden
Eye* (1941), and Amelia in *Ballad of a Sad Café* (1943). These
characters are McCullers' most sympathetic, and they often seem
to speak for her. Biff Brannon, when he sees Mick looking as much
like a boy as a girl, thinks to himself:

And on that subject why was it that the smartest people mostly missed that point? By nature all people are of both sexes. So that marriage and the bed is not all by any means. The proof? Real youth and old age. Because often old men's voices grow high and reedy and they take on a mincing walk. And old women sometimes grow fat and their voices get rough and deep and they grow dark little mustaches. And he even proved it himself—the part of him that sometimes wished he was a mother and that Mick and Baby were his kids. (274)

Biff, who is one of the strongest and most self-sufficient characters in McCullers' fiction, is shown becoming so after his wife dies. He takes over some of her "feminine" habits, discarding the clearly defined role which had previously confined him. If Mc-Cullers implies any solution besides racial equality to the social injustice and personal isolation and despair she portrays in her novels, it is a move toward the loosening of conventional gender roles, toward the more androgynous world Frankie envisions when she wishes people could "change back and forth from boys to girls."

But the critics who discuss McCullers' androgynous characters conclude that "there is something frightening about them." McCullers fails to present women who are happily female and "men who are men (i.e. Gary Cooper)," and Biff Brannon is a "sexual deviate."[23] The next step is devaluation of McCullers' reputation as a writer. Fiedler dismisses her as a "chic" writer supported by New York homosexuals. A. S. Knowles less readily equates androgyny and homosexuality but finds either one "frightening." In his reassessment of McCullers' literary reputation Knowles expresses distaste for the "By nature all people are of both sexes" passage quoted above; he is horrified that McCullers actually "means what she seems to be saying" in this passage. He concludes that McCullers links "sensitivity" with "sexual abnormality" and is thus a less important novelist than she first appeared to be.[24]

Ironically, the recognition of the importance of gender in McCullers' fiction has been no more productive than the ignoring of gender and search for "universal" themes we noted earlier. The main import of the Fiedler approach is a sinister message for potential novelists. If the "universalist" critics imply that novelists should avoid writing about female adolescence because it is not universal enough, the Fiedlerites proclaim loudly, "Do not write about female adolescence if you criticize the current gender system. Those who criticize the gender system are homosexuals, and homosexuals cannot be important novelists."

The universalists have tried to produce comprehensive interpretations of *The Member of the Wedding*, but to the Fiedlerites a fuller understanding of the novel seems to have been a secondary concern. The readings they have come up with are distorted and partial; we are left to figure out for ourselves why Frankie Addams should be lusting after Berenice or her brother. Frankie's attitude toward sex provides a specific example where both critical approaches have resulted in misreadings. Everyone recognizes that Frankie resists even the knowledge of sexual intercourse. It is not only that she does not understand, or try to understand, such incidents mentioned earlier as her "sin" with Barney MacKean and her glimpse of the boarder "having a fit"; she also conveniently "forgets" both incidents. After Frankie has misinterpreted the purpose of her date with a soldier and has had to fend off his advances, she fleetingly remembers these earlier bits of knowledge. But, significantly, she does not "let these separate glimpses fall together" (761); she prefers to think of the soldier as an anomaly, a "crazy man."

To the Fiedlerites, as we have seen, Frankie's resistance means that she is a lesbian or a "deviate." To the universalists it is either "pointless" or symbolic of the course of initiation in the modern world—Frankie's failure to gain "insight into sexual experience" shows that initiation no longer entails knowledge and commitment.[25] In fact, there is no evidence in *The Member of the Wedding* that Frankie is homosexual (or heterosexual, bisexual, or asexual). In the play she adapted from the novel McCullers presents Frankie in the last scene swooning over Barney MacKean, the boy she previously hated. In the novel we are given no clue as to what her sexual preference will eventually be. But Frankie does not fail to gain insight into heterosexual experience. Although she manages for a while to keep her "separate glimpses" of sex from falling together, near the end of the novel she gets a sudden flash of understanding (782). Significantly, her moment of recognition comes after her plan to join the wedding has failed; it is associated with her consequent feelings of helplessness and resignation—she "might as well" ask the soldier to marry her.

Frankie's attitude toward sex is not unusual. The adolescent heroines we have met so far, even the sensuous Charity Royall, fear and resist sexual experience; as we will see, resistance to sex is almost universal in novels of female adolescence. The reason is always the same: adolescent heroines view sex as domination by a man (not until very recently are they even aware of the possibility of sex with women). They may, like Mick Kelly, worry about losing their virginity (the woman is traditionally spoken of as "losing" her virginity when she "submits" or "yields" to a man); but they fear most strongly, as Mick does, losing their autonomy.[26]

In his survey of novels of adolescence James Johnson puzzles over Frankie's encounter with the soldier, wondering why her experience lacks the "positive quality" of Stephen Dedalus' sexual initiation.[27] If we look at Stephen's first sexual experience in *A Portrait of the Artist as a Young Man*, we find that his behavior is the opposite of Frankie's. Stephen, hardly the "man's man," Gary Cooper, "suddenly become[s] strong and fearless and sure of himself."[28] Frankie, on the other hand, does not "know how to refuse" the soldier's invitation to his room; she thinks she is unable to leave, and when he grabs her, she feels "paralyzed" (760). In other words, Stephen receives a sudden influx of power, while Frankie feels loss of power.

McCullers treats an adolescent girl's association of sexual intercourse with male domination and loss of personal choice and power in an early short story entitled "Like That." The thirteen-year-old narrator of the story, an early version of Mick and Frankie, bemoans the change that has come over her older sister. Previously she and Sis had had fun together, but one night after a date with her boyfriend, Sis began to act differently. The present Sis has lost weight, cries a lot, and spends her time sitting by herself or writing her boyfriend. The unnamed narrator, whom I will call N., declares, "I wouldn't like any boy in the world as much as she does Tuck. I'd never let any boy or any thing make me act like she does." She thinks of Sis as "dead."[29]

Although N. does not understand the cause of Sis's behavior, she associates the change with her sister's first menstruation which

she had "forgotten" for several years because she "hadn't wanted
to remember." N. thus connects becoming a woman with giving
up of self and being oriented toward and dominated by a man. N.
does not want to let "anything really change me," so she either
conveniently "forgets" or refuses to listen to information about
sex. N. concludes:

One afternoon the kids all got quiet in the gym basement and then started
telling certain things—about being married and all—I got up quick so I
wouldn't hear and went up and played basketball. And when some of the
kids said they were going to start wearing lipstick and stockings I said I
wouldn't for a hundred dollars. You see I'd never be like Sis is now. I
wouldn't. Anybody could know that if they knew me. I just wouldn't,
that's all. I don't want to grow up—if it's like that.[30]

   N. seems more conscious than Frankie of her motives in avoiding
discussion of sexual facts and "forgetting" those facts she cannot
avoid. McCullers has Frankie express her conflicts in fantasies, as
with her dream of a world where people could instantly change
sexes. Frankie knows this dream is impossible. She finds society's
condemnation of androgyny, which we saw expressed by literary
critics, reflected in her own world; after all, one of the freaks at
the fair is the Half-Man Half-Woman. Frankie thus projects all
her desires and fears into a fantasy that she imagines might be
more socially acceptable—she will join her brother and his fiancee
and become "a member of the wedding." Those readers who have
stressed the theme of spiritual isolation in McCullers' works have
noted that joining the wedding would allow Frankie to escape her
own separate identity, to become, as Frankie says, a "we" person
instead of an "I" person. But paradoxically, Frankie's plan to join
the wedding is also a desperate attempt to *preserve* her identity.
Her wedding fantasy is a symbolic way of resolving her conflict of
wanting to be an adult but not wanting to be a woman, not wanting
to "grow up—if it's like that."
   Weddings are, traditionally, the destiny of girls, and with marriage a girl officially becomes an adult. But Frankie has changed
her female destiny, for this wedding does not entail any of the
restrictions that she has perceived in womanhood. Her proposed

marriage is not to one man because in her society that implies submission; the marriage is for the same reason sexless. Nor does Frankie attempt to acquire in her brother and sister-in-law a new set of parents,[31] for then she would be a child again. Frankie dreams of being neither a *wife* nor a *child* but an adult *equal*. In reality Frankie is already a member of something—she has "the terrible summer *we* of her and John Henry and Berenice"; but "that was the last *we* in the world she wanted" (646), because a black woman and a child do not raise her status. Her brother Jarvis is a soldier, one of those envied beings who gets to see the world; his fiancee, whom Frankie has met only briefly, at least has the distinction of being "small and pretty" (630). According to Frankie's plan, the three JA's will travel together. She will no longer be trapped in her kitchen but can climb glaciers in Alaska and ride camels in Africa. Frankie will be able to fly planes and win medals, and all three JA's will be equally famous and successful (737–38). This fantasy makes Frankie feel "lightness" in place of that old constriction in her chest; it gives her a sense of "power" and "entitlement" (663).

But Frankie's plan to join the wedding is a non-realistic way of solving her conflict, a "flight from reality" more elaborately imagined than the ones Simone de Beauvoir describes. When Frankie is dragged screaming from the honeymoon car, her dream is crushed. She realizes that "all that came about [at the wedding] occurred in a world beyond her power" (768); she feels powerless (772). When she runs away from home after the wedding, Frankie merely goes through the motions of protest and attempted escape. She knows before she reaches the street corner that her father has awakened and will soon be after her. Her plan of hopping a box car seems unreal even to her. "It is easy to talk about hopping a freight train, but how did bums and people really do it?" (778). She admits to herself that she is "too scared to go into the world alone" (782).

Frankie now resigns herself—the world seems too "enormous" and "powerful" for her to fight. "Between herself and all the places there was a space like an enormous canyon she could not hope to bridge or cross" (784). When Frankie suddenly puts together the sexual facts she previously refused to connect and thinks she might as well ask the soldier to marry her, we realize that she is giving up her rebellion and submitting to her female fate. At this point the jail image, part of the motif of constriction in the novel, recurs. Frankie wishes the policeman who comes to fetch her would take her to jail, for "it was better to be in a jail where you could bang the walls than in a jail you could not see" (784).

Had McCullers ended *The Member of the Wedding* here, it would have been difficult for anyone to see the novel as "cute" and "sentimental," a *Tom Sawyer* as opposed to McCullers' *Huckleberry Finn*, *The Heart Is a Lonely Hunter*.[32] However, she includes a few pages showing Frankie several months later. John Henry has died of meningitis, Honey is in jail, Berenice plans to marry T. T., but Frankie is content. She has found a friend and model in the older Mary Littlejohn, a modern Good Good Girl with long blonde hair, pale white complexion, and ladylike habits; Mary encourages Frankie to collect paintings by Michelangelo and read Tennyson. The novel ends as Frankie, with "an instant shock of happiness," hears Mary at the front door (791).

Twentieth-century novelists rarely leave their characters in a state of euphoria, and those critics who have not thereby consigned *Member* to the rank of sentimental popular novels about adolescence have tended to focus on Frankie's "successful" initiation. That is, the "happy ending" means that Frankie is "accepting reality and responsibility."[33] Louise Gossett contends that McCullers often leaves adults "physically and emotionally ruined" but "brings her adolescents to a healthy measure of maturity." Her adolescents'

ability to achieve wholeness distinguishes their growth from that of many young people in twentieth century literature about the suffering adolescent. The struggle of the adolescent who appears in the fiction of William Goyen or Truman Capote injures or defeats him with a deadly finality. Mrs. McCullers prefers to educate rather than to destroy her adolescents.

Unlike these other adolescent protagonists, Frankie is not "injured or crippled emotionally" by her experiences.[34] Indeed, Frankie does not retreat to a fantasy world (Joel Knox of Capote's *Other Voices, Other Rooms*), end up in a mental institution (Holden Caulfield), or commit suicide (Peyton Loftis of Styron's *Lie Down in Darkness*). But the very point of McCullers' epilogue is to show that, while Frankie has "adjusted" to growing up and is undergoing a "normal" adolescence, she has been severely "crippled." Frankie has not merely replaced her old aspirations with new ones just as impossible;[35] she has changed the very nature of her dreams. Frankie's old dreams, of flying planes, of being able to switch genders whenever she wished, of joining the wedding, were protests against the secondary status of women. They were projections of her desire to be an autonomous adult. Now Frankie, or Frances, as she is finally called, wants to write poetry and travel with Mary Littlejohn. Her new dreams are socially acceptable and easily within her reach. Although she will not climb glaciers and ride camels with Mary Littlejohn, she may tour Europe under the aegis of Mary and her mother. It is permissible for Frankie to go "around the world" but not into it (790).

Frankie now lives in a permanent "daytime" state (790), or what Mick Kelly would call the "outside room." To Mick her "outside room" is "school and the family and the things that happened every day" and her "inside room" a "very private place" full of "plans" and "music"—in other words, her inner self (303). When Mick gives up composing to work at the five and ten and stops resisting womanhood to become "ladylike and delicate" (496), she is barred from the inside room: she loses her self. Although we leave Frankie at a younger age, it is clear that she has already sacrificed her "inner room." Her life is "filled with . . . school and Mary Littlejohn" (the outside room), and her summer of plans is almost forgotten. The very kitchen where Frankie thought about "who she was" and resisted "what she was going to be in the world" has been whitewashed.

Immediately after Honey's imprisonment and John Henry's death Frankie would feel a "hush" when she thought of them, and she had nightmares about John Henry. "But the dreams came only once or twice" and "it was seldom now that she felt his presence" (790). Although Berenice appears in the last few pages of the novel, Frankie hardly feels her presence either; she ignores her in anticipation of being with Mary Littlejohn and seems indifferent to Berenice's departure. The fates of Berenice, Honey, and John Henry reflect on Frankie's own situation. The formerly lively Berenice, who once towered over the Addams kitchen, is subdued; she sits sad and "idle" in a chair, "her limp arms hanging at her sides" (786). Honey is in prison as the result of drugging himself. John Henry's death seems fitting. Through most of the novel, as Frankie vacillated between childhood and adulthood, she alternately avoided and clung to him. Now, as part of her childhood and her "inner room," he is appropriately dead.

In reporting John Henry's death McCullers juxtaposes accounts of his terrible suffering with descriptions of the "golden" autumn weather—the chilled air and the clear green-blue sky filled with light (789).[36] The effect is to make Frankie seem a bit callous, for the cool weather reflects her joyous mood; she can hardly feel John Henry's death. Like Edith Wharton's *Summer*, *The Member of the Wedding* portrays an adolescent girl's hot summer, which at the very end of the novel gives way to a chilly autumn. But the passage to autumn has a different import in McCullers' novel. Although Frankie, unlike Charity, loves the cold, there is no glimmer of promise in *Member* because Frankie has not experienced any of the positive growth Charity has. The seasonal motif suggests the possibility of renewal; perhaps "spring will return" for Frankie as well as Charity, but Berenice, Honey, and John Henry are irrevocably lost. At the end of *The Member of the Wedding* Frankie seems better off than Charity. She is certainly happy, having released the tension of not "belonging"; but the final irony of the novel is that having gained her membership, Frankie has lost her self.

McCullers does not blame Frankie, any more than she does Mick, for this loss of self. As the critical comments stressing her new "maturity" imply, Frankie has done exactly what has been expected of her, what she has been educated to do. In this context Louise Gossett's remarks on her environment seem ironic. Frankie's environment, says Gossett, is less menacing than Holden Caulfield's:

His displacement is more radical than Frankie's because his society has no place for him, whereas the community of Frankie or of Mick, less large and competitive, defines what is acceptable in the stages through which the girls grow and also superintends their progress.[37]

It is, of course, the problem rather than the solution that Frankie's and Mick's society has a "place" for them and "superintends" them into it. That same society has a place for Honey Brown. *The Member of the Wedding* is less a novel of initiation into "acceptance of *human* limits"[38] than a novel of initiation into acceptance of *female* limits. Frankie's desire to be a soldier or a pilot, or Mick's to be an inventor or a composer, could be fulfilled by a boy; these goals are simply defined as unacceptable for girls. Nor is Frankie's ambition to travel and gain experience in the world unattainable for a boy. Gossett's comparison of Frankie with Holden Caulfield has relevance here. Holden's basic conflict resembles Frankie's—he does not want to remain a child but has reservations about the "phoniness" of adults (he projects these doubts into his dream of being "catcher in the rye" and catching children before they fall over the "cliff" into adulthood). But if Holden's "displacement" appears greater than Frankie's, it is merely a measure of his greater freedom. He can at least venture into the world and test it by experience. James Johnson includes Frankie and Holden as examples of modern adolescent characters who flee their homes and undertake journeys.[39] Yet Frankie's hour of running away hardly measures up to Holden's experience or that of Johnson's other examples, Eugene Gant, Nick Adams, or Stephen Dedalus, all inveterate wanderers.

The barriers to Frankie's entering the world are not solely external, any more than they are for Ruth Suckow's adolescent heroines. Frankie and Mick are "protected" (that is, banned) from experience in the way of Suckow's "nice girls," and Mick especially is expected to preserve close ties to the family. But, in large part, the girls fail to journey into the world because of their own passivity. Frankie and Mick, like Marjorie Schoessel, wait for "something to happen" to them—they do not think in terms of making something happen. They dream but seldom act. Even Frankie's desire to be a "member" stresses identification with the world rather than participation in it. When Frankie tries to run away from home, she discovers that she does not have the necessary resources to leave by herself. The details of "hopping a freight," for instance, lie outside the realm of her preparatory experience. She does not have to be prevented from hopping freights; her

greatest restriction is that she does not know how or really want
to.

Frankie's and Mick's passivity becomes striking when we compare them with the male adolescent protagonist of one of Mc-
Cullers' early versions of *The Heart Is a Lonely Hunter*. Andrew
has the same background as Frankie and Mick; he lives in a small
Georgia town with a jeweller father, a sister Sara, a little sister
Mick, and a Black cook Vitalis. Interestingly, much of this draft
deals with Andrew's recollections of his sister Sara's troubled adolescence and her attempts to "try to act like a boy" and run away
from home. McCullers had not yet determined her true focus, the
adolescent girl, and this early draft is confused because the protagonist, Andrew, is not really the center of interest. We discover
enough about him, however, to see how his character and fate
differ from that of Sara-Mick-Frankie.

Andrew resembles the female adolescent in being "lonesome"
and apprehensive about the future. "He was getting to be a man
and he did not know what was going to come. And always he was
hungry and always he felt that something was just about to happen."[40] The difference is that Andrew himself causes the event to
happen. He takes a walk by Vitalis' house, says he is hungry,
follows her into the house, and seduces her. Afterwards, Andrew
feels guilty and leaves town permanently for New York City. It
seems to him that his experience with Vitalis was "accidental,"
but it is clear from his seeking her out and claiming to be hungry
that he at least unconsciously sought sexual contact. Although
Andrew's experience involves some loss of control, as his bodily
desires overcome his conscious plans, it contrasts with Mick's and
Frankie's in that Andrew acts throughout. It is he who has the
desire, seeks out Vitalis, and initiates the sexual encounter. He
makes a decision to leave town and then follows through with his
decision.

Andrew is an early version of Harry Minowitz, and his two sisters
later merge into the figure of Mick Kelly. In *The Heart Is a Lonely
Hunter* Harry will be presented as more active than Mick; his
situation will also differ from hers in terms of his greater economic
opportunity and freedom of movement. Still, Harry ends up a
minor character, his function being to highlight the restrictions
placed on Mick. Like Ruth Suckow, McCullers includes male ad-

olescents in her fiction but reserves center stage for girls. Not until their last novels, Suckow's *The John Wood Case* (1959) and McCullers' *Clock without Hands* (1961), do they make a boy the protagonist, and they do not provide him with a female counterpart. There are, however, a number of novels which give equal development to the experiences of a pair of protagonists and thus allow us to see a female adolescent character compared more extensively with a male character. Charlotte Goodman calls this form the "male-female double *Bildungsroman*" and notes that it has been "particularly congenial to the woman novelist who wishes to emphasize the way in which a society that rigidly differentiates between male and female gender roles limits the full development of women and men alike."[41] One such novelist is Jean Stafford, an important writer who, like Suckow, has been undeservedly neglected. Stafford made adolescence the focus of much of her fiction, and in *The Mountain Lion*, the subject of the next chapter, she contrasts the evolution of two young protagonists, one female and one male.

INITIATION IN JEAN STAFFORD'S *THE MOUNTAIN LION*

During her lifetime Jean Stafford produced several collections of short stories and three novels: *Boston Adventure* (1944), *The Mountain Lion* (1947), and *The Catherine Wheel* (1952). Although she is not well known today,[1] her *Collected Stories* (1969) won a Pulitzer Prize and her novels were very favorably reviewed. All three are about initiation into adulthood. *Boston Adventure* tells the story of a young girl's growth to womanhood, while the youth in *The Catherine Wheel* is a boy whose growing pains have an impact on the older woman who befriends him. In *The Mountain Lion* two adolescent characters face initiation.

The plot of *The Mountain Lion* is simple. The protagonists, Molly and Ralph Fawcett, are introduced at ages nine and eleven, respectively, and taken to ages thirteen and fifteen. At the beginning of the novel they live with their widowed mother and older sisters in California and respond to the influence of two grandfathers. Their home is a shrine to Mrs. Fawcett's deceased father, Grandfather Bonney, who was a genteel merchant; each year they receive a visit from her stepfather Kenyon, a crude rancher. After Grandfather Kenyon dies, Ralph and Molly spend several summers at his son Claude's ranch. Here Ralph is gradually initiated into adulthood and Molly refuses initiation. At the end of the novel Ralph kills Molly in a hunting "accident."

The reviewers and critics who have discussed *The Mountain Lion* agree in their basic interpretation of the novel. They see two symbolic schemes. First, Grandfather Bonney and the Fawcett home over which his image presides stand for everything bourgeois and stifling. Ralph and Molly reject the Bonney world for that represented by Grandfather Kenyon and Uncle Claude's ranch—a natural world of freedom. The second set of contrasting symbols is formed by Ralph and Molly themselves. They supposedly represent two different ways of reacting to adulthood, the ways of alienation and integration; Ralph illustrates acceptance and Molly resistance to growth. The novel concludes appropriately because Ralph symbolically rejects childhood when he not-so-accidentally kills Molly. Molly's end is also fitting because if she won't grow up she must die.[2]

Within this general outline there is some room for disagreement. What is the symbolic meaning of the mountain lion Ralph misses as he shoots Molly? What values can be assigned to Molly's refusal of adulthood and Ralph's acceptance of it? Should one stress Molly's nobility in the face of a society which rejects "misfits" and "freaks," or should one dismiss Molly as a hopeless neurotic and emphasize Ralph's successful growth to "maturity"? There is no limit to speculation because the answers depend on readers projecting their own attitudes on the worth of the society the initiate faces.

The problem is that the novel itself does not focus on these questions. It does not simply assume x, an adolescent resistant to initiation, and y, an adolescent accepting of initiation, and move on to other matters. Stafford's primary concern is why one adolescent rejects what the other can accept. What makes Molly a misfit and Ralph a candidate for initiation? The standard interpretation of *The Mountain Lion* is reminiscent of critical response to McCullers' *The Member of the Wedding*; it strives for "universality" so that Molly and Ralph become "symbols" and their gender is ignored. If Molly and Ralph symbolize contrasting reactions to adulthood, they might just as well be two girls or two boys. But, as we shall see, the action of the novel would not make sense if this were the case—it is essential that Molly is female and Ralph male. Stafford shows that, because Molly and Ralph are of different genders, the conditions of their lives and the fates they may expect also differ.

It is generally assumed that Molly and Ralph start out the same and only later grow apart. They are ugly, sickly, and precocious children who do not get along with other people. They band together against the rest of the world and are so close they suffer nosebleeds at the same time. Both children resist the prospect of adulthood; for example, they refuse knowledge of sexual intercourse—schoolmates "had said things and hinted at others so awful that Ralph and Molly had to fight them."[3] In one sense they are treated similarly by their mother. She obviously prefers her two older daughters, who are attractive and well-behaved, and denies Molly and Ralph love. In a typical instance the children come home with nosebleeds, and Mrs. Fawcett "chooses" to act anxious rather than angry, embracing them "carefully so that she would not stain her white smocked shirtwaist" (12–13).

Even at the beginning of the book, however, there are important differences in Ralph's and Molly's views and in the treatment afforded them. Mrs. Fawcett may withhold affection from both children, but she is less harsh with Ralph. When Ralph offends her and Molly stands up for him, she sends Ralph from the room but slaps Molly's face and locks her in the closet. Mrs. Fawcett sees Ralph as more significant than Molly and as deserving of some respect just because he is a boy. When the neighbors sympathize with her after Grandfather Kenyon's death, she says, "First my father, then my husband, and now Mr. Kenyon. But I have my son" (54). Because only men count, Ralph is "all I have left in the world" (120).

Even Ralph at age eleven recognizes his superior position. Molly may be his best friend, but she is not an equal. She should stop trying to imitate him, thinks Ralph:

It was natural for her to want to be a boy (who *wouldn't!*) but he knew for a fact that she couldn't be. Last week, he had had to speak sharply to her about wearing one of his outgrown Boy Scout shirts: he was glad enough for her to have it, but she had not taken the 'Be Prepared' thing off the pocket and he had to come out and say brutally, 'Having that on a girl is like dragging the American flag in the dirt.' (30)

Stafford thus accentuates Ralph's learned belief in male supremacy. And Molly is intelligent enough to know that girls are being compared to dirt.

Not only is Molly made aware of the inferior status of women,

but she is also instructed in the types of things women are expected
to do. It is Molly, not Ralph, who is sent on household errands
and made to sew and cook. Ralph takes an interest in dogs, prize-
fights, and beards. The children's areas of activity have already
been marked out for them. Molly tries to copy Ralph, for she
prefers his world to that of her mother and sisters. The sisters,
Leah and Rachel, resemble Mick Kelly's older sisters; they are
Good Good girls who seem to step from the pages of a nineteenth-
century novel. They are considered beautiful because of their golden
hair, their fair skin which Mrs. Fawcett carefully protects from
sunburn and freckles, their delicate oval faces, and their small-
boned bodies. Leah and Rachel seek the company of grownups
and always behave like "perfect ladies." Later in the novel they
attend boarding school in the East where they study French, music,
elocution, and dancing. (Mrs. Fawcett intends that Ralph go to
college.) Although Molly sometimes envies her sisters' good looks,
especially when she enters adolescence and becomes increasingly
concerned with her appearance, she basically dislikes the "femininity" her sisters represent; she refers to them contemptuously
as Elsie Dinsmores.

The low status of women and their typical pursuits is already
evident to Molly. Ralph may be a "freak" also, but he recognizes
his "superiority" in gender; he is preferred by his mother, he is
not unfavorably compared to his sisters, and he is held out, even
before adolescence, the possibility of a fate different from Molly's.
Certainly the implications of accepting or rejecting initiation into
adulthood are different when we begin not just with x and y but
with a girl who has an inkling of belonging to an inferior group
and being accorded an unwanted fate and a boy who may have to
give up some things to become an adult but anticipates a more
palatable destiny.

Just as Molly and Ralph have been seen as tokens symbolizing
two opposing reactions to adulthood, so have their Bonney and
Kenyon heritages been regarded as contrasting symbols. The theory is that when Ralph and Molly visit Claude Kenyon's ranch
they enter an environment superior to their Bonney-dominated
home, a freer environment which gives the children a chance to
develop and be initiated into adulthood. The Kenyon ranch sup-

posedly offers great opportunities of which only Ralph takes advantage, while Molly proves herself a "true freak" who can fit into neither world. There are two assumptions here that need to be examined: one that the Kenyon world is opposite from and superior to the Bonney world and the other that entrance into the Kenyon world provides Ralph and Molly with equal opportunity for development.

Critics speak of Uncle Claude's ranch in glowing terms. It offers "freedom and the natural world" as opposed to the "stuffy, conventional world of Grandfather Bonney"; it represents the "idyllic past" and even a "lost pastoral Eden."[4] Certainly any new environment would seem a welcome change after the coldness and snobbery of Mrs. Fawcett and her friend Reverend Follansbee. When they visit the ranch, Ralph and Molly are no longer overprotected by their mother or harassed by Follansbee, and they at least have space and fresh air.

Gradually, however, Stafford makes it clear that Grandfather Kenyon's world, the West,[5] is no Eden. The Bonney home may indeed be associated with deadness (Mrs. Fawcett wants to poison the children's cat and Reverend Follansbee's hobby is taxidermy), but it is hard to support the contention that the Kenyon world is vital in comparison. Stafford describes the Western towns near Claude's ranch as "exactly the same." The buildings are faded and the streets filled with undernourished dogs. Ghost towns have "sagging, rotten" houses and saloons and gambling dens "as haggard as death itself." The names of the saloons—"The Golden Horn," "The Silver Dollar," etc.—have become ironic. When Ralph goes driving with Uncle Claude, he does not find the "green world" of Charity Royall; instead, he sees "dreary, unpainted farmhouses that stood here and there along the road, unprotected by any trees, bleak and dusty in a grassless field" (103).

If this is not the Romantic "West," neither are the inhabitants Natty Bumppos and Chingachgooks. The men are freer than the Bonney types only in the sense of being externally more lawless. They get drunk with abandon, "behaving exactly as drunk people in the movies did" (97), and they get drunk every Saturday night. Molly perceives the conventionality of their behavior, and Stafford continues from her point of view the movie analogy previously introduced by the narrative voice.

Uncle Claude had bought a lot of grain alcohol and rotgut (*rotgut!* People ought to be put in jail for using words like that) and kept saying that they would all 'get stinko and then I'm gonna trim every jack man of you at Red Dog.' It was not hard to imagine. They would all pile up to the gallery and clank their silver dollars together, acting as if they were in a movie. (214–15)

The Westerners follow their own internal laws, which are different from Grandfather Bonney's, but just as stringent.

Stafford includes in *The Mountain Lion* two descriptions of dinner conversations, one a typical Bonney dinner conversation and the other a Kenyon one. Mrs. Fawcett recalls nostalgically dinners with Grandfather Bonney, where he "directed table talk as adroitly and interestingly as a professional forum leader. . . . They talked of everything under the sun, often examining such concepts as 'justice,' 'charity,' and 'truth.' Some of Mrs. Fawcett's most cherished values had been developed at that table" (22). The satiric thrust of this passage is obvious, but supper at the Kenyon ranch hardly seems superior. It has some advantages; for instance, no forum leader type presides over the table talk. Yet conversation is so undirected that no one pays heed to anyone else. Each man speaks when he feels like it, and no one listens. While the subject matter is not intellectually and ethically pretentious, it is limited and unvaried—the men give their opinions on hunting, drinking, breeding bulls, and auctioning horses.

It seems that in many ways there is not much difference between the Kenyon and Bonney worlds after all. The ranchers gossip as much and act as concerned with appearances and one-up-manship as the Follansbees and other Bonney types. Only the topics differ, so that while the Bonneys criticize people's table manners the Westerners gossip about who can drink more, what so-and-so did when he was drunk, who has the best horses, and who cheated whom out of a horse (153). One of the outstanding defects of the Bonney world is hypocrisy; the Kenyonites are masters of "the lie direct" (Ralph feels disillusioned when he discovers that many of his cherished Grandfather Kenyon stories were tall tales). While the Bonneyites make a pretense of caring about other people, the Kenyons openly don't care—they are frankly more interested in animals. There is a parallel between Mrs. Fawcett's being oversolicitous of Ralph's health and Uncle Claude's making him give up wearing his glasses. Neither one thinks of Ralph as a human being and considers his true welfare.

Perhaps readers have ignored Stafford's presentation of the West in non-idyllic terms because they have focused on the way Ralph sees it through most of the book. Ralph sets up a dichotomy between the Kenyon and Bonney worlds:

> Looking at the portrait of his Grandfather Bonney, Ralph *read into* his face vacuity and self-pride; he *saw* the plump hands as indolent and useless and *believed* that in a handclasp they would be flaccid. . . . He *decided* that the world was made up of two groups of people. The first he called the 'Kenyon men' and this included those, who, like Uncle Claude, knew the habits of animals and subjected themselves to the government of the seasons and who, with age, became neither fat and bald like Grandfather Bonney nor bony and ragged like Mr. Follansbee. The other group he called 'Bonney merchants' and this included everyone he had ever known with the exception of the people at the Bar K, Grandpa, and Molly. The fundamental distinction between the two groups was, he *thought*, their attitude toward horses and, vice versa, the attitude of horses toward them. (114, my emphasis)

The words I have emphasized make it clear that this is Ralph's perception. When he makes his observation, he is twelve or thirteen years old; even if he were an adult one might question type of handshake and attitude toward horses as the best criteria for judging people.

Moreover, as Ralph grows older and becomes more intimately acquainted with Kenyon life, his perceptions change. He still prefers Kenyon over Bonney, but he no longer idolizes the Kenyon men. He is troubled by Uncle Claude's scornful reaction to a sick bull and sees in Claude's face "a certain ponderous stupidity, a sort of virile opacity, an undeviating dedication to the sickness and health and the breeding of animals" (168). If Claude has contempt for a sick bull, what would be his reaction to an infirm person? When Ralph is greeted by Claude on his last trip to the ranch, he "distrusts the enthusiasm in his uncle's voice, so boylike that it actually cracked" (169). Uncle Claude, the epitome of the Kenyon man, now seems more like a boy. Previously Ralph had considered him the most independent person in the world. Now he realizes that Uncle Claude demands company on his hunting and fishing expeditions because he can't stand to be alone. Ralph has a new understanding of the noble hunt for the mountain lion: "He [Uncle Claude] had never grown up and his hunt for Goldilocks [the childish name he gives the lion] was a childhood game; his men indulged and protected him like an innocent. They wanted him to be happy and so they wanted him to have the mountain lion" (199).

It is not surprising that American literary critics could overlook the childishness of Kenyon men when young Ralph finally comes to recognize it. American myths make it difficult for critics to treat very objectively a novel which juxtaposes civilized and relatively uncivilized worlds and includes a boy's hunt for a wild animal. We are under the shadow of Huck Finn escaping from Aunt Polly and Ike McCaslin hunting bear. As Leslie Fiedler has repeatedly pointed out, the classic American novels seem "innocent, unfallen in a disturbing way, almost juvenile." The protagonists (and usually the authors, one might add) are possessed by a dream of being "free—uncommitted and unbound by history or moral responsibility."[6] In the national imagination, Fiedler says, two boys with fishing poles, who live in a "mythicized rural hinterland of America," are continually on the lam from Aunt Polly, Aunt Sally, Widow Douglas, Miss Wilson, Becky Thatcher and all the female symbols of religion and "sivilization." The "good, good place" in canonical American literature is almost exclusively masculine. In fact, it is a condition of its being ideal that it is masculine, an escape from women. It is not only Huck and Tom fleeing Aunt Polly but, as Fiedler puts it, Jake Barnes shaking off the "queers and the women and the Jews" to "cut loose" with "good old Bill."[7]

In *The Mountain Lion* the only women at the Kenyon ranch are Mrs. Brotherman and her daughter, Winifred. Mrs. Brotherman, as the housekeeper, performs services for the men that they would prefer not to do themselves. Winifred, when she is not waiting on the men at the dinner table, is a "tomboy"; she does not look or act like a girl. The ranchers concern themselves solely with the traditionally male occupations of animal breeding, hunting, drinking, and gambling; they value knowledge of the above activities, aggressiveness, and physical courage. Since the Kenyon world is uncivilized and heavily masculine in comparison to the Bonney world, it is possible to see it as "idyllic," another "mythicized rural hinterland," until one realizes that Stafford is debunking rather than following the myth.[8]

As we have noted, the corollary to the assumption of Kenyon superiority is the view that by moving to the ranch Ralph and Molly receive an equal chance to mature into adulthood. The children's growth is said to be facilitated by their leaving their mother and entering the environment of their Grandfather Kenyon and Uncle Claude. Molly, out of sheer perversity, or maybe because she has already made an irrevocable decision not to be initiated, fails to take advantage of this opportunity. However, Stafford shows us that only Ralph's growth is made possible by entering the Kenyon world. Molly's growth is further hindered.

If we examine Ralph's attitude toward adulthood, we will see that, like the female adolescents we have encountered, he is in conflict about becoming an adult. He does not want to be treated as a child, and he craves the privileges of adulthood. Yet he sees that he will have to compromise his integrity, will have to give in to and perhaps even become the things he hates about the Follansbees and Grandfather Bonney. In the beginning of the novel Ralph has a pact with Molly that they will not compromise themselves—they will always "hate the right ones." Ralph even wants an operation to drain off his Bonney blood. What is it about the Kenyon world that makes Ralph change his mind, while Molly continues to refuse initiation?

We know that "the vitality and freedom of the Kenyon ranch" cannot be an accurate answer because the Kenyon world is presented as only different from, not more vital and free than, the Bonney world. As we have also noted, however, the Kenyon ranch is masculine: it is free from women and what are considered female concerns and values. It is the masculinity of the Kenyon world and the implications of this masculinity that allow Ralph to accept adulthood.

We have seen that Ralph does not have to face the discrimination Molly encounters and that, even before he makes his first trip to the ranch, he has begun to recognize the superior position of his sex. He also shows an interest in growing up which, as critics have noted, expresses itself in his resentment of Molly's copying him.

But this desire for independence means independence from Molly in particular, for Ralph has begun to seek out male companionship. When Grandfather Kenyon visits, Ralph creeps downstairs in his stocking feet in the morning so he won't wake his mother and sisters and can have breakfast alone with Grandfather Kenyon; he even considers the fragrance of Grandfather Kenyon's coffee "manly and stimulating" (56).

Stafford points up Ralph's concern with masculinity by using either the word "manly" or terms strongly suggesting masculinity whenever he thinks of his grandfather or Uncle Claude. So when Grandfather Kenyon arrives Ralph thinks he makes the family chauffeur look small and "somehow womanly" (33). Ralph believes it impossible that Mr. Kenyon has ever kissed anyone, and when he shakes hands and greets Ralph, Ralph feels "personally, privately addressed, man to man" (34). After Grandfather Kenyon dies of a heart attack (Ralph worries that his collapse is unmanly), Ralph transfers his attentions to Uncle Claude, whom he also views as masculine. Claude looks like his father and has "massive, bullish" shoulders and heavy arms that terminate in the biggest hands Ralph has ever seen. Ralph feels embarrassed about his "sissy life" in front of this animal-like man and resolves to win his respect.

Ralph's first necessity is to detach himself as much as possible from Molly. He convinces himself that Molly is "going crazy" and accepts Uncle Claude's invitation to the ranch only for himself, because "maybe something is going to happen to Molly" (82). (This suggests, of course, that he wants something to happen to her, and foreshadows the ending of the book.) Although Ralph cannot prevent Molly's being sent to the ranch with him, he can separate himself from her at the ranch. For the next few years, then, Ralph allies himself with Molly at home while ignoring her at the Bar K. He intends that Molly and Winifred be friends so that he can more conveniently spend all his time with Uncle Claude.

Ralph understands that Molly should be taking Winifred as a female "role model" just as he takes Uncle Claude as a male model. Although he pities Molly when he looks at Winifred and notes Molly's comparative plainness (she may not be able to successfully imitate Winifred), he believes he can live up to Uncle Claude. Late in the novel Ralph recalls that his friendship with Uncle Claude began with a look. His first evening at the ranch he saw Claude looking at him and "read the look as a question of his worth or of his manliness" (92–93). Ralph has learned to equate worth and manliness.

Claude Kenyon may have little to teach Ralph about becoming an adult (if Ralph himself comes to perceive Uncle Claude as childish), but Claude can initiate his nephew into male activities. Ralph learns to work "like a grown man"; he learns to ride and shoot and butcher animals. On Claude's suggestion he stops wearing his glasses, even though he is sick for a while and can never see as well without them. Although Claude at first laughs at Ralph's blunders, he occasionally praises him so that his confidence grows. Finally they become constant companions, spending their free time talking of hunting and horses. Through Uncle Claude Ralph also comes to knowledge of sex. Earlier he had joined with Molly in refusing such knowledge. Now when Claude takes him to see a cow calving, he feels a "painful exultation." Although he knows it to be "bad," he gets a warm feeling (119).

By the time Ralph is fourteen and preparing to spend his last year at the ranch he has begun to view his mother and sisters in a different way, that is, as objects. He is so conscious of his older sisters' sexuality that he is frequently overcome by the desire to kiss their necks, and he has sexual daydreams about them. He can see nothing but their physical beauty: "Looking at his older sisters with their fine, tender faces, their shining hair, their dresses of flowered pongee, catching their clean, delicious smell of soap and talcum powder, he wished Molly had never been born" (144). Since he has reached adolescence Ralph's attitudes have changed so dramatically that whereas he previously admired Molly and felt contempt for his other sisters, he now scorns Molly instead. Ralph shows how thoroughly he has absorbed the values of his society in the way he judges female beauty. He covets Leah and Rachel because of their whiteness and blondness: he appreciates their faces because they are "doll-like and china-white" (151).

Ralph's discovery of sex does not come without conflict, however. Like Ruth Suckow's adolescent boys, he sometimes hates his body because of the rapid changes taking place in it; his exultation at the sight of the cows calving is also "painful," and his sexual desire for his sisters brings him anxiety and guilt as well as pleasure. When Ralph finally alienates Molly for good by asking her to tell him all the dirty words she knows, his guilt is almost as great as her anger. In his guilt feelings Ralph resembles Suckow's Carl Ferguson and Warren Bonney, and his dilemma might be similarly interpreted as an "Oedipus complex." Much of Ralph's guilt stems from his abandoning his mother and sisters for strict identification with Uncle Claude. He has transferred his allegiance so that he now relates to them as though they were merely sexual objects.

Ralph has some bad moments in making this transference. He feels "terrified" when he remembers that Grandmother Bonney-Kenyon died giving birth to Claude, and when Reverend Follansbee lectures him about the love that binds a son to his mother, he becomes embarrassed and agitated. "He tried in vain to envisage Uncle Claude, but could see, in his mind's eye, nothing but his mother, bending over anxiously as he lay sick of scarlet fever, the neck of her gray silk blouse open so that her breasts showed" (122). Here Mrs. Fawcett is both the nursing mother of childhood and an object of sexual desire, and Ralph tries in vain to blot her out for Uncle Claude.

Whatever debilitating effects his guilt feelings may have in the future, Ralph is shown in the space of the novel to make the adjustments required for growing up. He can do so, while Molly cannot, for two reasons. First, he receives positive reinforcement from adults. Claude praises and encourages him, and the more Ralph learns about manhood at the ranch the better things become for him at home. Mrs. Fawcett approves Ralph's having "normal interests" and admits that "it was right for him to enjoy the company of a grown man—and, moreover, he was beginning to look . . . well, to put it bluntly, to look like a human being" (123). She now considers him worthy of love and makes affectionate gestures.

Secondly, although he may have a few reservations, Ralph likes what he has discovered manhood will mean. He is pleased when his mother and sisters receive libidinous stares; while he feels some guilt, he likes the fact of women being prey. (One wonders whether he wishes increasingly that Molly were dead because he feels sorry for her or because, in not accepting womanhood, she is a threat to the existing order.) Ralph has learned that men have power and, even though he will not be able to exercise Claude's power in the Bonney world, where external violence is subdued, he has at least been promised the role of "man of the family" as he gets his college education in the East.

In many ways Ralph's initiation process at the Kenyon ranch resembles boys' initiation as it has taken place in so-called primitive cultures. Stafford portrays Ralph as being separated from women and having a male sponsor who takes the novice into his circle. This part of the initiation process has been explained as follows:

> Realizing that it is not until the boy 'outgrows the popular idyll of the mother breast' and turns to face the world of specialized adult action, the sphere of the father, that he can be considered to be a mature adult, tribal elders forcibly introduce the boy into a society of men and totally exclude him from the society of women, especially his mother. Deprived of maternal solicitation, he is bound closer to all men—including his father; his unconscious Oedipal hostility to his father is converted into friendliness.[9]

Claude comes to mind as Ralph's father figure, but he is also the initiator, and it may not be too far-fetched to consider Grandfather Bonney as the father figure whom Ralph learns to accept because of their common manhood. The sequence of ordeals the youth goes through is supposed to establish the authority of the elders, and "the initiate is shown that if he demonstrates the proper humility and respect for this authority, he will become one of the privileged ones himself."[10] The ordeals Ralph meets range from his learning to go without glasses to his conquering his fear of horses and guns, and finally culminate in his actually hunting the mountain lion.

In the hunt of the mountain lion Stafford draws not only upon the extensive practice of trial by hunting in primitive cultures but also upon this practice as it has been presented as a motif in American literature. American initiation stories often include ritual trappings, as in Faulkner's "The Bear," and they presuppose the same values implied in the primitive practice of trial by hunting. Most American initiation stories involving a hunt have as an unstated premise that physical courage is the prime value and that it determines "masculinity," a requirement for maturity. Francis MacComber, for instance, "comes of age" or gains maturity by becoming a "man" in mastering his physical cowardice. Thus it is quite natural that, just as they followed traditional American literary patterns in assuming a neat polarity between the Kenyon and Bonney worlds, critics should place positive value on Ralph's hunt for the mountain lion. The killing of the mountain lion would be a final trophy for Ralph, a symbolic indication that he has come to adulthood.

But Stafford treats the hunt ironically. As in the case of the East versus the West, or Bonney versus Kenyon, she departs from the traditional romantic pattern. As we have already noted, Claude's obsession with the hunt is finally viewed as childish. Instead of a deadly serious adult ritual in which an innocent youth gets to partake, the hunt is a "childhood game" in which Claude, the supposed initiator, is himself an "innocent." Nor does Uncle Claude serve as an intermediary between the boy and nature, like Sam Fathers. His only power is secular (he reserves the lion for himself by threatening to fire any of his men who shoot at it), and his natural integrity is called into question when he, like Ralph, breaks their pact that neither should hunt the lion when alone. Stafford not only questions the assumption that the hunt determines maturity, but she also makes explicit other premises of the hunt as an initiation ritual, that the hunt is an exclusively male activity[11] and that it involves an assertion of power over the female.

Only men hunt at the Kenyon ranch (Ralph thinks it "natural" that girls would be uninterested in hunting). But Stafford does not allow us to forget that the hunted, the mountain lion, is female. Claude names her "Goldilocks" because she looks "blond as a movie star" (170). Both Claude and Ralph never fail to refer to the lion as a "she" or a "bitch." Interestingly, Ralph has fantasies about killing a mountain lion even before Goldilocks is sighted. He automatically assumes that the lion will be female and imagines shooting "the mother and the cubs" and then bringing Uncle Claude to see (113). In other words, by killing the mountain lion, the embodiment of femininity, Ralph would be conquering the female and proving his fitness to take power in the world of men. His unconscious desire to kill Molly probably stems from the same source. As Chester Eisinger states, "She comes to represent for him, all unknowingly, the feminine principle that stands as the obstacle to the full expression of maleness."[12]

In many initiation stories involving a hunt the protagonist destroys a "feminine principle," perhaps in himself or perhaps a part of nature conceived of as feminine. As in the case of "The Short Happy Life of Francis MacComber" and Walter Van Tilburg Clark's *The Track of the Cat*, the hero thus proves his fitness to dominate an actual woman. In *The Mountain Lion* the pattern is so exaggerated that Ralph's hunt leads to the killing of the mountain lion as the symbol of femininity, the loss of any "feminine principle" within himself, and the death of Molly. If Ralph's initiation is costly to him, in that his becoming thoroughly masculinized entails denying part of his humanity, its effect on Molly is to destroy her altogether.

Initially Molly seems as happy as Ralph to escape her Bonney home and visit Uncle Claude's ranch. But, as we have seen, the Kenyon ranch turns out to be a male refuge, where the role of women is to be silent hardworking servants to the men. The housekeeper, Mrs. Brotherman, hates the West and can hardly wait to return to New England; Mrs. Brotherman's predecessor, Mrs. Fawcett, "buried herself alive" for ten years keeping house while Grandfather Kenyon travelled; Mrs. Fawcett's predecessor, Grandmother Bonney-Kenyon, was "humorless," "beaten," and "unhappy" (22, 167). Other women in the West are worse off than the Bar K women. Each year that Ralph and Molly travel to the ranch they see a number of gaunt young women with several small children. "Years of hard work and bad food had given the women a canine look in the mouth and eyes." They have rotten teeth and hair like dirty strings, and they always leave the train at some "bleak, treeless town" (149–50).

While Uncle Claude enthusiastically adopts the role of Ralph's initiator, he gives Molly the same kind of treatment she received at home. He considers her "bookish and unhealthy" (167) and takes offense at her ironic comments on the "ride 'em cowboy" behavior of the ranch men. At first Molly makes an effort to win Uncle Claude's favor. She too stops wearing glasses, but her eyes are worse than Ralph's and she is almost blind without them. Finally, as Ralph recognizes, Claude acts "so mean to Molly" that she avoids their outings and stays inside to write (104–5).

Molly initially clings to Ralph, keeping a diary of everything he says and taking vicarious pleasure in his accomplishments, but the

ranch life pushes them further and further apart. Molly blames
Uncle Claude for destroying her close relationship with her brother,
the only person with whom she has been able to communicate.
She pours acid on her hand when she realizes that Ralph is repudiating her in favor of Claude. Molly no longer feels sure that
she prefers the ranch to home. She gradually changes her mind
about the superiority of the Kenyon world and revises her list of
heroic figures to include only her father and Grandfather Kenyon,
who are both dead.

Home life, while it gets better for Ralph, becomes worse for
Molly as she enters her teens. Mrs. Fawcett thinks the ranch has
improved Ralph, but she considers Molly more of a freak than
ever. Although she makes affectionate gestures to Ralph, she remembers to stroke Molly only "as a sop to her conscience" (124).
Molly has never completely relinquished her desire to gain attention and love from her mother. The acid-pouring incident should
probably be seen as an attempt to gain Mrs. Fawcett's attention
as well as to punish Ralph for his defection. Yet it becomes increasingly difficult for Molly to win her mother's favor because,
as an adolescent, she is supposed to become more "feminine" in
her appearance and behavior. When she refuses to conform to this
expectation, she seems more and more eccentric to those around
her.

Much of Mrs. Fawcett's new approval of Ralph concerns his
looks. He has begun to look "like a human being" to her while
Molly appears the same as she did when she was eight. The growing
discrepancy in the protagonists' looks has been seen as a "motif
to point up their respective movements toward integration and
alienation."[13] This view is the result of seeing Ralph and Molly as
mere x and y tokens. Actually the looks motif reveals the differences in what is expected of them according to their gender. It is
significant that Ralph and Molly look much alike: they have the
same coarse, straight hair, heavy eyebrows, and prominent nose;
but, as Ralph notes, "in a girl such ruggedness was not handsome
as it was in him and Uncle Claude" (144). It makes little difference
what type of hair and features Ralph has so long as he looks healthy
and strong. But Molly is doomed because the ideal for girls is curly
golden hair and delicate, rather than prominent, features.

When Molly adds her own name to her list of "unforgivable"

people, she is looking at herself in the mirror. She cries and cries as she watches herself "getting uglier and uglier until she looked like an Airedale" (217). (She does not look like a cat, the golden mountain lion.) It would be surprising if Molly did not hate herself, considering the overriding importance her family places on good looks in women. In her short story "The End of a Career," Stafford demonstrates the connection of looks and self-acceptance for women. Angelica Early, one of the most beautiful women in the world, has always lived by her looks; she fends off the effects of aging by spending months each year having her face lifted and receiving other beauty care. When her doctor tells her that the only solution for wrinkled hands is gloves, she takes to her bed and dies. The doctor had argued that "amour-propre" is more important than looks, but Angelica thinks, "How could she achieve amour-propre when what she had most respected in herself was now irretrievably lost? And if she had not amour-propre, how could she possibly find anyone else to love her? Were not these the things she should have been told when she was a girl growing up?"[14]

But as a girl growing up Molly learns that beauty is supreme. Intellectual attainments, on the other hand, are worthless in women. Molly's predominant virtue,[15] her sharp intelligence, counts for nothing in both the Bonney and Kenyon worlds. Reverend Follansbee ridicules intelligence in women, while Mrs. Fawcett feels ashamed of Molly's interest in books and embarrassed by her bright comments. "Everyone said that she had the brains of the family, but as Mrs. Fawcett was not interested in brains, she thought this a handicap rather than otherwise and often told Molly that there were other things in life besides books" (143–44). At the ranch it is even worse for Molly because no one there reads. The Bonney world values intellect in a man (Grandfather Bonney's knowledge of literature is a plus), but the Kenyon world places no value at all on intellectual attainments. Molly earns Claude's scorn partly because she is "bookish." As for Ralph, when he and Molly were younger he admired her quickness and learning; when he becomes an adolescent he begins to resent her greater intelligence.

Just as Molly's braininess and love for books are scorned, so are the possible vocations she imagines for herself. Her dreams are more specific than those of Ruth Suckow's heroines and more attainable (for a girl) than Frankie Addams' or Mick Kelly's. Molly longs for a scientific career and collects hibernating ladybugs to send to the local agricultural college. While her expectation that her name will appear in a scientific journal may be naive, it is interesting that the protagonist of an earlier novel of adolescence, Gene Stratton Porter's *A Girl of the Limberlost* (1909), managed to put herself through school with earnings from her butterfly collecting. Porter's heroine received encouragement and support from other people, but Claude and Ralph make fun of Molly. They label her enterprise "absurd" and "cranky," and "they said they imagined her boxes of ladybugs had given rise to all sorts of jokes in the laboratory" (208).

Molly's family also considers her writing a silly pursuit and ignores her fledgling attempts. Ralph is the only person who agrees to read some of her creations, and he does not understand them. Early in the novel Molly shows Ralph a poem she has written which goes "Gravel, gravel on the ground/ Lying there so safe and sound,/ Why is it you look so dead?/ Is it because you have no head?" (31). Ralph regards the poem as evidence that Molly is "going crazy," and at least one literary critic seems to agree, claiming that the poem reveals Molly's fear of sexual assault and her subconscious choice of death over life.[16] Perhaps this interpretation can be supported, but it is interesting to know that Stafford herself wrote the poem when she was six.[17]

Because Molly does not want to adopt the roles prescribed for her she is assumed to be "crazy," and therefore everything she shows interest in is "crazy" and to be discouraged or actively scorned. To complete the circle, Molly reacts to the lack of choices presented her by acting crazier. Her writings at the end of the novel are more curious than the gravel poem and quite openly hostile. She ends up writing one story about an aristocrat who has wasted away to the point where all is left of him is a tooth, and another about two men who have been pared down, respectively, to a right ear lobe and a bit of hair.

Molly manages to withstand public criticism of her interests and abilities without turning her anger on herself until she loses Winifred as a model. Winifred is one of the few bright spots in Molly's vacations at the ranch. Molly greatly admires this "tomboy" who wears blue jeans with dung on them. But when Ralph and Molly arrive at the ranch for their last stay, they discover that Winifred has changed:

> She was plump now and so mature and feminine that Ralph could not recognize in her the shooting companion of earlier summers, that rather negative and taciturn person who, without playing a role, had seemed like another boy. Now she was a positive creature, self-assured, beautiful and glowing with an interior smile. (172)

The terms "negative" and "positive" indicate that Ralph approves of Winifred's transformation (she has become prey, like his sisters, and he has sexual daydreams about her too), but for Molly the change is a disaster. Because Winifred remained a "tomboy" through her early teens, Molly was given hope that she herself could grow up without becoming like her sisters. Now at sixteen or seventeen, Winifred is suddenly "demure" and "softspoken," wearing upon her lips an "enchanting" and "mysterious" smile. The new Winifred glows when Ralph tells her he heard she was a good dancer; when Molly counters by praising her ability to read Latin, Winifred frowns and casts down her eyes "as though her character had been impugned" (193).

Molly is disillusioned but does not give up on Winifred until Winifred writes back from college that "my sorority sisters are griped because I'm the only pledge who is dated up for the junior prom" (215). Molly had thought that Winifred went to college to study Cicero's essays. Stafford makes the content and style of Winifred's letter deliberately parallel to an earlier letter their sister sent Molly and Ralph when she left on a trip. Leah wrote of her engagement:

> Mother made me promise not to tell but she can't do anything now since by the time you read this I will be on my way to China!!!!! On the third finger of my left hand, I am now the proud wearer of a diamond ring! . . . The Donor of the Famous Engagement Ring is named Robert Appleton and he is a senior at Dartmouth. I'd give anything to see your faces when you read this. (147)

Molly's reaction was to pretend to vomit. Throughout the book she has been sickened by Leah's vapidity, and now Winifred, as evidenced by her letter from college, has become another Leah.

It is not surprising that Winifred leaves college after her first year in order to get married. A critic's contention that Molly irrationally turns against Winifred just because she joins a sorority at college[18] is true only in the symbolic sense. Winifred changes her looks, her manner, her activities, and her goals in becoming "mature and feminine." She thus joins a sorority Molly wants no part of.

Molly's distaste for the female roles prescribed for her explains the fact that she resists knowledge of sex. She refers to sex as "all that tommyrot with which people are trying to ruin my life" (182). When Ralph tells her about the cows calving, she calls him a liar and has a nosebleed. She insists that stallions and geldings are two different breeds of horses. Molly's elaborate preparations for bathing show her resistance to her own sexual development and her association of that development with the possibility of male attack. She locks herself in the bathroom by drawing the bolt and turning the key in the lock as well; she moves a chair in front of the keyhole to thwart any "Peeping Tom." Molly then puts on her wrapper while she removes her underclothes and gets into her bathing suit for the bath. In a bit of rather obvious Freudian symbolism, she does not sit in the tub while the water runs because a snake might come through the faucet.

Molly wants to deny the signs of her sexual maturity. She hates even the word "body," preferring to think of herself as a "long wooden box with a mind inside" (177); she decides she will never be "fat," that is, sexual, like Ralph and the adults she dislikes. Molly's refusal to accept "the facts of life" could be interpreted as support for Ralph's theory: she is "crazy."[19] However, we have seen that other adolescent heroines, like Charity Royall and Frankie Addams, fear sex also, connecting it with loss of autonomy. Ralph initially joined Molly in repudiating sex; he learned to accept it when he realized he would have power as a man. To Molly sex suggests the separation of the genders that makes her "inferior" and will thus "ruin her life." Her developing body is relentless proof that she is becoming a woman.

However "crazy" one may consider her, Molly resembles her predecessors in the novel of adolescence. If she seems a "freak," she would prefer, like Frankie, to be shorter, less "ugly," and blonde. She would like to measure up and win approval; at the same time she emphatically rejects the "femininity" expected of her and resists growing up. Molly is perforce a rebel but, again like Frankie, whatever types of rebellion she tries are essentially passive and even, as in the case of the acid incident, masochistic. Molly views herself as helpless just as Charity, Marjorie, and Frankie do.

When Molly and Ralph were younger their attempts to exercise control over their environment took the form of childish rituals; they would print Reverend Follansbee's name seven times on a piece of paper and then set fire to it in their Buddha incense burner. Ralph outgrows his belief in magic—not because it automatically disappears when he reaches adolescence but because he learns that he himself has power. Molly, on the other hand, uses the incense burner at the end of the novel just as she did at the beginning. As she sees fewer and fewer possibilities for action, she retreats into a dream world and isolates herself from those around her. If Frankie and Mick lost their "inner room," Molly loses her outer room and toward the end of the novel lives almost entirely in her own fantasies.

Because one can envision no viable alternatives for her, it seems as inevitable that Molly perish as it is that the mountain lion be shot. That Molly and Goldilocks are linked is suggested by their simultaneous death at the end of the novel. Molly identifies with the mountain lion, which has its own special meaning for her. She envies the lion for its freedom, beauty, and golden hair, but she hates it for being hunted. That is to say, the mountain lion has qualities of a mythical female selfhood that Molly dreams of: it is independent, beautiful, virginal, and untamed; yet in reality it is not free—it is hunted by man and will ultimately be destroyed. Molly and the lion are both prey.

The mountain lion may seem to be a goddess, a Diana roaming the woods, but it is a false god, one with limited power. While it is undeniably a dangerous animal, it also resembles the bull-roarer, a sacred object found in many primitive initiation rituals.[20] The bull-roarer when attached to a string and whirled about makes terrifying noises that supposedly represent the voice of the Sky God. When the male novice is initiated, he discovers that the bull-roarer is really harmless, and he is thus set apart from the women and children who fear it. "The unmasking of the gods is not merely the uncovering of a deceit, but the revelation of a truth which adult *men* can bear to know, namely, that the real power lies not in far-off gods of a sacred lake or mountain but in themselves."[21] Molly can light her incense and pray that the "god of the mountain" escape. Ralph, the new-born initiate, can act: he can hunt the lion down.

The revelation that "adult men" have the "real power" is the key to initiation in *The Mountain Lion*. As we have seen, Ralph's recognition of this fact leads him to overcome his repugnance to adulthood. But in Molly's case the dialectic between desire for adult status and resistance to it is weighted heavily to one side. The inducements for her to grow up are few because becoming an adult woman would mean accepting a state of powerlessness and, in fact, affirming her own "inferiority." It is thus misleading for critics to discuss initiation in general terms of entrance to "adult-hood," for adulthood has traditionally conferred a different status on men and women. Stafford does portray in her novel two adolescents reacting in opposite ways to the prospect of initiation. Her more central concern, however, is the *meaning* of initiation, which differs for each character. Ralph accepts initiation because manhood gives him privileges. Molly resists not growth in general, but growth to womanhood, a devalued state.

By including in her novel a relatively uncivilized setting and a traditional initiation rite, Stafford suggests parallels between adolescence in modern America and initiation in so-called primitive cultures. Whereas in Western societies the gender-role implications of initiation are often forgotten, in primitive cultures they are clear. The initiation ceremonies "emphasize the end of a period of life in which the distinctions between male and female character have not been clearly marked off. . . . These rites signalize that now masculine and feminine roles can be fully assumed."[22] As Bruno Bettelheim puts it, "Initiation rites of both boys and girls . . . serve to promote and symbolize full acceptance of the socially prescribed sexual role."[23] Although Western cultures do not have extensive communal rituals to mark passage from childhood to adulthood, the meaning of initiation remains the same: it is, by and large, the process in which the young person learns to adopt her or his gender role.

This process is painful for Ralph Fawcett; in order to assume the masculine role, he must "kill" the parts of himself society would define as "feminine." But, as we have seen, the reward for so doing—real power—is attractive enough to make Ralph's ambivalence relatively short-lived. A more severe conflict for Ralph stems from his doubts about the worth of the adult society he will enter. He wants adult privilege and male power, but he fears becoming a hypocrite, one of the "Bonney merchants" who seem to be ubiquitous. Ralph thereby resembles the two most famous adolescent heroes in American literature, Huckleberry Finn and Holden Caulfield, both of whom associate adulthood with phoniness.

Molly experiences the same conflict: she too has reservations about the Bonney world. But for Molly this conflict is secondary—almost a luxury, one might conclude—because she cannot accept her gender role. All the female novelists of adolescence I have considered thus far portray gender role conflict as fundamental in their heroine's growth to womanhood. No heroine wants to be a Bonney merchant; in fact, hypocrisy is one of the blights they object to in North Dormer, Massachusetts, Buena Vista, Iowa, Columbus, Georgia, and Covina, California. However, they are too preoccupied with fighting "femininity" to worry overmuch about the phoniness of adults. All the girls we have encountered want to be adults but not women. When they discover that women are defined as inferior, they become resentful and afraid. They fiercely resist whatever they see as evidence of women's secondary position in society (for instance, sex and marriage). If they are too much divided against themselves to rebel very consistently or effectively, they do rebel. McCullers' N. speaks for all: "I don't want to grow up if it's like that."

The adolescent heroines of Wharton, Suckow, McCullers, and Stafford have something else in common: they have not been received by literary critics with the same warmth as Huck Finn or Holden Caulfield. While Huck has been viewed as morally superior and Holden as typical, if not superior, Charity Royall seems morally "inferior." Margaret Ferguson has been called "pathological" and "devoid of brains and normal instincts" and Marjorie Schoessel "simple" and "emotionally and intellectually limited." Frankie Addams is a "monster" and Molly Fawcett a "misfit," "maladjusted personality," and "true freak."[24] Clearly these heroines

voice a protest that, unlike Huck's and Holden's, critics do not
want to hear. But the question remains—are they "freaks" compared with female protagonists in other novels of adolescence? Do
some novelists create adolescent girls who are more "normal"? In
the next chapter I try to answer this question with a broad survey
of novels of female adolescence from 1920 to 1972.

VII

THE ADOLESCENT HEROINE AND "GOD'S PLAN FOR GIRLS"

My survey of women's novels of adolescence from 1920 to 1972 is based on a reading of some two hundred novels published during the fifty-year period (see Bibliography for a list of the fiction). While much of this fiction must be considered of lesser quality than the works by Wharton, Suckow, McCullers, and Stafford I have already discussed, it clearly manifests the same themes. In reading the novels I tried to avoid imposing patterns upon them, recalling how frequently commentators on the novel of adolescence have distorted the female novels to make them fit their conclusions about the male. Yet however cautious one may try to be, it is difficult not to be struck by the similarities in novels of female adolescence.

There is a constant sense of *deja vu* when girls envy their brothers, when they express outrage at being molested by a man, when they try to avoid doing housework, or when they say they feel enclosed, imprisoned, stuffed in a sack, or under a bell jar. In novel after novel the protagonist is in conflict over her gender identity. Most likely she considers women inferior and wants to be male; she rejects the traditional roles and vocations of women, especially marriage, and reacts in a violently negative manner to sex. In her rebellion against growing up female the adolescent heroine is usually besieged from within and without. She is hampered both by the strength of social institutions designed to prepare her for a subordinate role and by her own inner conflicts and passivity.

While Jo March's "tomboyishness" is unusual in a fictional heroine of the nineteenth century, modern girls are often portrayed as "tomboys" in the early years of their adolescence.[1] Like McCullers' Frankie Addams and Mick Kelly, they dress in traditionally male clothes; they like to play baseball, basketball, and even football, and they sometimes compete vigorously with boys. Linda Bradley of Helen Woodbury's *The Misty Flats* (1925) breaks her leg proving herself a more courageous diver than her male neighbors. Peggy Goodin's Clem Kelley in *Clementine* (1946) beats up a boy her age in a fistfight. Both Linda and Clem express a desire to change their sex. Linda prays that God will turn her into a boy; Clem wants to be male because she "knew girls weren't good for much, and personally, she had never been reconciled to being one."[2]

The belief that girls are "not good for much" is sometimes shown as arising in the heroine's childhood, when she is affected by a preference shown by one or both parents for boys. The protagonists of Anzia Yezierska's *Bread Givers* (1925), Josephine Johnson's *Now in November* (1935), and Frances Frost's *Innocent Summer* (1936) learn early in life that their fathers feel cheated in having daughters rather than sons. In Agnes Smedley's *Daughter of Earth* (1929) Marie Rogers recalls her brother's birth. Her father was congratulated as though he had performed a great feat:

A *son* had been born! I felt neglected, and when I ran to my father and threw my arms around one of his pillar-like legs, he shook me off and told me to go away. There seemed something wrong with me . . . something too deep to even cry about.[3]

Lacy Cole of Jane Mayhall's *Cousin to Human* (1960) envies her older brother and tries to imitate him because her mother considers boys more important than girls. In grade school Lacy writes a poem entitled "Ambition," wherein she expresses a desire to transform herself from "just a silly girl" to a boy.[4] In high school she imagines changing into a boy and winning her mother's approval by protecting her from Mr. Cole's violent tantrums. She would be like herself but "stronger. She saw herself, a person like a boy, of muscles and fists and anger. She would beat down the world. Justice would be done. A nameless, suffocating desire came over her" (90).

If a girl's parents do not convince her of her inferiority with comments like "It's too bad you ain't a boy,"[5] she may be educated by her brother(s) or by other boys her age. Brothers are prone to making such statements as "You're a girl . . . you don't know from nothing"[6] (Louise Meriwether's *Daddy Was a Number Runner*, 1970). They often ignore their sisters because they are ashamed of being seen with them (Woodbury; Dorothy Day's *The Eleventh Virgin*, 1924; Betty Smith's *A Tree Grows in Brooklyn*, 1943). Like Ralph in *The Mountain Lion*, the boys seem to fear that associating with girls will impugn their manhood (high status). The protagonists of Woodbury's *Misty Flats*, Daphne Athas' *The Weather of the Heart* (1947), and Alix Kates Shulman's *Memoirs of an Ex-Prom Queen* (1972) all learn as soon as they go to school that there is a girls' side and a boys' side to the playground; boys have access to all areas, but girls are not allowed in "boys' territory."

Even very young boys seem confident of their superiority. In Elizabeth Pollet's *A Family Romance* (1950), seven-year-old Paul asks his adolescent sister, Marjorie, "Don't you wish you were a boy?" She feels "secretly angry" and "resentfully" tells him to leave her alone. "When a girl's getting dinner, she doesn't want little boys around bothering her."[7] Underlying this exchange is an obvious struggle for status—Paul asserts his "superiority" in gender and Marjorie reminds him of his "inferiority" in age. Her angry reaction suggests that she concurs with her brother's evaluation of the sexes.

Many heroines thus enter adolescence with the belief that Smedley's Marie Rogers expresses; there is "something," that is, their gender, that is deeply wrong with them. The few girls who have not consciously thought of themselves in terms of their sex receive a shock when they reach adolescence. When Courtney Farrell, the protagonist of Pamela Moore's *Chocolates for Breakfast* (1956), makes a conventional remark on women's inability to "think straight," a teacher points out that Courtney herself is female. Courtney suddenly realizes that she has always thought of herself as the boy her parents wanted—even in her dreams she appears as "herself but male"; now she must come to terms with her gender.[8]

Winifred Van Etten's Selma Temple of *I Am the Fox* (1936) is a happy "tomboy" until she begins to menstruate. Her mother then gives her a book entitled *God's Plan for Girls*, which tells Selma "what a beautiful and marvelous thing this was that had happened to her" and warns her "not to do anything to imperil the perfect functioning of this new power of womanhood that was in her." Selma's reaction to the book is worth quoting at length.

Selma felt pretty important and grown-up . . . but still was not reconciled. At present she had distinctly no use for the mystic and beautiful power conferred upon her. Nothing interested her less than her potentialities as a mother. She'd never liked dolls and she didn't like babies. She didn't see why she had to get ready to be a mother. . . . And the lady doctor said that basketball and all the wild, strenuous things she loved to do imperiled God's plan for girls. Selma wondered vaguely what God's plan for boys was. Apparently they didn't have any beautiful, mysterious power to safeguard, for they could take part in all the sports they liked. . . . If they didn't have to put up with a beautiful plan of this kind, she certainly was mad. . . . A feeling of hostility toward . . . all males in general took possession of her. . . . Men had all the fun.[9]

In Ruth Seid's *The Changelings* (1955), twelve-year-old Judy Vincent comes to recognize the implications of her gender when she loses her position as head of her neighborhood gang. Her second-in-command, a boy named Dave, announces that he will no longer be bossed by a girl. Girls have no right to be leaders; who do you think you are, he asks, a guy?

It was an accusation. She had never actually called herself a boy, but neither had she ever thought of herself as one of the girls she despised for their soft, plaintive weakness. She was simply Vincent, with the proud right to walk with the strong. She had proved it—in a thousand ways. As she turned away, with her old disdain, she was stunned to see that the other faces reflected Dave's ugly laughter.[10]

The male members of the gang need little urging from Dave to rip off Vincent's clothes and "prove" to her that she is "lacking" in being female.

Vincent's experience reminds us that "penis envy," taken in its literal sense, is an inadequate explanation for female adolescents' common desire to change their sex. In her days as head of the gang Vincent never missed a penis. She conceived of herself, in Simone de Beauvoir's terms, as a "subject"—"She was simply Vincent." It has to be demonstrated to her that her lack of a penis bars her from leadership. The adolescent protagonists I have been considering envy boys because they believe that girls are defined as "silly," that is, non-essential, and weak. Boys, they think, are considered more important and stronger—society's plan for boys is not to limit them but to make them leaders and bosses.

Adolescent heroines would no doubt find it easier to grow up female if they could admire and identify with adult women. However, the girls seldom want to pattern themselves after any of the women they know. Katherine Anne Porter gives a striking picture of the lack of acceptable models for female adolescents in her short novel *Old Mortality* (1938). Although this novel is usually interpreted in terms of Miranda's rejection of romantic myths of the Southern past, it is just as much about her rejection of all the traditional female types presented to her. As a child of eight, Miranda hopes she will some day resemble her aunt Amy, who has been canonized by the family as a great beauty and a veritable "angel."[11] But when Miranda breaks through the romantic haze surrounding her aunt's life and early death, she finds that Amy was unhappy in her role as Southern belle. Amy thought herself useless, did not want to marry, and rebelled against being a "nice girl." When she finally gave in and married Gabriel, she referred to her wedding as her funeral, and six weeks later committed suicide.

The fate of Uncle Gabriel's second wife seems to Miranda almost as bad as Amy's. Miss Honey, who Miranda first thinks is a racehorse from the way Gabriel speaks of her, is a defeated and embittered woman. She resents both the ghost of Amy and her dependence on her husband's fluctuating earnings; Gabriel notes offhandedly that she has been "gloomy for years" (149). Miranda's grandmother provides a more positive example of a wife, but we discover in another Miranda story that the grandmother was always ruled by men. Her married life was a "grim and terrible race of procreation," and in her widowhood she had "all the responsibilities of a man but . . . none of the privileges."[12] It is no wonder that, at age fourteen, Miranda decides she would like to be a nun.

But at convent school she comes to view the lives of nuns as "dull" and limited. While she had imagined that it would be romantic to be "immured" in a convent, her experience is to feel "hedged and confined" and "locked in" (139).

The final adult woman model available to Miranda is her aunt Eva, a Latin teacher and suffragist. As a child Miranda was taught to ridicule Eva as an ugly "old maid" and thus a "blot" on the family (115). At eighteen she is willing to suspend judgment and even admire Eva's courage in defying convention and fighting for women's rights. However, when Miranda actually meets her aunt, she is chilled by Eva's obvious loneliness, her melancholy, and her continuing jealousy of Amy. In Miranda's eyes Aunt Eva has had to give up too much for her independence from men. There is, finally, no woman she encounters whom Miranda can emulate. Belle, wife, nun, "old maid"—she rejects them all and feels that she has "no place" in the world (179).

Other adolescent heroines have the same experience as Miranda. In Sylvia Plath's *The Bell Jar* (1963) Esther Greenwood wants to avoid turning out like her boyfriend Buddy's mother or her own mother. Esther considers Buddy's mother a typical wife; she leads a "dreary and wasted life" cooking, cleaning, and washing from morning to night.[13] Although her own mother is a widow with a job outside the home, Esther, in contemplating the possibilities of her own future, considers this example "no help" at all. Her mother teaches shorthand and typing and "secretly she hated it" (32). Esther resists learning shorthand—"The trouble was, I hated the idea of serving men in any way. I wanted to dictate my own thrilling letters." Unfortunately all the women she encounters "serve men" in some role, and Esther feels "like a racehorse in a world without racetracks" (62).

In some novels of adolescence heroines do find female adults whom they respect and try to emulate. However, it usually happens that the girl becomes disillusioned about the woman's "superiority" or finds her vulnerable to the same pressures as other women. The protagonist of Susan Sherman's *Give Me Myself* (1961) worships a professor whom she believes "superior" because of her rank and academic achievements; but she soon discovers that in her personal life the professor is a weak alcoholic exploited by men. Goodin's Clem Kelley is furious when the drama teacher whom she has taken as a model quits teaching to become a housewife. Clem complains, "I can't imagine you staying home all the time just cooking and having babies and everything. It's okay for some people, but—" (142).

In Ann Petry's *Miss Muriel and Other Stories* (1971) the adolescent narrator who figures in several stories takes pride in her aunt Sophronia because she has become a certified pharmacist. But the narrator (N.) is disturbed that her aunt's profession does not make her immune to the disadvantages of her sex. Sophronia must wear a uniform in the drugstore so that people will not take her for a customer; she cannot work at night because it is considered improper for "ladies." It frightens N. that her aunt was the only woman in her pharmacy class—she says Sophronia's graduation picture reminds her of a group of male moths encircling a lone female moth. N. had assumed that a "lady druggist" would never be pressured to marry, but she learns that Sophronia's degree does not protect her from moths; even at work Sophronia is pursued by men who, to N.'s anger and disgust, make sexual advances and proposals of marriage.

N. is joined by a large number of adolescent heroines in her negative attitude toward marriage. We have already seen that "wife" is one of the alternatives rejected by Miranda, Clem Kelley, and Esther Greenwood. They think of marriage in the way Jean Winthrop of Helen Hull's *Quest* (1922) does: "I'm not going to get married! . . . I don't want to do housework and ask a man for money and everything!"[14] The protagonist of Katherine Dunn's *Truck* (1971) describes a wife in contemporary idiom as a woman who must "sit in a cozy fucking little house with a toaster bringing up sleazy brats."[15] Girls seem to be unanimous in their dislike of housework and child care, but the role of housewife and mother is the one they most frequently encounter.

Protagonists who are poor, like those of Dorothy Myra Page's *Gathering Storm* (1932) and Smedley's *Daughter of Earth*, have little opportunity to see any women other than their own mothers and neighboring wives and mothers. Page's Marge Crenshaw, who comes from a family of cotton mill workers, believes that once lower-class women marry and begin bearing children they have little hope of escaping a life of continuing poverty and misery. Marge vows never to marry, saying she would rather be ridiculed as an "old maid" than end up dependent and trapped like her mother.[16] Smedley's Marie Rogers also sees her mother as a victim of her child-rearing role, and she notes that her mother's economic dependence makes her a slave to her husband; her mother can "never toss her head proudly and freely and say, 'I'm payin' for my keep here!' " (38). Marie is disgusted because all the women she knows "seemed to agree that a woman had to 'mind' her husband" (57). Even when they succeed in acting obedient, they are often, like Marie's mother, severely beaten by their husbands.

Although adolescent heroines from the middle and upper classes do not have to watch their mothers struggling for economic survival, they also regard their mothers as subservient to their fathers. The wife's subordinate position seems to be a stronger factor in the girls' frequent rejection of marriage than the dullness they perceive in household duties and childrearing. Natalie Waite of Shirley Jackson's *Hangsaman* (1951) at first tries to ignore the way her smug college-professor father tyrannizes over her mother. She attributes to drunkenness her mother's complaint that he wants her to "hang around the house, cooking and saying, 'Yes, sir,' when he opens his fat mouth. All he wants is no one to think they can be the same as he, or equal to him, or something."[17] But when Natalie goes away to college and discovers the relationship of her English professor and his wife to parallel her parents', she begins to dread the thought of marriage.

In Dorothy Canfield Fisher's *The Deepening Stream* (1930) Matey Gilbert and her older sister both decide not to marry because they view their mother's experience as a constant struggle against being cast into oblivion by their powerful father. The mother attempts to assert herself by taking up various hobbies, such as art and dramatics, but the father

could see her, long in advance, getting ready to make one of her trys to get her share of importance, and when the moment came, he had all ready exactly the practiced blighting word and accent to reduce her kind of importance to nothing at all.[18]

The protagonist of Laura Beheler's *The Paper Dolls* (1956) feels that she hates women because "they weren't *anything*. All they could be was some ugly old husband's *wife*."[19] The "reduced importance" of the wife is what adolescent heroines who are older and more articulate call loss of identity. Van Etten's Selma, when she is eighteen, conceives of herself as a fox being hunted by a sportsman (her suitor); if she marries him, her identity will be killed. When he protests that marriage and death are unrelated, Selma replies that marriage is "another kind of dying, another way of corruption, of identity destroyed" (17). Some heroines create vivid metaphors for the loss of identity they fear in marriage. The protagonist of Dorothy Roberts' *A Durable Fire* (1945) believes that marriage has made her cousin "a swallowed creature who lived in [her husband] the way Jonah lived in the belly of the whale."[20] Plath's Esther Greenwood, as we have seen, initially dislikes the idea of marriage because a wife's housekeeping duties seem to take up all her time. But Esther is even more upset when her boyfriend tells her that when she marries and has children she won't even *want* time to write poems. Esther concludes, "When you were married and had children it was like being brainwashed, and afterward you went about numb as a slave in some private, totalitarian state" (69).

A large majority of female protagonists in the novel of adolescence dislike marriage, but almost all of them react negatively to sex. In early adolescence girls are often presented as seeking knowledge about sex and feeling frustrated when no one will answer their questions. This is the situation in Frances Newman's *The Hard-Boiled Virgin* (1926) and Dana Faralla's *The Madstone* (1958). In the latter novel Inger decides never to ask her mother about "these things" again "She gave us a silly little story, *Margery May's Twelfth Birthday*, to read, and it told us absolutely nothing at all. She didn't have enough courage to talk to us face to face as though it is something too shameful to be discussed."[21] But when they reach fourteen or fifteen many girls no longer want to know about sex. They are anxious and afraid in their ignorance, yet it seems worse to find out the truth than to continue to fear that they can get pregnant from kissing (Smith; Van Etten; Mildred Gilman's *Fig Leaves*, 1925) or from a boy's touching their breasts (Gladys Schmitt's *Alexandra*, 1947) or their vaginas (Meriwether). The protagonist of Dorshka Raphaelson's *Morning Song* (1948) thinks a virgin is a religious girl.

Some heroines resemble Frankie Addams in trying to keep their bits of knowledge separate from each other and unconscious. The narrator of Toni Morrison's *The Bluest Eye* (1970) understands that women menstruate and realizes they can get pregnant, but she refuses to connect the two facts. The adolescent characters in *Alexandra* are sixteen before they admit to themselves and each other their inner knowledge of intercourse, conception, and birth. "All the time we had known as much. Not plainly, not so that you could put it into words, but in some inward, obscure, and frightening manner."[22]

The popular assumption that adolescents require only a calm explanation of sex by a rational adult does not hold true for fictional girls. It is a recurrent situation in novels of adolescence for girls to try to escape explanations from understanding adults. In Sylvia Wilkinson's *Moss on the North Side* (1966) Cary runs away when her father begins to tell her how chickens lay eggs. The protagonists of Frost's *Innocent Summer* and Mary Ellen Chase's *Mary Peters* (1934) are upset and miserable when their mothers attempt to discuss sex in a matter-of-fact way. Mary Peters wants "desperately to escape"; her mother's words make her feel "hot all over," and she cannot help crying.[23] At times girls' reaction to information about sex is more extreme, as when Wilkinson's Cary and Smedley's Marie become nauseous.

There are obvious reasons why adolescent girls recoil from sex. The shame and secrecy with which our society has traditionally surrounded sex is clearly relevant; in several novels girls learn to be ashamed of their bodies and even to hate them. Sex is also associated with marriage, which, as we have seen, many adolescent heroines want to avoid, and with childbirth. Some girls are most afraid of the radical loss of status attendant on getting pregnant outside of marriage; others fear the physical pain of childbirth. In Day's *The Eleventh Virgin*, Victoria Lincoln's *Celia Amberley* (1947), and Elizabeth Madox Roberts' *The Time of Man* (1926), the protagonists' distaste for sex is traced to their having heard women screaming in childbirth. When Roberts' Ellen Chesser meets a pregnant woman, she is disturbed by this memory and actually "hate[s] the woman for the pain she was going to have."[24]

In *The Bell Jar* Esther Greenwood's witnessing of a woman

having a baby becomes a factor in her later mental breakdown.[25] Esther feels horrified at the woman's "unhuman" screaming and outraged when her boyfriend, Buddy Willard, tells her the woman has been given a drug which will make her later forget the pain. "I thought it sounded just like the sort of drug a man would invent. Here was a woman in terrible pain . . . and she would go straight home and start another baby, because the drug would make her forget how bad the pain had been" (53). After the birth Buddy wears a "satisfied expression," but Esther wonders if there are any other ways for women to have children (54).

Although Esther Greenwood is unusual in connecting childbirth with the oppression of women, many adolescent heroines associate sexual intercourse with male domination. In my discussion in Chapter V of Frankie Addams' resistance to sex I referred to Simone de Beauvoir's theory on this point. According to de Beauvoir, girls fear surrendering their subjecthood in intercourse; they cannot help being influenced by the conventional view of the sex act as conquest of the woman by the man. This contention is borne out in several novels of adolescence. The protagonist of Hope Field's *Stormy Present* (1942) becomes obsessed with the Biblical saying, "The wife hath no power of her own body," and vows that "no man shall have power over my body."[26] When the heroines of such novels as *Daughter of Earth*, Heather Ross Miller's *The Edge of the Woods* (1964), and Sara Mirliss Blake's *When Mist Clothes Dream and Song Runs Naked* (1965) accidentally view or hear intercourse, they assume that the woman is being attacked, humiliated, or used as an object. Pecola Breedlove of Morrison's *The Bluest Eye* fears that her father is in pain, but "terrible as his noises were, they were not nearly as bad as the no noise at all from her mother. It was as though she was not even there."[27]

Many girls do not need to rely on Biblical injunctions or observation of other women, for they have first-hand experience. Most adolescent protagonists must endure leers, "harmless" pinches, obscene name-calling, and sexual propositions from men, but what is startling is the large number of heroines who are physically assaulted. To give just a few examples, there is Judy Vincent, whose treatment by her former gang we have already seen, and Esther Greenwood, who is attacked by a misogynist date. In Theodora Keogh's *Meg* (1950) the twelve-year-old heroine has not even begun to menstruate, but she finds that her "initiation" into a club of four boys is to be "screwed" by the leader.

Jesse of Joanna Crawford's *Birch Interval* (1964) is tied to a tree by some neighbor boys, who touch and discuss her sex organs and then stick a pole up her vagina. This is merely a more extreme version of what Shulman's Sasha Davis refers to as "pantsing," the custom of a group of adolescent boys capturing a lone girl and tearing off her underpants to look at her sex organs. As she grows older, Sasha graduates to being forced to touch the penises of a gang of teenaged boys to a whole series of near rapes in parked cars. Adolescent girls in *Gathering Storm, When Mist Clothes Dream*, Lillian Halequa's *The Pearl Bastard* (1961), and Caroline Slade's *Sterile Sun* (1936) and *Margaret* (1946) are raped. In *Innocent Summer* and *A Family Romance* girls' fathers attempt to rape them, and in *The Bluest Eye*, Grace Metalious' *Peyton Place* (1956), and Joan Colebrook's *The Cross of Lassitude* (1967) they succeed.

The adolescent heroines who are sexually assaulted react with furious anger, but they also feel humiliated and ashamed and tend to keep the incidents secret. In many cases it is the main purpose of the attacking man or men to degrade the girl and make clear to her her "inferiority." Thus it is pointed out to Esther Greenwood that she is nothing but a "slut," like all women, and to Judy Vincent and Crawford's Jesse that they are "lacking" in not having penises. These girls resent being humiliated more than they do being physically hurt.

Almost every aspect of sex reminds adolescent heroines of a future they dread. Intercourse suggests to them domination and exploitation by men, menarche curtailment of their activity, childbearing severe pain and a restricted role as housewife and mother. We may note that, except for pain in childbirth, these concomitants of menstruation, intercourse, and childbearing are not necessary ones for female humans but are the result of social custom; for instance, menstruation does not actually entail restriction of girls' activity—the author of *God's Plan for Girls* merely states that it should. However, adolescent heroines seldom have any way to distinguish God's plan from society's plan. They are simply aware that they do not want to grow up limited by their female sex organs.

Thus, when Mary Peters listens to her mother's explanation of sex, she sees the "shining, quiet days of her past" being "shut out of sight" and feels that she is being forced to face an unwanted future (75). In *Fig Leaves* Lydia Carter's physical development brings her "nothing but terror." It creates a "definite wall between the present and the past" and portends a future which she thinks will be "too awful" to bear. Lydia, like many adolescent protagonists, thinks, "I don't want to grow up."[28]

If adolescent heroines try to resist growing up, however, or reject traditional roles of women, they come in conflict with social institutions. The function of these institutions, notably the family and the school, is to "prepare" girls for a subordinate role (usually wife and mother), and the methods they most often use are indoctrination and constant surveillance. Should a girl persist in being a "tomboy" past the "normal" age, she must be reminded that she is a girl, not a boy, and given further instruction in cooking and sewing (Woodbury). A mother must discourage her daughter from playing football, buy her a new dress or a golden-haired doll, and "talk vaguely about the future joys of home and babies" (Goodin, 13). When a female adolescent expresses a desire to be a composer, she should be humored and told that she can "marry a rich guy someday and never have to worry" (Rosemary Wells's *The Fog Comes on Little Pig Feet*, 1972).[29] If she wants to be a jockey or a fireman or a writer, she is to be reminded that girls do not become jockeys and firemen and that women writers are "queer" (Potter, Woodbury).

Parents and school officials are frequently portrayed as trying to control female adolescents' reading. In the early part of the twentieth century it was difficult for a girl to find in her reading "any references to adolescence, or anything to explain why life was so unreasonably difficult and why she was so unhappy."[30] Protagonists of more contemporary novels are given books on adolescence. In addition to *God's Plan for Girls*, there are the following: *In Defense of Chastity* (Plath), *Youth Faces Life* (Nancy Hale's *Secrets*, 1971), *Your Daughter and Nature* (Daphne Athas' *Entering Ephesus*, 1971), and *The Adolescent Girl* (Harriette Simpson Arnow's *The Weedkiller's Daughter*, 1970). But these books only prescribe how girls should act. As Esther Greenwood puts it, the one thing they fail to consider is "how a girl felt" (66). When heroines try to read on their own, they often run into opposition. In answer to her request for a novel like Upton Sinclair's *The Jungle*, Page's Marge Crenshaw receives a lecture from the librarian and a copy of *Elsie Dinsmore*. The protagonist of Ann Chidester's *Young Pandora* (1942) has to lie to obtain a Dreiser novel. Courtney Farrell of *Chocolates for Breakfast* is punished for reading *Finnegan's Wake* because it is not on her school's approved book list. Protagonists are restricted not only in the type but in the amount of their reading. They are warned that too much reading can interfere with household duties or scare away prospective boyfriends (Day; Woodbury; Shirley Ann Grau's *The House on Coliseum Street*, 1961).[31]

The surveillance of girls seems to penetrate every corner of their lives. Mothers are especially watchful, like Sheilah Miller's mother in Olive Higgins Prouty's *Conflict* (1927), who insists that daughters must never withhold any of their thoughts from their mothers. In quite a few novels the protagonists respond by keeping secret journals and diaries that they are hard pressed to hide from adults. Psychoanalyst Helene Deutsch, in attempting to explain the penchant of adolescent girls for secrets, resorts to the theory that they are getting revenge for all the secrets their parents previously kept from them.[32] But the fictional girls seem merely to be protecting themselves against adults' invasion of their privacy.

Boarding schools and colleges try to match the vigilance of parents by instituting detailed and complicated systems of rules. In novels where adolescent heroines go away to school there is usually, in fact, more emphasis on the girls' collision with restrictive rules than on their experiences in the classroom or in extracurricular activities.[33] In Kathleen Millay's *Against the Wall* (1929) the protagonist must memorize a whole book of regulations; in Carman Barnes's *Schoolgirl* (1930) she is punished for going to the library without stockings. Pamela Moore's Courtney Farrell can be penalized for offenses ranging from being late to dinner to not having her galoshes and polo coat at the foot of her bed at lights-out time. The galoshes are to stamp out ashes in case of fire and the polo coat to cover up the girls' pajamas—apparently female modesty must be preserved even in emergencies.

In many cases school regulations are designed specifically to mold girls to a "nice girl" ideal. Some of the rules for women at Lydia Carter's university in *Fig Leaves* are "not going on picnics alone with a man, wearing a hat when going into town, . . . avoiding the use of bubbling fountains in conspicuous places, staying off campus at night, not riding unchaperoned in automobiles after nine o'clock." Lydia wonders, as the reader might, why drinking fountains should be taboo. She thinks, "It couldn't be germs. Possibly it pulled your skirt up as you leaned over! What a silly lot of rules!" (161).

For enforcement of the rules some schools have so-called "honor systems," where students are supposed to spy on each other. Others use housemothers and deans to watch for girls who deviate from the norm. The lectures and "pep talks" of these parent substitutes are occasionally presented as more absurd than the college rules. The heroine of Margery Latimer's *This Is My Body* (1930) is warned by the Dean of Women that she must learn to be a "good sport" and "adjust" herself to college traditions. "It is not pleasant," the Dean says. "Nothing is pleasant. I mean to say, nothing unpleasant is pleasant."[34] In Wells's *The Fog Comes on Little Pig Feet* a lecture from the headmistress is only the first step for girls who persist in breaking rules. The protagonist, Rachel Sasakian, learns that her boarding school has a "special" dormitory, separated from the rest of the school by a moat, for "social problems or mental problems or something that doesn't fit in" (63).

In the more recent novels of adolescence the authority figure in the background may be a psychiatrist; he or she replaces the parent, the school principal, or the minister in demanding girls' confidence and explaining the "adjustments" they must make. Although the heroines of *The Bell Jar* and Joanna Greenberg's *I Never Promised You a Rose Garden* (1964) are finally helped by sympathetic psychiatrists,[35] the psychiatrist is often portrayed as purely an agent of social force. The doctor in Wells's novel, for instance, seems unable to comprehend the word "free." When Rachel tells him she wants to leave school for the "free world," he responds, "How long have you had these feelings about Communists chasing you?" (56).

Susan Schnitzer's psychologist in *The Weedkiller's Daughter* is a "Grand Inquisitor" who uses the royal "we" when he talks and hides a tape recorder in his office.[36] He claims that "the main desire of the normal girl is hunting and holding a mate"; if her intelligence and achievement test scores are too high, she must be "seeking . . . compensation for lack of popularity" (360). Susan quickly decides to conceal her true feelings. If the "normal" adolescent girl is supposed to hate her mother, "jealous of her mate-catching, her childbearing abilities," Susan asks, "How would this—this psychologist evaluate me if I—were to say I pitied my mother?" (75).

In Nora Johnson's *The World of Henry Orient* (1958) Marian Gilbert sees her friend Val's psychiatrist as part of a conspiracy to check Val's rebellion. Marian gets angry when the psychiatrist explains that Val must learn "good manners," "outgrow" her close attachments to other girls, and become interested in boys.[37] Marian contends that she can understand Val's problems better than the psychiatrist or any other adult. "I shared her fate; it was my world as well as hers, we would grow up into it at the same time, and it was shocking to see how it was already treating another of my generation" (207).

In his survey of novels of adolescence W. Tasker Witham states that the female protagonists seem to be less rebellious than the male.[38] Certainly they are less open in their rebellion. Adolescent girls are seldom portrayed as violent or in trouble with the police; they tend instead toward passive resistance and secret disobedience. When female protagonists try more direct means of revolt, they usually find themselves shuttling back and forth between restrictive institutions. They rebel against one institution by embracing another, which turns out to be just as limiting. Thus girls may try to escape an oppressive home by going to school or to escape an oppressive school by going home. They may marry to elude their families or remain at home to avoid marriage. But whatever they do they cannot get away from social pressure to accept a subordinate role.

The experience of Millay's Rebecca in *Against the Wall* is a case in point. Rebecca can hardly wait to leave her small-town home to attend college. She resents being a "nice girl," who cannot go out alone at night or frequent the bars and dancehalls her brother enjoys. At home she has the choice of marrying her suitor and being a housewife or continuing to work in a butcher shop. Yet when Rebecca finally gets to college she discovers that she does not have the freedom she anticipated. Not only is she hemmed in by a plethora of rules, but the school holds the same assumptions about women's place that she was trying to escape. The purpose of women's colleges, Rebecca decides, is

to teach girls and to keep them from knowing anything at the same time. A simple task, that. Let 'em learn Psychology Physicology Family History Astronomy Biology Anything—but never let them *think!* Never let them apply their learning to their own brains. To their own bodies. Let them praise God and get married—to the only man they've ever kissed—and hate him, maybe, but have lots of babies. And keep his house clean.[39]

It is easy to see the difficulties girls confront in trying to rebel if we consider what happens when they react against the double standard of sexual behavior for men and women. It might appear that since adolescent heroines have such an aversion to sex, they would consistently seek to avoid it; yet several protagonists hurry to lose their virginity. The key to this seeming contradiction is that they are rebelling against being Good Good girls. To remain "pure" or a "nice girl" means, in their view, to comply with the restrictions society places on women but not men. When she discovers that her boyfriend has had an affair, Esther Greenwood wants to lose her virginity as soon as possible because "I couldn't stand the idea of a woman having to have a single, pure life and a man being able to have a double life, one pure and one not" (66). To be a "nice girl" is to objectify oneself. As Millay's Rebecca puts it, "Nice girls had to be owned. Had to belong to any man they wanted. Possessed. Tagged. And put away for safe keeping" (306).

The conflict between resistance to sex and resistance to being a "nice girl" is openly expressed by Smedley's Marie Rogers. Marie shrinks from sex—"Sex meant violence, marriage, or prostitution, and marriage meant children, weeping and nagging women and . . . unhappiness"; yet, at the same time, she feels uncomfortable about being a virgin at nineteen. "I resented virginity, and the so-called 'purity' of women, and reacted violently to any suggestion about it. It had always shamed me that men judged women by such a standard" (157). Thus, when a protagonist attempts to rebel, she is caught between two evils. If she resists sex, the girl sees herself as complying with the double standard and waiting to be "owned." If she defies society and tries sex outside of marriage, she risks punishment and exposure to the domination she fears. Furthermore, the girl does not change society's valuation of women; she merely switches from one object status to another, from "nice girl" to "whore." In connection with this point it is notable that when adolescent heroines do make an active rebellion against adult authority, it is generally in terms of sex: they lose their virginity, have sex with a number of men, or, in delinquency novels, become prostitutes. Ironically, in attempting to do something as bad as possible to show their contempt for the society that limits them, girls can only respond as sexual beings. It would take more awareness and sophistication than they possess for them to realize that with this type of rebellion they only confirm society's equation of women with their sex organs.[40]

It is thus difficult for adolescent heroines to put up any effective opposition to society's plan for girls. If they are stubborn enough to resist indoctrination and clever enough to escape constant surveillance, they may attempt to rebel against accepting a subordinate role in society. But the restrictions placed on women are so pervasive and so thoroughly institutionalized that girls' revolt can easily be contained. Moreover, adolescent heroines have to contend with what is probably the greatest hindrance to girls' rebellion—their own internal conflict. Many protagonists find it hard to trust their own feelings and perceptions; they suspect that *God's Plan for Girls* and *In Defense of Chastity* are "right" and they are "wrong." As I have noted, adolescent protagonists very seldom meet adult women who have not accepted their position as the "second sex," and until very recently rebellious women have been all but absent from history books. Hence it often seems to the girl that she stands alone in her predicament, and she fears being "abnormal."

Sasha of *Memoirs of an Ex-Prom Queen* resembles Frankie Addams in her anxiety about being a "freak." Esther Greenwood thinks she must be "abnormal" because she seems to lack a maternal instinct and prefers studying to dating. Wells's Rachel worries that she ought to learn to dance and meet boys instead of

spending her time by herself thinking and writing in her diary.
Being a "loner," she says, is

> all very fine for cowboys, but probably not so fine for teen-age girls. People
> who talk to themselves are supposed to be crazy. Having a diary is 'normal,'
> but in a way it is talking to myself. I am afraid, at times, that I shall be
> the first in my family to go mad. (12)

After Rachel is sent to a psychiatrist for breaking school rules, she
is convinced that she must be "crazy."[41] The protagonists of *Hangsaman* and Jessamyn West's *Cress Delahanty* (1945), who are both
secretly rebellious and uneasy about their futures as women, think
of themselves not only as "freaks" but as criminals. Natalie and
Cress have fantasies where they imagine themselves being questioned by a detective about some unspecified crime.

In their horror of being abnormal, crazy, or criminal, girls often
begin experimenting part-time with doing what they know is expected of them, that is, concerning themselves with their looks
and showing interest in love and romance. Thus they often seem
to be two people at the same time. The protagonist of Josephine
Carson's *Drives My Green Age* (1957) is sometimes "Miss Boy"
and sometimes "Miss Lady." Clem Kelley plays football with the
boys and also tries out her mother's lipstick and giggles over love
stories in *Ladies' Home Journal*. West's Cress Delahanty and Anne
Nall Stallworth's Florrie Birdsong of *This Time Next Year* (1971)
spend part of their time in boys' clothes and part in their mothers'
dresses and high heels. When dressed up, both girls are torn between pride at their "grown-up" looks and resentment of the constraints of women's clothing; Cress's hat and high heels cause her
pain, while Florrie considers bras "medieval torture instru-
ments."[42] Their ambivalent feelings toward adult women's dress
mirror a basic conflict of adolescent protagonists: they want to be
"grown-up," but they do not want to be restricted as women.

In their relations with boys, adolescent heroines often develop
"crushes" and make a trial at being "in love," but young adolescents tend to pick a man who is much older and, ideally, one who
is married. They can thus prove themselves "normal" (interested
in romance) and at the same time avoid actual contact with the
man. In *Cress Delahanty* and *Celia Amberly* the protagonists, just

to be extra safe, choose middle-aged married men whom they believe to be dying. Older adolescents, such as Esther Greenwood, Sasha Davis, and Lydia Carter, acquire a boyfriend as a sort of shield. Like many of Suckow's female adolescents, they do not particularly like the boy, but his attentions ward off their own and society's worry that they are not properly "feminine."

It is obviously a formidable task for girls to try to reject the female roles offered them and at the same time prove they can live up to these roles. They are reduced to striving to be "feminine" and "non-feminine" simultaneously. Adolescent protagonists are also hampered by their internalization of society's low estimation of women. As we have seen, girls learn very early that females "aren't good for much." Although they may protest this valuation during adolescence, they seldom succeed in discarding a deeply ingrained belief in women's inferiority. Even writers like Agnes Smedley and Sylvia Plath, who make their heroines fully aware that women are forced into inferior positions, portray them as crippled by hatred of women and therefore self-hatred.

Marie Rogers, for instance, is constantly outraged at discrimination against women, but at the same time she despises women for their complicity in oppression and says she hates herself "for having been born a woman" (119). So, when girls attempt to rebel against society, they often end up turning their anger against themselves. Courtney Farrell deliberately loses her virginity in defiance of "nice girl" standards, but she then slashes one of her fingers with a razor blade to remind herself that she is "guilty" (119). When a boy tries to kiss her, Wilkinson's Cary, who has resolved to keep free of men, punishes *herself* by beating a splinter into her hand.

Heroines' inner conflict between wanting to protest society's low valuation of women and despising women (including themselves) is often reflected in their attitudes toward their parents. A girl may hate her father and appoint herself her mother's protector, like Sara Solinsky in Anzia Yezierska's *Bread Givers*, and still wonder why her mother submits. If she is not inferior, how did she end up a servant? Sara demands of her mother, "How could you have married such a crazy lunatic as Father?"[43] Not until she returns home to her mother's deathbed, in a pattern familiar from Ruth

Suckow's novels, does she decide that she failed to appreciate her mother's strengths. In several novels the adolescent heroine feels torn between her mother and her father. Natalie Waite of *Hangsaman* becomes a pawn in her parents' private battle. Her father encourages her to model herself after him and scorn her mother as a moron who should be restricted to the kitchen. Natalie's mother counters by acting as though "she and Natalie were associated in some sort of mother-daughter relationship that might, by means of small female catchwords and feminine innuendoes, separate . . . the family into women against men" (16). Although Natalie frantically resists her mother's efforts, since she would rather be a professor and writer like her father than a kitchen slave, she cannot forget her mother's situation. Throughout the novel she vacillates between identifying with her father and identifying with her mother.

Ellen Webb of Mildred Walker's *Winter Wheat* (1943) also feels "pulled two ways" in her relationship with her parents.[44] In childhood and early adolescence Ellen admires her primitive and intuitive mother and wants to resemble her. But when she discovers that her mother faked pregnancy in order to get her father to the altar, Ellen is deeply ashamed. She says, "I'm not like you, Mom, so I'd do anything to get a man to marry me" (314), and begins to view herself as more like her father. Yet Ellen cannot turn her back on her mother; she still feels hurt and angry when people "act as though Mom weren't quite . . . quite equal to Dad" (6, Walker's ellipsis).

Natalie and Ellen resemble Ruth Suckow's protagonists in their inability to identify comfortably with either father or mother. They have good reason to try to resemble, or at least to please, their fathers, who hold privileged positions in society; the girls all dread ending up with their mothers' fate. Yet they cannot entirely abandon their early identification with the mother and their feeling that she *should* be equal. The desire to champion the mother remains as strong as the impulse to deny her. Many girls want to fight for their mothers (and themselves) by, as Mayhall's Lacy Cole puts it, "beating down the world" and "doing justice."

It would be hard to imagine any group less equipped to "beat down the world" than the heroines of novels of adolescence. Even if the social forces arrayed against them were less formidable and the girls were not quite so divided against themselves, they would still be victims of their female upbringing. That is to say, any attempt to "do justice" is usually doomed before it starts because the girls have already learned to be passive. I noted in discussion of *The Member of the Wedding* that Frankie is more passive than McCullers' male adolescents and thus greatly limited in her rebellion. But, in comparison with many female adolescent protagonists, Frankie seems a dynamo.

There is Elizabeth Pollet's Marjorie, for instance, who is inwardly defiant but outwardly acquiescent almost beyond the realm of credibility. Although she dislikes the man who pursues her and secretly resents his emphasis on her looks and his ordering her around, Marjorie behaves "like a helpless little puppy on a leash" (19). She simply waits for "what would happen next" and obeys her lover as he tells her when it is time for her to eat dinner, to sit beside him quietly while he works, or to submit to him sexually (118–19).

Some protagonists seem to spend most of their time prone. Shulman's Sasha Davis dislikes sex but allows her boyfriend to "work out" on her whenever he wants.[45] In Anne Tyler's *A Slipping-Down Life* (1970) the heroine idles away her days either sleeping or lying down while eating and reading romances. In the evening she manages to sit at her window "gazing into darkness so heavy and still that it seemed something was about to happen, but nothing ever did."[46] Even those girls who most clearly recognize the oppression of women are passive. Marge Crenshaw of the radical *Gathering Storm* points out the injustice of its being easier for boys to leave the cotton mills and make their way in the world, but she never even attempts to escape. Van Etten's Selma considers herself "helpless" (192). Plath's Esther overflows with sarcastic remarks about Buddy Willard, but it "never occurred to her to say no" to his plans for her (78).

These heroines have already begun to lose their autonomy. In Simone de Beauvoir's terms they are learning to regard themselves as "objects" rather than "subjects." Pollet's Marjorie often thinks she is nothing more than an ornament. In *The Weather of the Heart* Eliza Wall views herself as a "top" and her boyfriend as "the power that made her spin about."[47] Cress Delahanty splits herself in two in her imagination so that she can look at herself as object. She stands in front of a mirror surveying her body:

And because she regarded herself, thinking of him, he who was yet to come, it was as if he too, saw her. She loaned him her eyes so that he might see her, and to her flesh she gave this gift of his seeing. She raised her arms and slowly turned and her flesh was warm with his seeing. Somberly and quietly she turned and swayed and gravely touched now thigh, now breast, now cheek, and looked and looked with the eyes she had given him.[48]

This splitting effect also appears in *The Time of Man* and *Hangsaman*. Roberts' Ellen Chesser believes she is "ugly" and "useless" in herself, but she can endow her body with beauty and importance by pretending that she is a man admiring it (123). Natalie Waite continually steps back and tries to view herself as an object of male eyes.

Like many female adolescent protagonists, Natalie occupies her time dreaming rather than acting. Girls have fantasies of leaving home, travelling around the world, becoming famous writers or actresses, even of protesting the efforts of parents or suitors to control their behavior. But they seldom take any steps toward realizing their dreams. Some adolescent heroines gradually withdraw from the real world. The protagonist of Grau's *The House on Coliseum Street* thinks she is part of a play where "nothing was going to happen; nothing was real."[49] Pollet's Marjorie says, "I spend all my time daydreaming" (which perhaps explains her willingness to let her boyfriend control her outer movements) (102). The protagonists of Laura Beheler's *The Paper Dolls*, Josephine Johnson's *Wildwood* (1945) and Jean Stafford's *Boston Adventure* (1944) retreat entirely to the realm of their imaginations.

With such a passive orientation toward the world it is no wonder that girls' rebellion is often what de Beauvoir calls "symbolic." They set fires (Colebrook, Wilkinson), run away from home when sure to be caught (Athas, Blake, E. M. Roberts), and perform masochistic actions like cutting or burning themselves (Moore, Tyler, Wilkinson). In attempt to exercise some control over their futures, girls rely on some imaginary passive force instead of their own initiative. Thus many adolescent protagonists follow the example of Molly Fawcett who, unlike her brother Ralph, clings to her childhood belief in magic. Girls wait for the prince or the fairy godmother to come and save them. Marian Gilbert can only "hope against hope that some sort of magic would take us [she and her friend, Val] back to where we had been before life got so vastly complicated" (172).

Adolescent heroines seemingly lack the resources they would need to do battle with the world; they are only, as I said of Frankie Addams in Chapter V, "struggling in their cages rather than trying to get out." Significantly, the image of the cage, or the trap, is the most common image in novels of female adolescence. Woodbury's Linda Bradley is "stifled," even "enclosed and suffocated" in her parents' home.[50] The protagonists of Johnson's *Now in November* and Dunn's *Truck* feel "trapped,"[51] and it seems to Latimer's Megan Foster "as if everything was pushing her into a small space" (16). Sheilah of Prouty's *Conflict* perceives herself as "a wild animal caught in a trap";[52] she believes, changing the metaphor, that she is "caught in a net—a soft, clinging net, and every effort she made to get out of it, simply seemed to bind the meshes closer and closer" (13).

Sometimes the trap image dominates the entire novel. Selma Temple of *I Am the Fox* thinks of herself throughout as a fox who has been hunted down and caught in a trap. In Kathleen Millay's and Sylvia Plath's novels the protagonists are represented, in accordance with the titles, as "against the wall" and under a "bell jar." The latter makes an especially effective image of constriction, for the bell jar is a trap which also conveys the sense of suffocation many protagonists have. Plath extends its reference beyond her particular heroine. She suggests that Esther's situation of "sitting under the . . . glass bell jar, stewing in . . . sour air" (152) is not merely the result of her own "neuroticism" or "madness" but is the general state of adolescent girls. Esther says, "What was there about us, in Belsize [mental institution], so different from the girls playing bridge and gossiping and studying in the college to which I would return? These girls, too, sat under bell jars of a sort" (194).[53]

In examining pre–1920 novels with girl protagonists I noted the existence of a few "socialist-feminist" works in which girls were allowed to escape their bell jars. Heroines were shown actively challenging paternal authority, escaping from home, meeting feminist guides, and becoming strong and independent. However, modern novelists of adolescence, even those who are radical or openly didactic, seldom depict their heroines taking such a course. Their protagonists tend to rebel secretly and haphazardly; if they escape one institution or female role, it is usually for another just as restrictive; strong women guides are conspicuously absent. The modern girl is presented with few positive alternatives, and her future seems bleak.

"Comic" novels of adolescence, those which portray adolescent antics from a nostalgic or patronizing point of view, usually end with the protagonists giving up their protests and accepting womanhood. But, although the author may imply that she is thus providing a "happy ending," she generally shows some ambivalence by stressing the heroine's resultant loss of identity. Jessamyn West identifies most of the time with Cress Delahanty's parents and breathes a sigh of relief when she brings Cress to the threshold of adulthood properly "feminine." Still, she has Cress point out near the end of the novel:

It was strange how women lost, as they grew up, their own private, special look.... Girls flashed signals as to who they were, jumped, screamed, cried: they let you know. But grown-up women like Mrs. Agnew [her mother's friend]? What could you tell about her? Except that she was grown-up. She was round, she was gray, she was grown-up. She had crawled in under a smooth shell. (211–12)

In *Clementine* Peggy Goodin describes the exact point at which Clem stops resisting womanhood. When she loses a wrestling match with a boy named Hank, Clem indulges in a fit of crying.

She cried for ... her wrist that hurt and for the traitor who had said 'I give.' She cried for something else that hurt more than all the twisted wrists in the world, something she could do nothing about. It was a man's world—a dirty doggone man's world. (81)

After this incident Clem changes. She worries about her appearance, tries to like cooking and knitting, and pretends to be stupid at geometry so Hank can feel superior. Although she earlier rejected *Little Women* to read *The Red-headed Outfielder*, she now

pours over *Man's Love Life—What He Expects and Wants.* Goodin's official attitude seems to be that Clem's transformation is "cute"
and that she has won a victory when she gets Hank to go steady.
However, it is hardly possible to portray loss of self more directly.
Everything Clem does after the crying incident is pretense in order
to acquire Hank: she has adopted a fake identity.

In novels where the adolescent heroine does not clearly lose her
identity, her ultimate fate is usually left undefined; she remains in
conflict with society and divided within herself. The reader does
not know whether the protagonist will be reconciled to growing
up, like Cress and Clem, whether she will adjust outwardly and
continue to rebel inwardly, or whether she will become mentally
ill. The latter possibility is not at all uncommon, for those novelists
who present their heroines as emphatically rejecting womanhood
usually give them a choice of madness or death. While I think
critics should exercise great caution in referring to characters as
"mad,"[54] it is clear that some girls are incapacitated. They are
portrayed as withdrawn so far into their own dream worlds that
they can hardly function in everyday tasks (Beheler, Grau, Green,
Jackson, Johnson, Latimer, Morrison, Plath, Pollet).

At the conclusions of *The Bell Jar* and *I Never Promised You a
Rose Garden* Esther Greenwood and Deborah Blau prepare to
return to society, but other characters seem headed for the hos-
pitals Esther and Deborah are leaving. Some, like Shirley Jackson's
Natalie, are just managing to avoid suicide. In Beheler's *The Paper
Dolls* and Barbara Probst Solomon's *The Beat of Life* (1960) the
protagonists commit suicide at the end of the novel; Kerrin of
Josephine Johnson's *Now in November* tries to kill her tyrannical
father and then kills herself. In a final note of irony regarding the
adolescent girl's predicament, Kerrin's father is outraged at her
"unnatural" act. Girls, he claims, do not have the right to commit
suicide (201).

In describing the main characteristics of novels of female adolescence, I have naturally emphasized the strong similarities in
protagonists' characters and experiences. However, the novels obviously reflect the wide differences in the writers' individual circumstances—the age in which the author writes, the section of the
country where she lives, her political and social orientation, and

her class and race. For example, the college Kathleen Millay depicts in the 1920's is, as we might expect, more rigid in its expectations of women than the ones presented fifty years later in Marilyn Hoff's *Dink's Blues* (1966) and Hortense Calisher's *Queenie* (1971). Southern writers often portray their heroines as especially limited because they must bear the weight of specifically Southern ideals of womanhood; Porter's Miranda would never be allowed to work outside in the fields and grow strong and sunburned like the Midwestern protagonist of *Winter Wheat*. If the author's experience has been in a large city, she is likely to make her protagonist grow up quickly; the numerous heroines from New York City cannot postpone their knowledge (and in most cases experience) of sex until they are sixteen, like the small-town protagonists of Schmitt's *Alexandra*. Nor do they take solace in nature in the manner of some country girls, like Stallworth's Florrie Birdsong.

One could document many such variations in novels of adolescence, according to the author's period and region; but, for the most part, they are differences in specification which make the novels diverse in texture rather than theme. Protagonists are shown reacting to womanhood in much the same fashion. No matter what their local version, female education, the "nice girl" standard, and sexual initiation are all resisted as portents of an unwanted future. If we turn our attention to the novelists' political and social beliefs, we can see very clearly that their portrayal of gender role conflict transcends their differences.

Although some writers I have considered manifest explicitly radical or feminist attitudes, others seem as pious and conventional as the creator of Elsie Dinsmore. We have just encountered the conservatism of Peggy Goodin and Jessamyn West; while they show some ambivalence, they express approval of their protagonists' acceptance of traditional female roles. A more extreme conservative than Goodin or West is Dorothy Grant, who in *Devil's Food* (1949) has her adolescent heroine rebel against her mother by accepting a scholarship at a small "liberal" college. The entire college population consists of Communists, sex maniacs, and bigamous professors, one of whom seduces the protagonist; eventually she repents and returns home to her mother where Grant says she belongs.

But, interestingly enough, before being chastened at the end of

the book, Grant's heroine differs little from the defiant protagonists of socialist-feminist novels like *A Daughter of Earth* and *Memoirs of an Ex-Prom Queen*. The basic contrast between the
conservative novel of adolescence and the explicitly feminist one
lies in the author's attitude toward her protagonist's rebellion.
While the conservative writer identifies with the girl's parent(s)
and eventually punishes her, the feminist identifies with the protagonist and either has her continue to rebel or expresses sorrow
over her defeat at the end of the novel. But both types of authors,
in the course of the novel, present their heroines in flight from
womanhood.

This theme also transcends differences in class and race. The
experience of poor protagonists obviously departs in many ways
from that of middle-class or rich girls. Some of the circumstances
I discussed earlier do not even apply to lower-class heroines. They
do not face the attempts of colleges and boarding schools to guide
them into female roles because their education has been cut short.
They are not in a position to scorn being a teacher (Van Etten)
or a secretary (Plath) because these vocations are seldom open to
them. To the heroine who is poor, adolescence generally means
being old enough to help support the family. It is an initiation into
hard work and portends a future of hard work.

But this does not mean that the poor protagonist has no awareness of her sex. If anything, she seems to be more disturbed by
her approaching womanhood than other heroines because she fears
her gender will doom her to a life of continued poverty. All the
white protagonists who are clearly poor, in that their families must
struggle for a minimum of food, shelter, and health care, express
a strong desire to be male. As I noted earlier, Page's Marge Crenshaw complains that boys have it easier because they are mobile
and employable and can escape their backgrounds; girls are soon
introduced to a constant round of childbearing and must bear the
brunt of poverty.

The two types of adult women lower-class heroines most often
encounter are defeated wives and mothers, made old before their
time, and prostitutes, the objects of social scorn. The only way for
a girl to avoid these fates is seemingly to "marry up"; but to
Smedley's Marie Rogers, who refuses a chance to do so, this alternative seems no better, and perhaps worse, than prostitution.

The prostitute "made her living in the same way as they [married women] made theirs, except that she made a better living and had more rights over her body and soul" (118). One of the young prostitutes in Caroline Slade's *Sterile Sun* claims that married women must "work their bodies" just as prostitutes do, only they "cover it up with God" (99).

Poor girls are thus defined even more than middle-class girls in terms of their sex organs. It would seem that their possession of a vagina and a uterus restricts them to two choices: they may use their vagina to make money or their uterus to make children. This observation about lower-class heroines also applies to many black protagonists. However, black adolescents find themselves in a particularly vulnerable position because they are barred even from the traditional compensation of womanhood, that is, from being a *valued* sexual object.

In Toni Morrison's *The Bluest Eye* Claudia receives a blue-eyed, blonde-haired doll for Christmas. Adults consider the doll beautiful, but Claudia hates it because it represents a white model of womanhood she can never live up to. The white "nice girl" standard, when pressed upon black adolescent heroines, is especially insidious. In Meriwether's *Daddy Was a Number Runner* and Paule Marshall's *Brown Girl, Brownstones* (1959) the protagonists are admonished by their parents to be "ladies"; ladies do not act like boys and fight, nor do they let boys touch them. But this warning becomes ironic in terms of the girls' actual experience. They are not treated with respect no matter how they act, and if they do not fight they will constantly be touched.

The life of twelve-year-old Francie Coffin in *Daddy Was a Number Runner* is a constant struggle against sexual abuse by men of all ages and colors. She cannot leave her Harlem tenement without being assailed with nasty epithets and remarks about her body, and physical attack is almost a daily occurrence. Whenever Francie goes to the movies, she is followed by a man who exposes himself and tries to reach inside her pants; in order to get meat from the butcher or rolls from the baker, she must allow them to "feel" her; she is nearly raped by an adolescent boy next door. Nor is Francie's experience unusual. In *The Bluest Eye* Claudia's friend Pecola is insulted and stoned by a gang of street boys, beaten up by a middle-class adolescent, and raped by her father.

Acting like a "lady" would seem to yield few rewards to the black adolescent. It does not save Francie from being perceived solely as a body or magically endow Claudia with the blue eyes and blonde hair which would make her at least a socially valued body. Moreover, black protagonists who get a chance to emulate those blue-eyed, blonde white girls often find that being a "nice girl" involves loss of identity.[55] In Zora Neale Hurston's *Their Eyes Were Watching God* (1937) the heroine's grandmother tries to protect her from sexual exploitation. She tells Janie: "[Neither] de menfolks white or black is makin' a spit cup outa you," and pressures her to make an early marriage with a well-off farmer. But Janie soon regrets her marriage. She is respectable and financially secure, "just like white folks," but she considers her life empty and fears she may have bartered her soul.[56]

Selina Boyce of *Brown Girl, Brownstones* realizes that many other West Indian girls act more "ladylike" than she does.They have been able to attend school and get decent jobs and can successfully imitate white girls. Yet "the way their gloved hands lay lifelessly in their laps" scares Selina. The girls' faces seem to have lost their "individual mold" and to be marked by "evasiveness" and "docility."[57] Selina considers her gender a greater handicap than her race. When she hears that all girls must grow breasts and menstruate, "an inexplicable revulsion gripped her and her face screwed up with disgust. 'It's never gonna happen to me,' she said proudly." When her friend points out that sexual development is inevitable, Selina feels a "sullen despairing anger" (61). To Selina womanhood means that she will have to "suffer" like her mother and her mother's friends (46). She is furious when one of these women touches her breasts and remarks that she is growing up. "It was the rite which made her one with Florrie's weighty bosom and Virgie Farnum's perennially burgeoning stomach. It meant that she would always have vestiges of Iris Hurley's malice and the mother's gorgeous rage" (78). Selina feels "trapped" within her body (62).

If some black authors, like Paule Marshall and Ann Petry, stress their heroines' gender identity, others place more emphasis on race and class identity. The main theme of Florence Crannell Means's *Shuttered Windows* (1938) and Barbara Anderson's *Southbound* (1949) is the middle-class Northern protagonists' ambivalence concerning their ties with poor blacks in the South. However, in most cases the writer does not separate gender and race. The black adolescent heroine is portrayed as in double jeopardy; to grow up black and female is to be twice limited. As Morrison's Claudia remarks, black girls must "edge into life from the back door. . . . Everybody in the world was in a position to give them orders" (108).

Claudia resents the gift of the blue-eyed doll not only because the doll is white but because it is a doll. "What was I supposed to do with it? Pretend I was its mother? I had no interest in babies or the concept of motherhood" (13). When in Jessie Redmon Fauset's *Plum Bun* (1929) the light-skinned Angela Murray goes to New York and passes for white, she at first feels exuberant at being "free." If she were male, Angela thinks, she could be president; she then laughs bitterly "for the 'if' itself proclaimed a limitation." Angela tries to convince herself that there are "sweeter, more beautiful gifts for women" than the "power, greatness, and authority" reserved for men, but "she knew that men had a better time of it than women, coloured men than coloured women; white men than white women."[58] Angela cannot "pass" as a man.

In his introduction to *Daddy Was a Number Runner*, James Baldwin discusses the limitations placed on Francie because of her race. He contends that if we compare her with the heroine of *A Tree Grows in Brooklyn*, who also lives in a New York slum, we will see

to what extent poverty wears a color—and also . . . arrives at an *attitude*. By this time, the heroine of *Tree* (whose name was also Francie, if I remember correctly) is among those troubled Americans, that silent (!) majority which wonders what black Francie wants, and why she's so unreliable as a maid.[59]

In one sense Baldwin is right. If he had wanted to pursue the comparison in more detail, he could have noted that to white Francie a "junkie" is a person who gives her pennies for old rags. Furthermore, while white Francie can get an office job to help her finish high school, black Francie is told that she cannot be a secretary when she grows up. A white teacher advises her to improve her sewing instead, because "there aren't very many jobs for Negroes in [the secretarial] field" (131).

But Baldwin ignores part of black Francie's predicament, or perhaps he *is* part of her predicament. According to Baldwin, Francie stands "on the edge of a terrifying womanhood" because black men, her "only hope," have been "cut down" and cannot "save" her.[60] However, in the novel Francie is portrayed as wanting to save herself. She perceives male pride as one cause of women's suffering: it makes her father forbid her mother to accept any assistance which would ease her burden; it induces a neighbor's husband to buy a car while the children go hungry. Francie's father says, "A man's got to have something like that car . . . so he knows he's a man" (61).

It seems to Francie that the men already have more than the women. Her father's life as a gambler and philanderer who has time for pleasure does not seem unattractive to her. It is the fate of her mother, a hardworking janitress and laundress, which Francie particularly wishes to avoid. In fact, when she says she would like to be a secretary, she knows hardly anything about secretarial work. Her ambition is a protest against the few choices available to black girls. At the end of the novel Francie and her friend Sukie are left in tears, fearing that they will end up just like their mothers and sisters. "Either you was a whore . . . or you worked in a laundry . . . or had a baby every year" (187).

Racism makes Francie more vulnerable than the white heroine of *A Tree Grows in Brooklyn*. But in wanting to reject the limited female roles offered her, she resembles her namesake. The two Francies have many common feelings and experiences.[61] They are hurt because their brothers receive preferential treatment in the family; they dislike housework, cooking, and sewing and resent being pressured to act "ladylike." Both girls are frequently assaulted by men; they resist knowledge of sex and think they never want sexual experience. Although they worry about their looks and have romantic daydreams about handsome movie stars, they do not look forward to marriage. The two Francies feel torn between an attractive playboy father and an overworked janitress mother: they want to deny the mother in favor of the father, and thus try to avoid her fate, but at the same time they identify with the mother and strive to protect her.

If the above description sounds familiar by now, it is because adolescent heroines are in many ways so similar. As I remarked at the beginning of this chapter, one has a constant sense of *deja vu* in reading novels of female adolescence. This holds true whether the author is black or white, whether she comes from New England or New Orleans, whether she writes for *Ms.* or *Ladies' Home Journal.* The two characteristics which unite the novelists are their strong emphasis on the protagonist's gender and their representation of its constraints. When they write about adolescence, women writers seem concerned, above all, with portraying their heroines' reaction to womanhood. In most of the novels from 1920 to 1972 this reaction has been overwhelmingly negative.

But what about more recent fiction? Has the contemporary resurgence of feminism had any impact on the novel of adolescence, perhaps influencing novelists to portray growing up female in a more positive light? In order to explore this question, I will discuss the novels of the past ten years as a separate group. In the next and last chapter I extend my survey to the present, observing the effects of the current women's movement. I also consider the future of the novel of female adolescence and the role of literary criticism in helping shape that future.

VIII   THE NEW GIRLS

For a future I didn't want a split-level home with a station wagon,
pastel refrigerator, and a houseful of blonde children. . . . I didn't
even want a husband or any man for that matter. I wanted to go
my own way. That's all I think I ever wanted, to go my own way
and maybe find some love here and there. Love, but not the now
and forever kind with chains around your vagina and a short circuit
in your brain. I'd rather be alone.[1]

So declares sixteen-year-old Molly Bolt, the protagonist of Rita
Mae Brown's *Rubyfruit Jungle* (1973). Except for her rejection of
the now and forever kind of love, Molly sounds much like the
heroines discussed in the last chapter. As a young adolescent she
resembles them in her insistence on being a tomboy; she hates
wearing dresses and doing housework and resists her mother's
attempts to make her a "lady"—she wants to be president of the
United States or a great film director. As an older adolescent in
college Molly chafes against the abundant discriminatory rules,
and her rebellion makes her a candidate for the school psychiatrist.
She feels trapped in her adolescence: "There was no place to go
back to. No place to go to" (96).

But in 1973 Molly was as much a new kind of heroine as Wharton's Charity Royall in 1917. It is not her words that make her
different but her actions. When her mother decides to curtail sports
and reading in favor of cooking, cleaning, and sewing, Molly locks
her in the cellar. In college she reacts to the girls' curfew by bribing

172 Growing Up Female

the guards to let her stay out late. After her affair with her room-
mate is reported to the dean, she openly acknowledges being a
lesbian, even though her admission means the loss of her scholarship. Molly leaves college and hitchhikes to New York with
$14.61 in her pocket. There she manages to graduate *summa cum
laude* and Phi Beta Kappa from NYU, all the time working to
support herself and resisting being kept by wealthy lesbians. At
the end of the novel Molly has even reconciled with her mother
and made a film. Despite the discrimination she faces as a woman
and as a lesbian, she approaches the future with confidence and
seems well on the way to achieving her adolescent goal of becoming
a film director. The novel ends: "One way or another I'll make
those movies and I don't feel like having to fight until I'm fifty.
But if it does take that long then watch out world because I'm
going to be the hottest fifty-year-old this side of the Mississippi"
(217).

Does Molly's willingness to fight, her active orientation toward
the world, and her success in preserving her autonomy indicate a
new trend in novels of female adolescence? *Rubyfruit Jungle* was
the first publication of the avowedly feminist press Daughters, Inc.,
an early product of the current women's movement. One might
well assume that the resurgence of feminism has had some effect
on recent novels of adolescence by women. Whenever I give talks
on the novel of adolescence people make this assumption; they
expect the adolescent heroines of the 1970's and 1980's to be less
"depressing," more like Molly Bolt than Stafford's Molly Fawcett.
But in 1973, the year *Rubyfruit Jungle* appeared, Daughters also
published Pat Burch's *Early Losses* and Blanche Boyd's *Nerves*.
While these novels are as consciously feminist as Rita Mae Brown's,
the protagonists bear no kinship to Molly Bolt.

Burch's heroine rejects the two alternatives she sees for herself,
college and marriage, and ends up at home being waited on by
her mother. In contrast to Molly, she is pathologically passive,
viewing "every activity (that was not lying down while reading and
eating) as immensely exhausting."[2] Diane Hamilton of *Nerves* is
a modern Frankie Addams. She too labels herself a "freak" and
a "criminal" and divides her time between being a tomboy and
dressing up in an orange chiffon dress.[3] Diane finds that high heels,
earrings, and mascara hurt, just as all the women she knows lead

painful lives. Her mother feels that her identity has been "erased" in marriage and is hospitalized with bad "nerves"; her mother's friend leaves her husband only to commit suicide; her widowed aunt lives a miserably lonely existence. Diane suffers anxiety attacks when she ponders these adult models. The refrain she repeats to herself, "I will never be crazy. I will never get killed. I have to grow up," indicates that she associates female adulthood with madness and death (158). Diane is left turning her anger on herself— cutting herself with a knife and murmuring magic spells to ward off the future.

Diane Hamilton is more typical of recent adolescent heroines than Molly Bolt. In fact, ten years after *Rubyfruit Jungle* Molly remains an anomaly. The novels of adolescence of the past decade resemble their predecessors so closely that I could legitimately have discussed them with earlier novels in Chapter VII. There are some changes, which I will explore in the first part of this chapter— notably, the preoccupation of many novelists with sex, the modern feminist consciousness of others, and their disposition to treat issues raised by the current women's movement, including lesbianism. However, these developments have not made the recent novels different from the earlier ones in theme or characterization of the heroine. Substantial change in the fiction of female adolescence may have to await extensive social change; it is certainly revealing that contemporary novelists who try to present more positive images of growing up female have difficulty staying within the realistic tradition of the adolescent novel. I pursue this point in the remainder of the chapter as I consider the future of the novel of adolescence.

Ironically, the most striking development in novels of female adolescence does not have to do with feminism and is often at odds with feminist goals. This is the more explicit treatment of sex, a change that can be traced to the "sexual revolution" and new permissiveness in publishing rather than the influence of the women's movement. Heroines of the 1970's and 1980's no longer worry about getting pregnant from kissing; they "fuck" and receive diaphragms from their parents as Christmas presents (Norma Klein's *Domestic Arrangements*, 1981). In Sonia Pilcer's *Teen Angel* (1978) thirteen-year-old Sonny Palovsky has to acquire a condom full of semen as her initiation into a teen gang. Sometimes the novelist's treatment of sex forms a bizarre contrast to the tone of the rest of the work. Ruth Doan MacDougall's *The Cheerleader* (1973) is a sentimental novel, the first half of which might have been written in 1900. The protagonist and her friends seem as wholesome as Rebecca of Sunnybrook Farm in their preoccupation with cheerleading, Latin class, and junior prom decorations. The reader wonders why the book was not classified for young adults—that is until after the prom when our Good Good heroine is found giving the football captain "his second blow job of the evening."[4]

Girls' increased sexual activity does not mean that they like sex any more than their predecessors did. Most consider it "disgusting"[5] and wonder why the boys enjoy it. Nor do the protagonists yet feel sufficiently knowledgeable about sex. In Joyce Maynard's *Baby Love* (1981), a novel about adolescent mothers, all the characters remain ignorant despite their experience. To one girl, "Going all the way did not seem to be a very big deal—it happened so fast she is still not too clear about the details but feels dumb asking, since obviously she is a mother, and should know."[6] Even Pilcer's Sonny Palovsky, a walking catalog of dirty jokes and sexual positions, feels frightened by a mysterious discharge which seems like "an albino period." Sonny knows all the words but has no idea how to behave: "She didn't want him to think she was *easy* or *horny* or a *nymphomaniac*. . . . She began to feel like maybe she was coming off like a *prude* which was worse than being a *tramp*. So she let herself be held. . . . But she wriggled uncomfortably."[7]

Sonny is typical of recent heroines in being completely preoccupied by sex. In several novels, including Klein's, Maynard's, Pilcer's second novel of adolescence *Maiden Rites* (1982), Josephine Carson's *Where You Goin, Girlie* (1975), and Louise Blecher Rose's *The Launching of Barbara Fabrikant* (1974), the emphasis on sex is so strong that it dominates every other aspect of the heroine's development. Rose's protagonist refers to sex as "my white whale, ship, ocean, adventure, and metaphor."[8] In this respect the adolescent heroine has come full circle. At the beginnings of American fiction nearly two hundred years ago girls' initiation was likewise viewed solely in terms of sexual experience: sex was also Charlotte Temple's white whale.

Even though the so-called sexual revolution has had a more

pronounced effect than the feminist revolution on recent novels of adolescence, we cannot conclude that the women's movement has failed to influence the fiction of the last decade. John Lyons' contention in his update of *The College Novel in America* that the "feminists' crusade . . . has not touched the form"[9] does not hold true for the novel of adolescence (nor for college novels with female protagonists). One finds direct references to "sexism," the "movement," and "women's lib." More significantly, there is an increased feminist consciousness on the part of many authors and an inclination to pursue new topics that have gained currency within the women's movement. With the exception of Rita Mae Brown, feminist authors do not invent heroines and plots substantially different from non-feminist creations. The difference lies in the directness of the feminists, their tendency to make very clear connections between their heroines' individual predicaments and the general status of women.

For example, almost all novels of female adolescence from 1920 to the present, whether by feminists, non-feminists, socialists, conservatives, etc., include scenes of male sexual harassment or violence; at best the heroine encounters a man who exposes himself and at worst she or one of her friends is beaten or raped. But the contemporary feminist authors give their protagonists a greater understanding of their situation. Thus the heroines of Fannie Flagg's *Coming Attractions* (1981) and Sharon Isabell's *Yesterday's Lessons* (1974) recognize that it is socially permissible for fathers to rape daughters: "No one would do anything about that."[10] Rape is considered the woman's fault, even by the victim herself, so that one character realizes her friend "was ashamed of being raped, as if the very fact of her femaleness permitting it was her fault."[11]

Many recent heroines are able to provide some analysis of circumstances familiar to us from earlier novels of adolescence. They may understand the reasons for being torn between mother and father. Angela of Linsey Abrams' *Charting by the Stars* (1979) examines her preference for her wandering father, who deserted the family, over her prosaic mother; even as she envies his "immense strength" and "vast freedom," she sees that she is allowing him to "grow in my mind to the proportions of a giant," whereas "he's everything wrong with the world. . . . He left my mother holding the bag."[12] Some characters now recognize that they suffer from a lack of adult female models and perceive the lack as a cultural problem. In Marge Piercy's *Braided Lives* (1982) the protagonist struggles to find women to add to the list of famous people she admires. In Jill Robinson's *Perdido* (1978) an adolescent movie buff, who does not want to marry, studies women's film roles and complains that "there aren't any middle-aged unmarried women in movies who aren't crazy."[13] Even novels of adolescence seem to provide models for boys but not for girls. Emily Howard of Susan Ries Lukas' *Fat Emily* (1974) eagerly reads *A Portrait of the Artist as a Young Man*, which her boy friend recommends as a handbook for adolescents; Emily finds the novel irrelevant to her situation, in her words full of "bullshit."[14]

Emily's speech and feminist insights are inconsistent with the fact that she is supposed to be growing up during the Eisenhower administration. Those novelists who endow their characters with a post-women's-movement consciousness often run into difficulties with point of view, a problem I will discuss later in this chapter. Other feminist authors create heroines with less awareness but provide a context in which their experience can only be understood from a feminist perspective. Often they exaggerate patterns common to earlier novels of adolescence. Natalie Petesch, in *The Odyssey of Katinou Kalokovich* (1974), gives "Returning Home to Take Care of a Sick Parent" a chilling twist which vividly illustrates the lack of options for women. In high school Kate has a clear idea of "the sort of life she wished to escape from—a life so delimiting for a woman that nearly any act of independence violated some law."[15] This is the plight of her mother, Channa; her marriage to a tyrant "seemed to Kate the ultimate entrapment, and convicted Channa (in her daughter's view), of some genetic fault against which she, Kate, must be eternally vigilant" (54). At sixteen Kate runs away and marries an itinerant musician; a year or two later, after a divorce, abortion, and dead-end job, she feels relieved, like many earlier heroines, to be summoned home to nurse her mother. But her terminally ill mother soon goes to a sanitarium and Kate is left, permanently it seems, to care for the house and her parents' new baby. Through no "genetic fault" Kate at the end of the novel becomes her mother.

The familiar passivity of the adolescent heroine is taken to new extremes by Alice Hoffman in *White Horses* (1982). The protagonist not only fails to act but suffers from a mysterious sickness wherein she suddenly falls asleep and sleeps for days. This modern sleeping beauty's illness is traced to the expectation, passed to her by her mother, that she will be "rescued" by a man on a white horse. Female adolescence is portrayed in the novel as a period of waiting akin to the long sleep of the fairy tale. It results in a "perfect" woman, one who "had been waiting to be rescued for such a long time that it might be years before her tongue could form words, and even longer before she could conjure up the strength to say a word like no."[16] Other feminist novelists follow Hoffman in presenting adolescence as an artificially created state (rather than a "natural" stage in growing up) which performs a function for society. They make the same parallels between the teen years and old age that I discussed in Chapter I. Sometimes the protagonist feels she can communicate only with an elderly person (in Linsey Abrams' novel the friend is crippled to boot). Lynne Sharon Schwartz's *Balancing Acts* (1981) depicts the parallels between an old man's futile rebellion against old age and death and an adolescent girl's against growing up.

In recent novels of adolescence the influence of the women's movement can be seen not only in the feminist consciousness of authors like Alice Hoffman but also in their attention to issues which have been prominent in modern feminist theory. Some of these issues, such as the nature of mother-daughter relationships and the prevalence of rape and male violence, are not at all new to the novel of adolescence. Others were suggested by earlier writers but receive more explicit treatment in fiction of the 1970's and 1980's. For example, both Carson McCullers and Jean Stafford show an interest in adolescent eating habits; McCullers' heroines eat "greedily" and are always hungry, while Stafford's Molly Fawcett becomes obsessed with the fear of getting fat. In more recent novels girls suffer from eating diseases with a name. The protagonists of Beth Gutcheon's *The New Girls* (1979) and Anne Snyder's *Goodbye, Paper Doll* (1980) have "anorexia nervosa," while B. of Marianne Hauser's *The Talking Room* (1976) diagnoses herself as suffering from "Bulimia. A pathological craving for food."[17] The characters' eating disorders are uniformly connected with their reactions to approaching womanhood. The anorexics are portrayed as desperately trying to allay their suspicion that they are not "free and in control,"[18] and B. and Freda Zax of *Early Losses* fill themselves with food as a substitute for the experience and independence from which, as adolescent girls, they are being "protected."[19]

By far the most important development that has taken place in recent novels of adolescence as a result of the feminist movement is the emergence of lesbian themes and characters. One now finds openly lesbian adults who play vital roles in protagonists' development: mothers, as in Hauser's *The Talking Room*; teachers, as in Fanny Howe's *First Marriage* (1974) and Jane Logan's *The Very Nearest Room* (1973); and artists, as in Joan Lindau's *Mrs. Cooper's Boardinghouse* (1980). The latter novel, in which an elderly lesbian befriends the twelve-year-old protagonist, is one of the mere handful of contemporary novels in which the heroine has a positive adult female model. Recent adolescent heroines, unlike most of their predecessors, have at least some awareness of lesbianism, and several girls who seem headed toward heterosexuality, as in Shylah Boyd's *American Made* (1975), are allowed to have sex with their girl friends before they turn to men. Marge Piercy's Jill Stuart in *Braided Lives* acts on her love for girls until she hears that "not only were our games wicked . . . but they were worse than regular terrifying real sex."[20] Jill writes "Am I an L.?" in her notebook, "scared to spell out lesbian" (25). Significantly, a number of adolescent heroines, however scared they may be, are portrayed as openly lesbian. If Molly Bolt's assertive character has remained unique, her lesbianism has not.

I use the term "openly lesbian" because lesbianism has of course been portrayed indirectly in earlier novels of adolescence. The heroine may form an attachment to a woman that is neither described as sexual nor labelled lesbian but seems extremely close. Authors usually shroud the relationship in ambiguity. In Shirley Jackson's *Hangsaman*, for instance, it remains unclear whether Natalie Waite's female lover is saving her from madness or driving her mad, or even whether she is a real character or a product of Natalie's imagination. Lesbianism receives explicit treatment only in some boarding school, college, and prison novels that are cautionary tales about the "dangers" of girls living together without contact with men and boys. Characters end up hardened or destroyed by lesbian relationships in such novels as Carman Barnes's *Schoolgirl* (1930), Mary Lapsley's *The Parable of the Virgins* (1931),

Sara Harris' *The Wayward Ones* (1952), and Susan Sherman's *Give Me Myself* (1961). At best the novelists show ambivalence, like Ann Bannon in *Odd Girl Out* (1957). In this college novel Laura Landon has an affair with her sorority sister whom she eventually loses to a man. Laura is the more independent girl since she does not "need a man" and dares go off on her own to New York; nevertheless she has to proclaim the superiority of her former lover's choice of heterosexuality: "I've grown up emotionally as far as I can. But you can go farther, you can be better than that."[21] This same attitude appears in Barbra Ward's *The Short Year* (1967), in which a seemingly happy couple parts at the end because "we're not growing. We are stunted. We're trying to remain children."[22]

Most recent novelists present lesbianism as wholly positive and liberating. The question becomes not how the lesbian protagonist can be "cured" but how she can develop and act upon her love for women in a hostile environment. The negative attitudes once given to the heroine are transferred to socializing agents like mothers and psychiatrists who consider lesbians "freaks" and try to program girls for heterosexuality. Those protagonists who recognize their attraction to other girls in early adolescence are told that sex with women is a "stage" they will grow out of; it is just a preparation, as Piercy's Jill was told, for "regular" or "real" sex. If the girl resists this view, she is thereby refusing to grow. When the heroine of Sarah Aldridge's *All True Lovers* (1978) tries to explain that she loves a girl, her mother replies: "That is something a child might say. You keep reminding me that you are nearly a grown woman. Yet you can say such a silly thing when I am trying to talk to you as a grown woman."[23]

The association of lesbianism with a childish state puts the lesbian heroine in a tighter version of the adolescent bind discussed in the last chapter. Like all heroines she does not want to grow up to secondary status and male domination, and in her case there may be a greater loss involved since, according to adults, she will have to renounce her attraction to women. Yet she must grow up in order for her feelings to be taken at all seriously and for her to be independent enough to act on them.

Inez Riverfingers of Elana Nachman's *Riverfinger Women* (1974) reacts to this dilemma by attempting suicide. Other girls simply wait, feeling completely alone in their situation. Although Bonnie Zimmerman finds "coming out" the focus of many lesbian novels, the "rite of passage through which the lesbian establishes and affirms her self,"[24] there is seldom any question of most adolescent heroines coming out at an early age the way Molly Bolt does. Usually the authors take the protagonist into her early twenties and have her come out at the end of the novel. In her teen years she rarely has any sexual experience. If she does, she rationalizes it as a result of her love for a particular woman; as Abby River-fingers tells Inez, "I'm not lesbian, I just love you, Inny."[25] Molly Bolt, with her customary contempt for hypocrisy and self-deception, scorns this solution. She becomes furious when Carolyn, her high school lover, decides that lesbians "look like men and are ugly" but "I'm not like that at all. I just love Molly. That doesn't make me queer" (92–94). Molly rejects Carolyn's apologies and refuses to have anything more to do with her.

But most lesbian adolescents are incapable of dismissing a lover with Molly's final words on Carolyn: "She could take her prom queen tiara and shove it up her ass" (96). They lack not only Molly's toughness and certainty but also her ability to act. Thus the dominant image in recent lesbian novels of adolescence is, just as it was in earlier novels, the trap. In *All True Lovers* the heroine resembles "a bird capable of far-ranging flight enclosed in too small a cage" (84); in Maureen Brady's *Give Me Your Good Ear* (1979) she forms part of a "chain" of female oppression;[26] in Sharon Isabell's *Yesterday's Lessons* (1974) she can "hardly breathe" because she feels "like I was locked in a room and the walls were slowly going to crush me to death." She continues: "I wanted to leave ever sence [sic] I can remember. I was frightened. What was I going to do?" (74).

Isabell's protagonist lacks the money for college and the training for a good job. Finally she joins the army, which she finds as regimented and as hostile to her lesbianism as high school; one of the many sexist regulations is that women must wear lipstick when in uniform. Heroines who can escape to college find the rules even more restrictive than non-lesbians do because one of the rules is heterosexuality. When Inez Riverfingers attends a "progressive" college, she learns that freshmen have to live in dormitories unless they are married; when she tells the dean she and Abby consider themselves married, he prescribes psychiatric treatment. Lesbian heroines who make it through college are still at loose ends. Angela of Linsey Abrams' *Charting by the Stars* (1979) feels that "the world is on the other side of the fence, and if we choose to join it, it will be at our own risk. Many women spend their adult lives inside walls, behind fences, under cover" (108). Angela herself fears taking a risk—"beyond the realm of my fantasies I am a coward, a girl" (76), and when her lover leaves her to join the world she returns to the safety of home. At the end of the novel Angela is in limbo, oppressed by "a weight of womanhood" and waiting "to grow wings . . . to set me free" (256).

Although Angela sees no stars by which to chart her future, she does not end up dead or mad like so many earlier heroines; nor has she lost her "inner room" accommodating herself to female adulthood. Most recent novels of adolescence with lesbian heroines have comparatively positive endings. However tight the trap and however ineffectual the protagonists may seem in their struggle to escape, they have usually made some progress. In *All True Lovers* the heroine has been "disowned" by her family but is finally free to live with her lover. In *Give Me Your Good Ear* she comes out as a lesbian and succeeds in communicating with her mother, breaking a long tradition of silence. Harriet Springer of Kate Stimpson's *Class Notes* (1979) no longer considers the "exhilaration she had experienced . . . with other women" to be a "sin"; she vows to accept her body.[27]

Riverfinger Women and *Yesterday's Lessons* also have "happy endings," although they are not particularly convincing. Inez Riverfingers claims to be telling the story of how she and her friends "learned to change (acid on stone) who we thought we were doomed to be into who we are. Tough, strong, proud: free women" (16). Actually the girls drift from one painful encounter with homophobia and sexism to the next until the end of the novel when they suddenly receive enough money (from a magical drug sale and inheritance) to start a commune in Canada. *Yesterday's Lessons* concludes with a bloodbath, an apotheosis of the male violence that occurs throughout the book. After the protagonist's friend argues with a stranger in a bar, he breaks into her home and stabs her to death while her children look on. This incident overshadows the upbeat scene that follows. In the final paragraph the heroine takes a motorcycle ride that "gave me a freedom I never experienced before" (206). She feels she has "hope" for the future.

Positive endings occur more frequently in expressly feminist novels of adolescence, whether the protagonist be lesbian, heterosexual, or uncommitted. Moreover, the feminist novels with positive endings tend to be the same novels which are plagued with narrative inconsistencies. Not only do the endings often seem "tacked on," but the heroines' consciousness may be too modern for the era in which the action is set. Earlier in this context I mentioned Emily Howard of *Fat Emily*, the girl who pronounces *A Portrait of the Artist as a Young Man* "bullshit." At the end of the novel Emily, who "had always given in quickly" and "could never fully imagine leaving" her mother or her boyfriend, suddenly breaks away from both to live entirely on her own (77, 160). While Emily would be only marginally believable in the 1980's, the novel is set in the 1950's. The majority of recent novels of adolescence are set in an earlier time period, usually the 1930's, 1940's, or 1950's, no doubt to accommodate the authors' own adolescent memories. The less sophisticated novelists make obvious lapses. In *The Launching of Barbara Fabrikant*, for instance, the protagonist is supposed to be attending college in 1961, yet refers to "women's lib" (70).

More experienced writers like Marge Piercy devote some attention to the task of reconciling a 1980's consciousness with 1950's memories. Piercy begins and ends *Braided Lives* with reflections by the protagonist's mature self. Although the frame technique is not unusual in novels of adolescence, Piercy also includes throughout the novel italicized sections in which the mature self provides a feminist analysis of the action. In this way she explains occurrences that the adolescent Jill cannot understand—for example, why the one female participant in a college poetry reading is considered a lesser poet (149). But even with this (rather mechanical) innovation Piercy has difficulty keeping her heroine from being too aware for her age and time. Many of Jill's adolescent thoughts— for instance, that her mother "will not bond with me" (73)—seem inspired by a contemporary feminist library.

The feminist authors' difficulty has to do not only with time consistency, which careless non-feminists can violate as in *The Launching of Barbara Fabrikant*, but with their desire to pursue two different goals simultaneously. They want both to illustrate the gender-based restrictions that "trap" their protagonists and to provide some positive alternative, to show their heroines becoming, in the language of *Riverfinger Women*, "tough, strong, proud: free women." Part of the trap is that the girls are taught to be tender, weak, and humble, so that when they suddenly act "tough" the strength seems imposed upon them. We are not prepared for the previously meek Emily Howard's about face at the end of the novel.

One motif in feminist novels of adolescence that illustrates the authors' dilemma is the refusal of heroines to join girls' organizations. Lukas' Emily rejects sororities and Abrams' Angela runs away from her girl scout initiation ceremony. In Ella Leffland's *Rumors of Peace* (1979), a novel set in the 1940's, Suze Hanson turns down an invitation to join a high school girls' club; when told that the club gives girls power, she replies, "That's not power. . . . That's just going after men."[28] The symbolic value of this motif is obvious. In rejecting girls' clubs the protagonists announce their refusal to participate in accepting the traditional female role. Like Stafford's Molly Fawcett, they scorn the existing "sorority." However, Emily, Angela, and Suze are also portrayed as terribly anxious to please and belong in the world; while they are inwardly rebellious, they seldom say no. For these heroines to have negative feelings toward girls' clubs would be believable; for them to refuse to join seems out of character. In Kate Stimpson's more realistic *Class Notes* Harriet dreams of refusing the DAR Good Citizen award and publicly denouncing the Daughters as "a bunch of narrow-minded bigots"; when the time comes for her to act her fear of being "bad, disobedient, ungrateful, rude" makes her accept the award (61–62).

The question of whether heroic action belongs in the plot of the novel or the adolescent protagonist's daydreams recalls an earlier time in which feminists wrote novels clearly in the didactic tradition. Before the ascendence of the realistic mode, when such actions were relegated to dreams, feminist authors had their young heroines take twenty-mile walks through storms, rescue other characters, lead labor strikes, run farms and businesses, become famous writers, etc. In Chapter II I discussed socialist-feminist novels like Mary Johnston's *Hagar* (1913) and Zona Gale's *A Daughter of the*

Morning (1917), in which girls are shown becoming tough, strong, proud, and free. These girls, as I noted, are illustrations of the authors' theories on proper female education, and their experiences fall into patterns that I labelled "Challenging of Paternal Authority," "Escape from Home," "Meeting of Feminist Guides," and "Resistance to Temptations" (such as marrying a sexist or living the life of the rich). The modern feminist novelists have the same didactic impulse, but with one exception they have remained tied to the realistic form.

The exception follows the same patterns as the early feminist novels, the only difference being that the lesbian Molly Bolt's temptation is being "kept" by wealthy women rather than marrying a sexist. *Rubyfruit Jungle* has enjoyed great popularity: it is the most widely distributed novel, the closest approach to a "best-seller" published by a feminist press.[29] Critics, however, have received it with less enthusiasm because of its didacticism. In *Lesbian Images* (1975) Jane Rule criticizes the novel for being "too preachy" and labels it a "manifesto."[30] Carol Burr Megibow considers *Rubyfruit Jungle* "contemporary wish fulfillment." She complains that Rita Mae Brown fails to show how Molly gains her strength; Molly does not "make herself" but appears "ready-made" at the beginning. Brown provides "a stirring image without the guidelines to replicate it."[31] But for Molly to retain her zest and assertiveness, which the critics do appreciate, in a nonpreachy novelistic form might well be impossible. This point is illustrated rather graphically in the critical commentary of Ellen Morgan, one of the earliest feminist literary critics to discuss contemporary women's fiction and try to predict future trends.

In her 1972 article "Humanbecoming: Form & Focus in the Neo-Feminist Novel," Morgan argues that the *Bildungsroman* is the "most salient form for literature influenced by neo-feminism." Although it has previously been a male form, it seem well-suited to express women's emergence from social conditioning and "progress toward the goal of full personhood." Morgan anticipates a new type of heroine, one who grows up rather than down. She looks forward to "a realistic novel in which a heroine shows us what it is like to live as a free and fully human female being in a patriarchal society."[32]

One might expect some revision of this last phrase since it is a contradiction to be a free and fully human female being in a patriarchal society; but five years later in "The Feminist Novel of Androgynous Fantasy" (1977) Morgan has given up on the *Bildungsroman* and the "realistic novel" as well. She notes that most contemporary feminist novels have been realistic works that "explore the actual conflicts within women and between women and society that are taking place as patriarchal traditions undergo rejection." Yet, she continues,

at the heart of the feminist impulse is a fierce hunger for images of authentic female selfhood—images which might illuminate what a liberated female person would be like. And the social reality in which the realistic novel is grounded is still sufficiently patriarchal to make a realistic novel about a truly liberated woman very nearly a contradiction in terms.

Hence, Morgan concludes, fantasy must be the "primary vehicle" for the portrayal of women achieving authentic selfhood.[33]

In Morgan's view a change in social reality would be required to produce realistic novels with positive, "liberated" characters like Molly Bolt, and until significant social change occurs she recommends a change in form. Fantasy, the form she chooses, can "rearrange or transform society as a way of showing how more equitable treatment for women may be fostered" (40). Pamela Sargent, a feminist science fiction writer, attributes her choice of the form to her being less limited by "past facts or present-day realities" in which women of strength and achievement are exceptions to the rule; she notes that science fiction and fantasy allow her to "imagine and write about worlds where strong independent women *are* the rule."[34] Fantasy incorporates the didactic impulse but in a manner more acceptable to contemporary literary tastes than the feminist "manifestoes" of the early twentieth century.

However, it is not yet clear whether fantasy is a viable form for the portrayal of positive images of adolescence. Thus far most science fiction novels with female adolescent protagonists have been of the more sombre type. Instead of creating an equitable society with strong women, they point up existing inequities by projecting exaggerated versions of our own. In *The Two of Them* (1978) Joanna Russ portrays female adolescence in two different cultures as a time when the male rulers try to contain girls' ambitions by ruthlessly channelling them into "every woman's lifelong project of forming a feminine personality"; in these societies "you haven't a chance at seventeen, you haven't a chance as a girl."[35] Marge Piercy in her first novel of adolescence, *Dance the Eagle to Sleep* (1970), highlights the social function of adolescence, including its separation of the genders, by imagining a "Nineteenth Year of Servitude." During the year of servitude (or "service," as this future American society dubs it) adolescent boys have to join the army or street patrols and girls become nurses and teachers' aides.

Anthropologists praised the Nineteenth Year of Service for providing a rite of passage and sure enough, everybody could tell the nineteenth-year-olds from their younger brothers and sisters, because they all had their hair cut and wore uniforms. There was an absolute gap between kids and adults, a *before* and an *after* that could never meet. The sexes were segregated and sharply differentiated in function. The elders had no more trouble telling the boys from the girls and keeping them from joining their small differences. . . . The Nineteenth Year had bottled up the so-called Youth Revolution.[36]

The one science fiction novel I am aware of that portrays a girl growing up in a more equitable society, Elizabeth Lynn's *The Northern Girl* (1980), has a young heroine who is really a "miniature adult." Writers who create utopias with no discrimination against women are likely to eliminate adolescence as well. One might imagine a fantasy that depicts the transformation of a society from Russ and Piercy's to Lynn's, but so far this has not been done. The most intriguing glimpses of a different future appear here and there in realistic novels. For instance, in Beth Gutcheon's *The New Girls* the headmistress of a boarding school stops a student play because it includes the word "diaphragm." She is shocked at the girls' "rebellious fury."

Why were they so angry? When had she seen girls angry in a body before? Never. Alone she could handle them easily, as she had for decades, by manipulating their need for approval, by belittling them, by destroying their faith in their own judgment. But in a group? What if all the girls were angry at the same time at the same thing? What if they stuck together and stood their ground? . . . She glared at them and they glared at her, and each saw a vision of a new future that made them tremble. (296)

Apparently the "new future" is far off because the girls do not stand their ground. Despite Gutcheon's attempts to make them "new girls," they are really old ones. They have names like "Muffy," "Wheezy," "Cibby," "Gub-Gub," and "Peaches" and feel apprehensive about their futures as women; they leave school headed for unhappy marriages, multiple divorce, and suicide—fates much like those of Mary McCarthy's graduates in her fifties novel, *The Group*. If the "new girls" in novels of the 1970's and '80's are not so new, it may be that any changes beyond the small changes we have seen in recent novels will have to await a transformation in the status of women or the state of adolescence. Even if we assume that the experience of female adolescence is now changing as a result of the resurgence of feminism, we would have to wait another decade, as contemporary girls become novelists, to see the results in the novel of adolescence.

It may reasonably be objected that in tying prospects for significant innovations in the novel of adolescence so closely to social change I am exaggerating the extent to which literature tends to reflect life. That the realistic novel is "grounded in social reality," as Ellen Morgan puts it, does not mean that it depends totally on that reality or imitates it with accuracy. When I speak on the topic of novels of adolescence, someone always asks, "Is this really what it has been like to grow up female in America?" No doubt the question is one for historians and social scientists to answer, but it brings up some interesting issues regarding the formal requirements of the adolescent novel and the psychology of the authors.

The fact, for instance, that so many adolescent heroines are called home to care for a sick parent surely reflects social realities: the expectation that girls have a special duty to nurture their families and the belief that their activities are less important, and thus more interruptable, than boys'. Yet it also provides a convenient way for the novelists to reunite the protagonist and her parent(s) and carry out the theme of her relationship with her family and her separation or lack of separation from her childhood self. Heroines' universal scorn for motherhood, and in fact for any nurturing "female" activity, mirrors our society's exaltation of everything male; but perhaps it also reflects the authors' own adolescent ambition, not necessarily representative of all adolescent girls, for success in the "male" career of authorship.

That the authors succeeded in publishing at least one novel makes one wonder—did they have different, perhaps more conflicted, adolescent experiences than non-authors? Why, considering their ultimate success in at least one endeavor, do they create heroines who are so totally defeated? Ruth Suckow, Carson McCullers, and Jean Stafford all emerged from backgrounds not unlike their adolescent characters', yet their heroines must give up their ambitions and fade away or die. Edith Wharton's artist characters are always male; in *Reinventing Womanhood* (1979) Carolyn Heilbrun notes that Wharton never depicts female artists "whose lives might reflect her own struggle."[37] Heilbrun's point that women writers have failed to imagine women characters with the strength and autonomy they themselves achieved, instead revealing an "urge toward the destruction and denial of female destiny " (79), seems particularly true of novelists of adolescence.

In looking for reasons for this phenomenon or in simply recognizing the inevitable element of fantasy that will distort an author's actual experience of adolescence, it is possible to place one's emphasis solely on psychoanalyzing the novelist. This is Patricia Meyer Spacks's method in *The Adolescent Idea* (1981). While W. Tasker Witham assumes in his survey of novels of adolescence that real life adolescent problems can be confirmed through their appearance in fiction, Spacks takes the opposite approach suggested in her title and particularly her subtitle, "Myths of Youth and the Adult Imagination." Spacks concentrates on British novelists' fantasies about youth, "fantasy" being defined "as psychoanalysts do, to designate mental productions serving the purpose of wish fulfillment."[38] The principal fantasy she discusses is the fantasy of potentiality, novelists' view of youth as a time of freedom and unlimited opportunity so that they "always resent the young for being unlike themselves, value them for representing earlier versions of self, full of possibility" (107).

Nothing could seem more alien to the novels with which we have become acquainted. Our American novelists' view appears much closer to Marge Piercy's; her narrator expresses "stark terror lest somehow entering that mind I'll be trapped back in that skinny sixteen-year-old body. I hardly got through the first time. My idea of hell is to be young again" (3). Whatever wish American novelists of adolescence may be fulfilling it is hardly nostalgic identification with a youthful self full of potential. In fact, the only British heroines Spacks uses to illustrate this sort of projection are creations of men writers. Perhaps in recognition of this problem she decides to have it another way by contending that the fantasy of potentiality may "reverse itself" in the works of women writers (119). Presenting girls as victims allows the novelist to "express awareness of the self's vulnerability and pleasure in the possibility of transcending weakness" (195). This version, wherein the novelist projects a weak adolescent self to furnish a happy contrast with the transcendant mature writing self, provides a more convincing unconscious motive for novelists like Piercy and one possible explanation for the failure of women writers to recreate imaginatively their own strengths.

At the same time, Spacks's reverse fantasy of potentiality illustrates the dangers of going too far with the psychological approach. She refers to the "myth of adolescent weakness" throughout her book, as though adolescent weakness were entirely an invention of female authors. But, as I noted in my discussion of the rise of adolescence in Chapter I, adolescent weakness is not a myth—female adolescence is a social state characterized by weakness. It is one thing for a method to imply "a relative absence of concern with matters of fact" (13), as Spacks describes hers, and another for it to contradict matters of fact. Whether or not women writers exaggerate the victimization of adolescent girls, their failure to portray them as "full of possibility" cannot be attributed simply to individual wish fulfillment or even a shared cultural fantasy of adolescent weakness. The depiction of adolescent strength in *Rubyfruit Jungle* required an imaginative leap and, as we have seen, could not be contained within the form of the realistic novel.

In her attempt to account for the tendency of women writers to create weak heroines, Heilbrun emphasizes the social causes. She notes society's tolerance of a wider range of behavior for men than for women and points to the inhibiting effects of the widely held assumption that the male perspective is all encompassing and the female restricted. In the conventional view a strong and autonomous woman cannot "stand for the full range of human experience," nor can she possibly behave in an acceptable manner; any forthrightness or assertive action, any concentration of her energies on herself rather than service to others, is "condemned as offensive" (88). "In a world where such judgments continue to be made," Heilbrun concludes, "it is scarcely surprising that women writers have not attempted the struggle to present their own accomplishments as women fictively" (90).

The conventional judgments of women Heilbrun discusses are reminiscent of the critical judgments that have in fact been made about women's novels of adolescence. We recall that Wharton's Charity, Suckow's Margaret, McCullers' Frankie and Mick, and Stafford's Molly have all been viewed as "offensive" in some way. If these characters are not strong and autonomous, they have seemed threatening even in their passive rebellions. Moreover, while "the maturation of a young boy" is "the archetypal theme with which American novelists have been concerned,"[39] novels of female adolescence have been considered limited; works like *The Member of the Wedding* cover only "a narrow corner of human existence." As we have seen, the novels may be dismissed as "too feminine," as in the case of Ruth Suckow; or they can be made over to seem more universal by being about an abstraction like spiritual isolation or a male character—so that *Summer* is really about Lawyer Royall and *The Mountain Lion* emphasizes Ralph above Molly.

Novels of (male) adolescence have been popular with American literary critics, as I noted in the Preface, because they fit so well with the "archetypal" patterns (male) critics have perceived in (male) American literature. Thus in "The Cult of Adolescence in American Fiction" Barton Friedberg argues that "the innocence represented by these young protagonists in some way typifies the innocence and naivete of America itself."[40] The characters' ambiguous initiations represent the doubts and confusions of America in an age of increased responsibility. Or, as Leslie Fiedler and Ihab Hassan would have it, there is a "correspondence between the process of adolescence and that of American culture," and the experiences of the adolescent hero recapitulate twentieth-century America's loss of innocence, the modification of the American Dream by the fact of guilt.[41]

According to Hassan in his influential book, *Radical Innocence* (1961), the situation of the adolescent protagonist "reflects the predicament of the self in America." The image "he" presents is "the new image of man in contemporary fiction."⁴² The youthful hero, once portrayed as an initiate being confirmed into a viable mode of life in society, has been merging with the figure of the "rebel-victim," a combination of Prometheus and Sisyphus (33–35). His outstanding quality is radical innocence, "radical" meaning both deeply rooted and extreme and "innocence" the "innocence of a Self that refuses to accept the immitigable rule of reality, including death, an aboriginal Self the radical imperatives of whose freedom cannot be stifled" (6). The awareness of the hero or anti-hero is "supremely existential." He performs "gratuitous actions which refer to no accepted norm (the need to act precisely because action is no longer intrinsically meaningful)," makes "demonic gestures," and compulsively engages in violence as a form of world negation (19, 27).

Although one suspects that Hassan is talking about male heroes and anti-heroes, it may appear that we could apply his comments to female adolescent protagonists. Surely the young heroines I have discussed can be characterized as "rebel-victims" and, while they can hardly perform gratuitous actions until they learn how to act, they at least make gestures of protest. If, as Hassan suggests, schizophrenia is the ticket to modern herodom, female protagonists have earned their admission. However, the trouble with Hassan's theory in regard to female novels of adolescence is that girls' primary rebellion cannot be considered existential in the way he means. Hassan's modern hero makes an existential choice to be a rebel-victim. He becomes a victim only by taking a stance as a victim; he rebels against the "immitigable rule of reality," that is, the human condition. The young heroine, on the contrary, is a real victim; she rebels not because her human body is doomed, by immitigable rule of reality, to imperfection and death, but because her female body, by mitigable rule of society, dooms her to subservience.

The "loss of innocence" inevitable in growing up has a different implication for girls than for boy-existentialists. When, for instance, the protagonists of Sherwood Anderson's "I Want to Know Why" and Hemingway's "Indian Summer" discover the secrets of sex, they are disillusioned because they have to confront the fact of human mortality; but to adolescent heroines, as we have seen, sex implies being hunted and conquered by men. The "compulsive violence" of the hero may well be visited upon her. What Hassan calls the "typical insight" of the young hero, that "it is better to be the hunted than the hunter" (148), remains foreign to the female protagonist. This "insight" can only be enjoyed by a person in position to be hunter. For the girl, existential anguish is a luxury: she has no time for protesting the unchangeable.

But to suggest that adolescent heroines' main rebellion may not be existential, that their outstanding quality may not be "radical innocence," is to remove female novels of adolescence from the realm of the "universal" as construed by the American literary establishment. I chose Ihab Hassan's book for discussion because it so clearly defines what critics often look for, and in fact expect, in an important or "great" American novel with a youthful protagonist. In the nineteenth century the hero should be an "American Adam" nursing his innocence in the forest and in the twentieth century that same "aboriginal Self," now exiled to the city and feeding on his guilt.

A novel by a member of an oppressed group can be "great" insofar as it can be made to conform to this standard of "universality." In the case of Ralph Ellison's *Invisible Man* (1947), for example, the protagonist's race is often conveniently forgotten, except as it symbolizes exclusion and alienation, and the hero taken as the American Adam and the European-American Underground Man rolled into one.[43] Although such a pattern is harder to find in novels with female protagonists since Eve represents guilt, rather than innocence, and there is no prototypical Underground Woman, the situation is similar for women writers. So long as an author can be seen as depicting the existential predicament of modern "man," her literary reputation may be "elevated" to the level of male writers.

There is no room in this scheme for the emphasis on gender we have seen in women's novels of adolescence. Novels about a girl's response to growing up female seem "narrow"; for an established author to write such fiction makes her "less important than she first appeared to be." Apparently novels by women in which gender becomes an issue are not only limited but indistinguishable from one another. In *Bright Book of Life* (1971) Alfred Kazin discusses modern women novelists together in one chapter. He finds women's fiction alike in its "inordinate defensiveness against a society conceived as the special enemy of the sensitive"; the authors fail because they "start from the 'heroine' as a . . . victim of her position."[44] When in the late 1970's Maureen Brady tried to publish her (excellent) novel of adolescence, *Give Me Your Good Ear*, she was told that the market was "enormously resistant to novels of women's growth and development." The reason? Because "these novels are the same."[45] In her efforts to get published Brady continually had to face the assumption that novels of men's growth are more distinctive and more universal than those of women's growth. *"Give Me Your Good Ear thus is perceived as nothing substantially more than one woman's personal odyssey,* while a book like *Portnoy's Complaint* is a best seller with 'universal significance' "* (139).

Brady was advised to do something to "set her novel apart" in an "ever more crowded market of women's novels" (138). What this something might have been is unclear, unless she were to change her protagonist's gender. The not-so-hidden message of the literary establishment to the potential woman novelist of adolescence indeed seems to be "make your protagonist male." Perhaps the young novelist's predecessors, Wharton, Suckow, McCullers, and Stafford, were responding to this call when they turned in their later works to the exclusive portrayal of male adolescence.

Fortunately, the growth of a feminist literary criticism in the past decade has begun to provide a more supportive atmosphere for women writers. Feminist literary critics have attacked the "double standard of literary abilities," which assigns the most desirable qualities to male novelists and the least to female,[46] and challenged the assumption that men's preoccupations and point of view are universal and women's limited. Feminist critics point out that men have defined themselves as the universal in literature and literary criticism as well as other areas. Men have constructed, in Nina Baym's words, "the theories controlling our reading of American literature," theories that like Ihab Hassan's lead to the "exclusion of women authors from the canon."[47] Once critics are freed from the necessity of fitting every novel by a woman into one of these theories they can make fresher and more sympathetic readings of women's works; instead of denying the female experience presented by making it symbolic of some form of "universal" (male) experience, they can consider it on its own terms. Feminist critics obviously lack the power of the male literary establishment, and young writers like Maureen Brady must struggle with the dominant critical ethos. Still, the very existence of a body of critics and readers who do not have to ignore the relevance of gender must be considered a plus for the potential woman novelist of adolescence.

In one respect, however, as I have already implied, the expectations of feminist literary critics make her task more difficult. Feminist literary criticism, like all criticisms, has had from its beginnings a prescriptive as well as a descriptive function. As Cheri Register notes in her bibliographic essay on feminist literary criticism, it "attempts to set standards for literature that is 'good' from a feminist viewpoint."[48] What is "good" has come increasingly to mean that which portrays woman as an actor in the process of change rather than a victim of her powerlessness. Many critics look for "a vision of the future, a model of the positive process of change."[49] The assumption is that fiction should provide models for the reader because, as one writer puts it very straightforwardly, "literary techniques can and do influence the life from which they derive." She continues: "Confronted with a growing number of heroines who celebrate life instead of death, who struggle to develop their potentialities to the fullest, who survive and grow stronger despite their hardships, sensitive readers, particularly women, will begin to re-evaluate their own strengths and opportunities."[50]

This emphasis on strength, on what Ellen Morgan called "images of authentic female selfhood," has made certain types of fiction the favorites of feminist critics. One type is science fiction, Morgan's ultimate choice, which I have already discussed. The other is a version of the *Bildungsroman*, not Morgan's original choice with the traditional young protagonist, but a *Bildungsroman* expanded far beyond its usual definition to include much older heroines. According to Bonnie Hoover Braendlin, the "modern feminist bildungsroman" is a recasting of the form by women writers to show women's development toward a more viable existence free from predetermined roles. The new *Bildungsroman* may include adolescent memories, but "it focuses primarily upon the crisis occasioned by a woman's awakening, in her late twenties or early thirties."[51] Most of the novels Braendlin discusses, including Margaret Atwood's *Surfacing* (1972) and *Lady Oracle* (1976), Sheila Ballantyne's *Norma Jean the Termite Queen* (1975), and Lisa Alther's *Kinflicks* (1976), have protagonists who are or have been married and are "awakening" to the restrictions of their adult roles as wives and mothers.

In Annis Pratt's wide-ranging survey of women's fiction young heroines tend to appear in what she calls "novels of the enclosure"; the emphasis is on the stifling of their development in adolescence and marriage and motherhood. The more positive fiction, the "novels of rebirth and transformation," features heroines who are middleaged or older. Having lived through various roles and rejected many social expectations, these protagonists experience a transformation that "differentiates them from the younger heroes of the novel of development."[52] Pratt suggests a reason for the relative success of the older heroine in achieving strength and selfhood. The young protagonist seeks social integration, and her quest is aborted by society's refusal to assimilate her unmaimed; the older heroine has a more individual and "spiritual" goal; she wants "to integrate her self with herself and not with a society she has found inimical to her desires" (136). But whatever the reason for the older protagonist's success, the fact that she moves toward achieving "authentic female selfhood" makes the modern feminist *Bildungsroman* the most popular form of feminist fiction. The *Bildungsroman* with the older protagonist can incorporate positive images and stay within the realistic tradition of the novel.

I do not mean to imply that feminist critics' preference for active heroines over passive victims is at all a bad thing; nor do I think that in trying to foster the growth of feminist ideals in literature we critics have been foisting our preference for strong heroines on unwilling novelists. What Morgan calls the "*fierce hunger* for images of authentic female selfhood" (my italics) is shared by all feminists, be they critics, readers, or novelists; author Elana Nachman may not have succeeded in making her adolescent characters "tough, strong, proud, and free," but her sincere wish to do so cannot be questioned. Our desire for fiction to provide models for change may yet have positive effects on the female novel of adolescence. At the same time that it makes the novelist's task more difficult it offers a challenge that may lead to innovations in form from which the novel of adolescence could benefit. If most recent experiments, such as Marge Piercy's use of multiple narrators in *Braided Lives,* have not been entirely effective, there have already been a few successes. In *Give Me Your Good Ear,* for instance, Maureen Brady manages to combine the positive and the realistic by having a mature narrator recollect her adolescence and in the process free herself from the past and learn to be an actor rather than a victim; this novel ends with a mother-daughter reconciliation that is much more convincing than *Rubyfruit Jungle*'s.

In future novels of adolescence we may see more of this emphasis on positive development, on the process of growing "up" rather than "down." But I submit that there is still room for the bleaker social protest novel that the novel of adolescence has been to date. The novel of female adolescence has customarily been a symbolic vehicle for the exploration of gender issues, and it thereby serves an important function whether or not the novelist can imagine any way out of the restrictions that stifle the heroine. Furthermore, it is necessary to recall that novelists of adolescence have traditionally stressed conflict rather than development for good reason—because conflict has always been a vital part of the concept and reality of adolescence, especially female adolescence. Annis Pratt may well be right in maintaining that novelists can allow older heroines to achieve autonomy because the older heroine can more easily reject social expectations and seek "to integrate her self with herself" instead of a hostile society. But it is also true that a patriarchal society is less inimical to an independent woman past childbearing age and less hesitant to assimilate her or at least leave her alone to pursue a personal quest.

In my discussion of the beginnings of female adolescence I noted the strong, indeed exclusive, focus of social thinkers on adolescence as preparation for women's two key roles as wife and mother. G. Stanley Hall, we recall, felt that higher education, the most visible means of personal development for girls of his time, might prevent girls from marrying or weaken their progeny. Once a woman has already fulfilled or clearly failed to fulfill her primary function as a member of a patriarchal society, she becomes of less importance to that society. On the other hand, the adolescent girl, yet to fulfill her function, is crucial to the replication of the social system. Whatever her present goal, whether it be "social integration" or not, her society will insist on integrating *her*. Thus, I am suggesting, she cannot realistically be portrayed as ignoring social expectations to pursue her own goals; even the irrepressible Molly Bolt realizes that she may have to "fight until I'm fifty." So long as women's main function is conceived to be marriage and childbearing, and so long as wifehood and motherhood carry lower status than male pursuits, the adolescent girl will be in conflict with society.

The fact that the adolescent girl is more essential to the furtherance of patriarchy than the woman past childbearing age should make future novels of adolescence of particular interest to readers who look to fiction for reflection of social change. If the "second wave" of feminism has produced any real changes, it seems that we might find them reflected in the novels of adolescence of the 1990's. If, for instance, the range of occupations open to women has been widening and women have been entering positions of greater influence, might adolescent heroines be allowed the positive female models they have so far almost universally lacked? Perhaps the most crucial question is whether novelists of the future will conceive of womanhood in the overwhelmingly negative way of their predecessors. Will they continue to portray growing up female as a loss, as the entering of a tightly enclosed space that entails the death of the self?

Sheila Ballantyne includes a striking image in her 1982 novel of adolescence, *Imaginary Crimes*. In this novel, as in several earlier novels I mentioned in the last chapter, the gulf between girls' and boys' experience is symbolized by their separation on the school playground. Ballantyne's protagonist and her friends spend their recreation time atoning for the "imaginary crime" of being born female. They practice fainting, holding their breath until they lose consciousness, because they enjoy the sensation of coming to—it feels like being "reborn."

For hours we died and were reborn until the day one of the mothers across the street looked out her window and noticed the wide circle of boys at one end of the playground, playing basketball, and the tighter circle of girls at the other, fainting.[53]

In future novels of adolescence will girls still be enclosed in tighter circles than boys? Will they still feel the need to be reborn at twelve?

NOTES

Preface

1. See Frederic Carpenter, "The Adolescent in American Fiction," *English Journal*, 46 (Sept. 1957), 313–19; Barton Friedberg, "The Cult of Adolescence in American Fiction," *Nassau Review*, 1 (Spring 1964), 26–35; Ihab Hassan, "The Idea of Adolescence in American Fiction," *American Quarterly*, 10 (Fall 1958), 312–24; and James Johnson, "The Adolescent Hero: A Trend in Modern Fiction," *Twentieth Century Literature*, 5 (April 1959), 3–11. Hassan and Leslie Fiedler discuss adolescent protagonists in their respective books, *Radical Innocence* (1961) and *No! in Thunder* (1960).

2. Unpublished dissertations include William Agee, "The Initiation Theme in Selected Modern American Novels of Adolescence," Florida State University, 1966; Robert Bickham, "The Origins and Importance of the Initiation Story in Twentieth Century British and American Fiction," University of New Mexico, 1961; Stuart Burns, "The Novel of Adolescence in America: 1940–1963," University of Wisconsin, 1964; Helen White Childers, "American Novels about Adolescence, 1917–1953," George Peabody College, 1958; Mary Nell Griffin, "Coming to Manhood in America—A Study of Significant Initiation Novels, 1797–1970," Vanderbilt University, 1971; Ignatius Melito, "Themes of Adolescence: Studies in American Fiction of Adolescence," University of Denver, 1965; Isaac Sequeira, "The Theme of Initiation in Modern American Fiction," University of Utah, 1970; and Bernard Sherman, "The Fictive Jew, Jewish-American Education Novels: 1916–1964," Northwestern University, 1966. Some of these dissertations treat short fiction as well as novels. Most of the criticism on fiction of adolescence, however, emphasizes the novel. As a general rule I am restricting my remarks to the novel of

adolescence, but I introduce short stories when they seem particularly
relevant to the discussion.

Anthologies include William Coyle, *The Young Man in American Lit-
erature* (New York: Odyssey Press, 1969); Clyde Davis, *Eyes of Boyhood*
(Philadelphia: J. B. Lippincott, 1953); F. Anthony De Jovine, *The Young
Hero in American Fiction: A Motif for Teaching Literature* (New York:
Appleton-Century-Crofts, 1971); and Thomas Gregory, *Adolescence in
Literature* (New York: Longman, 1978). In his *The Adolescent Through
Fiction: A Psychological Approach* (New York: International Universities
Press, 1959), psychologist Norman Kiell illustrates adolescent problems
by quoting lengthy passages from novels.

3. In a typical study Mary Nell Griffin (above) considers thirty-six
works, one by a woman with a male hero and two by men with female
protagonists. Sometimes only male novelists and characters are included,
as in Friedberg's article, Melito's and Sherman's dissertations, and Davis'
and De Jovine's anthologies (although De Jovine claims to provide "a
syllabus that is comprehensive, unified, and pedagogically viable").

4. Melito, p. 1; John Lyons, *The College Novel in America* (Carbondale: Southern Illinois University Press, 1962), pp. 70–72. Likewise, in
Susanne Howe's classic account of the *Bildungsroman, Wilhelm Meister
and His English Kinsmen* (1930), the "hero" searches for the proper
"wife."

5. William Thrall, Addison Hibbard, and C. Hugh Holman, *A Handbook to Literature*, revised ed. (New York: Odyssey Press, 1960), p.
31. Italics mine.

6. Leslie Fiedler, *No! in Thunder* (New York: Stein and Day, 1972),
p. 286; Johnson, p. 6.

7. Lillian Schlissel, "Contemplating 'The American Eve,' " in *American Women and American Studies*, ed. Betty Chmaj (Pittsburgh: KNOW,
Inc., 1971), p. 258.

8. The emphasis of *The Voyage In: Fictions of Female Development*,
ed. Elizabeth Abel, Marianne Hirsch, and Elizabeth Langland (Hanover,
N.H.: University Press of New England, 1983) is on older heroines. *The
Voyage In* is the first collection of essays specifically on the female novel
of development. Other relevant essays are Bonnie Hoover Braendlin,
"Alther, Atwood, Ballantyne, and Gray: Secular Salvation in the Contemporary Feminist Bildungsroman," *Frontiers*, IV (Spring 1979), 18–22,
her "*Bildung* in Ethnic Women Writers," *Denver Quarterly*, 17 (Winter
1983), 75–87, and her "New Directions in the Contemporary Bildungsroman: Lisa Alther's *Kinflicks*," in *Gender and Literary Voice*, ed. Janet
Todd (New York: Holmes & Meier Publishers, 1980), pp. 160–71; Elaine
Ginsberg, "The Female Initiation Theme in American Fiction," *Studies
in American Fiction*, 3 (Spring 1975), 27–38; Ellen Morgan, "Human-

becoming: Form & Focus in the Neo-Feminist Novel," in *Images of Women in Fiction: Feminist Perspectives*, ed. Susan Koppelman Cornillon (Bowling Green, Ohio.: Bowling Green University Popular Press, 1972), pp. 183–205; and Annis Pratt and Barbara A. White, "The Novel of Development," in Pratt, *Archetypal Patterns in Women's Fiction* (Bloomington: Indiana University Press, 1981), pp. 29–37.

9. W. Tasker Witham, *The Adolescent in the American Novel, 1920–1960* (New York: Frederick Ungar Publishing Co., 1964), p. 1.

10. I have excluded British fiction, novels by male authors, and so-called "juvenile" or "youth" fiction, novels about adolescents written for children or adolescents, primarily because I needed to place some limits on a massive body of material. There are, however, important novels of female adolescence by British authors, such as Doris Lessing and Dorothy Richardson, that deserve more critical attention than they have so far received. Although the adolescent heroines of male authors often strike me as purely mythical creations based on what the writer fears (Faulkner's Eula Varner) or hopes (Herman Wouk's Marjorie Morningstar) a girl might be, there have been perceptive novels of adolescence by men with female protagonists; works like William Styron's *Lie Down in Darkness* (1951) and Philip Roth's *When She Was Good* (1967) deserve feminist analysis. Novels about adolescents written for adolescents tend, as one might expect, to differ in many ways from those written for adults. For several articles which discuss the portrayal of female adolescence in youth fiction, see Millicent Lenz and Ramona Mahood, eds., *Young Adult Literature: Background and Criticism* (Chicago: American Library Association, 1980).

11. Thus Childers, pp. 347–60, finds that novels of adolescence in the 1920's and 1930's tend to cover a longer span in the protagonist's life and portray the character in a broad social context, whereas the novels of the 1940's and 1950's concentrate on a shorter period of time and emphasize the psychological processes of the hero; point of view becomes progressively more limited. For more discussion of broad changes in form by decade, see Gregory, pp. xv-xvii, and Witham, pp. 14–17.

Chapter I. Introduction to the American Novel of Adolescence

1. Stuart Burns, "The Novel of Adolescence in America: 1940–1963," p. 3; Mordecai Marcus, "What Is an Initiation Story?" *Journal of Aesthetic and Art Criticism*, 19 (Winter 1960), 222. William Agee in "The Initiation Theme in Selected Modern American Novels of Adolescence" and Mary Nell Griffin in "Coming to Manhood in America—A Study of Significant Initiation Novels, 1797–1970" see the novel of adolescence as an "initiation novel."

2. My characterization of the *Bildungsroman* here and on pp. 13–14 is based on the following sources: Jerome Buckley, *Season of Youth: The Bildungsroman from Dickens to Golding* (Cambridge, Mass.: Harvard University Press, 1974), pp. 13–27; Marianne Hirsch, "The Novel of Formation as Genre: Between Great Expectations and Lost Illusions," *Genre*, XII (Fall 1979), 293–311; Susanne Howe, *Wilhelm Meister and His English Kinsmen* (New York: AMS Press, 1966), pp. 4–7; Roy Pascal, *The German Novel* (Manchester, Eng.: Manchester University Press, 1956), pp. 1–29; and G. B. Tennyson, "The *Bildungsroman* in Nineteenth-Century English Literature," in *Medieval Epic to the "Epic Theater" of Brecht*, ed. Rosario Armato and John Spalek, I (Los Angeles: University of Southern California Press, 1968), pp. 135–46.

3. Helen White Childers, "American Novels About Adolescence, 1917–1953," p. 4; Griffin, p. 4. As I will explain in later chapters, this pattern is more typical of the male novel of adolescence than the female.

4. John Lyons, *The College Novel in America*, pp. 103–4. "The Everlasting No" is a reference to Thomas Carlyle's *Sartor Resartus* (1833–37). Carlyle is credited with introducing the *Bildungsroman* into English literature; also, in 1824 he translated Goethe's *Wilhelm Meister*, the prototype of the *Bildungsroman*.

5. W. Tasker Witham, *The Adolescent in the American Novel, 1920–1960*, p. 3.

6. Childers, p. 5.

7. Witham, p. 3.

8. Edgar Friedenberg, *The Vanishing Adolescent* (New York: Dell, 1959), p. 20.

9. See, for instance, Nathan Miller, *The Child in Primitive Society* (New York: Brentano's, 1928), pp. 181–219; and Margaret Mead, "Adolescence in Primitive and Modern Society," in *The New Generation*, ed. V. F. Calverton and Samuel Schmalhausen (New York: Macaulay Co., 1930), 169–88.

10. Philippe Ariès, *Centuries of Childhood*, trans. Robert Baldick (New York: Vintage, 1962), p. 29. Further references are noted in parentheses within the text.

11. John Demos and Virginia Demos, "Adolescence in Historical Perspective," *Journal of Marriage and the Family*, 31 (Nov. 1969), 632–33; Joseph Kett, *Rites of Passage: Adolescence in America 1790 to the Present* (New York: Basic Books, 1977), pp. 31, 36. See also Kenneth Keniston, "Youth: A 'New' Stage of Life," *American Scholar*, XXXIX (1970), 631–32. For an argument that the notions of "miniature adulthood" and absence of adolescence are exaggerations, see Ross Beales, "In Search of the Historical Child: Miniature Adulthood and Youth in Colonial New England," *American Quarterly*, 27 (Oct. 1975), 379–98.

12. Kett, p. 151. Further references are noted in parentheses within the text.

13. G. Stanley Hall, *Adolescence* (New York: D. Appleton and Co., 1924), II, 232. Further references are noted in parentheses within the text.

14. Demos and Demos, p. 636.

15. Alexis de Tocqueville, *Democracy in America* [1840] (New York: Alfred A. Knopf, 1945), II, 192–93. Tocqueville says: "In America there is, strictly speaking, no adolescence: at the close of boyhood the man appears and begins to trace out his own path."

16. Richard Kalish, "The Old and the New as Generation Gap Allies," in *Readings in Human Socialization*, ed. Elton McNeil (Belmont, Calif.: Brooks/Cole Co., 1971), p. 255.

17. Friedenberg, pp. 32, 199.

18. See Daniel Guillory, "The Mystique of Childhood in American Literature," *Tulane Studies in English*, 23 (1978), 229–47; Horace Scudder, *Childhood in Literature and Art* (Boston and New York: Houghton, Mifflin and Co., 1894); and Philip Stewart, "The Child Comes of Age," *Yale French Studies*, No. 40 (1968), 134–41.

19. James Johnson, "The Adolescent Hero: A Trend in Modern Fiction," 3–4.

20. Witham, p. 274.

21. Howe, p. 14.

22. Ihab Hassan believes this to be characteristic of the novel of adolescence. See his *Radical Innocence* (Princeton, N.J.: Princeton University Press, 1961), p. 274.

23. Johnson, pp. 6–7; Stuart Burns, "The Novel of Adolescence in America: 1940–1963," p. 10.

24. Ariès, p. 332. Simone de Beauvoir contends that this precocity, which can be found even today, is due to the limited nature of woman's traditional role.

It is not a far cry from child to housekeeper. A man expert in his trade is separated from the stage of childhood by his years of apprenticeship. Thus the little boy finds his father's activities quite mysterious, and the man he is to become is hardly sketched out in him at all. On the contrary, the mother's activities are quite accessible to the girl; "she is already a little woman," as her parents say; and it is sometimes held that she is more precocious than the boy. In truth, if she is nearer to the adult stage it is because this stage in most women remains traditionally more or less infantile. *The Second Sex* (New York: Bantam, 1952), p. 266.

25. Mary Chadwick, *Adolescent Girlhood* (New York: John Day Co., 1933), p. 89. In *A New England Girlhood* (Boston: Houghton Mifflin

Co., 1889), p. 78 and pp. 166–67, Lucy Larcom recalls being told that infancy lasted for twelve years and that at age thirteen she was a woman.

26. Ellen Morgan, "Humanbecoming: Form & Focus in the Neo-Feminist Novel," p. 184.

27. Joseph Kett, "Adolescence and Youth in Nineteenth-Century America," in *The Family in History: Interdisciplinary Essays*, ed. Theodore Rabb and Robert Rotberg (New York: Harper & Row, 1973), pp. 107–8. Further references are noted in parentheses within the text.

28. Carroll Smith-Rosenberg, "Puberty to Menopause: The Cycle of Femininity in Nineteenth-Century America," in *Clio's Consciousness Raised*, ed. Mary S. Hartman and Lois Banner (New York: Octagon Books, 1976), pp. 24–25.

29. Carroll Smith-Rosenberg, "The Hysterical Woman: Sex Roles and Role Conflict in Nineteenth-Century America," *Social Research*, 39 (1972), 656.

30. Sharon O'Brien, "Tomboyism and Adolescent Conflict: Three Nineteenth-Century Case Studies," in *Woman's Being, Woman's Place: Female Identity and Vocation in American History*, ed. Mary Kelley (Boston: G. K. Hall & Co., 1979), p. 352. Further references are noted in parentheses within the text.

31. Shulamith Firestone, *The Dialectic of Sex* (New York: Bantam, 1971), p. 81.

32. Morton Hunt, *Her Infinite Variety* (New York: Harper & Row, 1962), p. 51.

Chapter II. The Girl Protagonist before 1920

1. John Lyons, *The College Novel in America*, p. 47.

2. W. Tasker Witham, *The Adolescent in the American Novel, 1920–1960*, p. 18.

3. Lillie Deming Loshe, *The Early American Novel* (New York: Columbia University Press, 1907), p. 7.

4. *The Female American; or, the Adventures of Unca Eliza Winkfield* (Ridgewood, N.J.: Gregg Press, 1970), pp. 46–47.

5. Maria S. Cummins, *Mabel Vaughan* (Boston: John Jewett, 1857), p. 18.

6. Herbert Brown, *The Sentimental Novel in America, 1789–1860* (Durham, N.C.: Duke University Press, 1940), p. 130.

7. Helen Waite Papashvily, *All the Happy Endings* (New York: Harper, 1956), p. 102. Papashvily notes that it was not unusual for female authors to begin their careers at fifteen or sixteen; Isabella MacDonald Alden ("Pansy") was first published at the age of ten.

8. Leslie Fiedler, *Love and Death in the American Novel* (New York: Dell, 1966), p. 262.

9. Martha Finley, *Elsie Dinsmore* (New York: Dodd, Mead, and Co., 1893), pp. 35–36. Further references are noted in parentheses within the text.

10. Leslie Fiedler, *No! in Thunder*, pp. 259–76.

11. Henri Petter, *The Early American Novel* (Columbus: Ohio State University, 1971), p. 29.

12. Alexander Cowie, *The Rise of the American Novel* (New York: American Book Co., 1948), pp. 414–15.

13. Susan Warner, *The Wide, Wide World* (Philadelphia: J. B. Lippincott, 1885), p. 219.

14. Maria S. Cummins, *The Lamplighter* (Boston: John Jewett, 1854), p. 134.

15. Ruth Suckow, "Literary Soubrettes," *Bookman*, 63 (July 1926), 517–19.

16. Fiedler, above, would disagree with my contention that there are girl protagonists in the nineteenth century, outside of seduction novels, who are not entirely Good Good. This is because he tends to view women only in terms of their sex organs—girls are Good when they preserve their virginity and Bad when they lose it. Fiedler's premise carried to its logical conclusion ends up as Norman Mailer's contention in *Advertisements for Myself* (1959) that there will never be a great novel by a woman until the first prostitute tells her story.

17. Papashvily, p. xvii. Dee Garrison and Ann Douglas agree with Papashvily's rebellion thesis; Alexander Cowie and Barbara Welter emphasize conservatism and conformity in the sentimental novel. For an overview of the disagreement on this issue, see Mary Kelley, "The Sentimentalists: Promise and Betrayal in the Home," *Signs*, 4 (Spring 1979), 434–46. Kelley herself takes a middle position, as do Nina Baym in *Woman's Fiction: A Guide to Novels by and about Women in America, 1820–1870* (Ithaca, N.Y.: Cornell University Press, 1978), and Jane P. Tompkins, "Sentimental Power: *Uncle Tom's Cabin* and the Politics of Literary History," *Glyph*, 8 (1981), 79–102.

18. For a full account of one author's use of religion as a feminist weapon, see Christine Stansell, "Elizabeth Stuart Phelps: A Study in Female Rebellion," in *Woman: An Issue*, ed. Lee R. Edwards, Mary Heath and Lisa Baskin (Boston: Little, Brown and Co., 1972), pp. 239–56. Papashvily, pp. 104–7, and Baym, pp. 41–44, also discuss the subversive possibilities of the religious theme.

19. Grace Greenwood [Sara Clark Lippincott] in "Zelma's Vow," *Atlantic Monthly*, 4 (July 1859), 73–84, tries to make the protagonist herself a "bad" girl. The dark and exotic Zelma is a younger version of Haw-

thorne's Zenobia. But, although she is said to have "nomadic and lawless instincts" (75), Zelma never acts on them. She becomes an actress and dies of a broken heart when her husband leaves her. In *The Morgesons* (1862) Elizabeth Stoddard has her rebellious heroine flirt with real badness. Bored with school, sewing, and reading the Bible, Cassandra Morgeson falls in love with her married cousin, Charles. But before they can do anything beyond declaring their love, Stoddard kills off Charles in an accident and has Cassandra become Good Good.

For an interesting discussion of the bad girl foil (the "shadow figure") in popular women's fiction, see Sally Allen McNall, *Who Is in the House? A Psychological Study of Two Centuries of Women's Fiction in America, 1795 to the Present* (New York: Elsevier, 1981), pp. 45–49.

20. Hannah Foster, *The Coquette; or, the History of Eliza Wharton* (Boston: William Febridge, 1855), p. 168. Further references are noted in parentheses within the text.

21. Susanna Haswell Rowson, *Charlotte Temple* (New York: Twayne, 1964), p. 61.

22. Quoted in Brown, p. 121.

23. E.D.E.N. Southworth, *The Hidden Hand* (New York: Grosset and Dunlap, [1880?]), p. 40. Further references are noted in parentheses within the text.

24. Louisa May Alcott, *Little Women* (Garden City, N.Y.: Literary Guild, 1950), pp. 5–6. Further references are noted in parentheses within the text. *Little Women* has come to be considered, like *Huckleberry Finn*, a book for children or adolescents; however, I regard it, along with Kate Douglas Wiggin's *Rebecca of Sunnybrook Farm* (1903), as also a novel for adults.

25. *Louisa May Alcott: Her Life, Letters, and Journals*, ed. Ednah Cheney (Boston: Little, Brown, and Co., 1910), p. 192.

26. Willa Cather, *My Ántonia* (Boston: Houghton Mifflin, 1949), p. 187.

27. Sarah Orne Jewett, "Farmer Finch," in *A White Heron and Other Stories* (Boston: Houghton Mifflin, 1886), p. 52. Further references are noted in parentheses within the text.

28. Mary Wilkins Freeman, "Louisa," in *A New England Nun and Other Stories* (New York: Harper, 1891), p. 405. Cather's Ántonia also works in the fields. To most of the characters she is thus "poor Ántonia." Jim Burden complains that farm work has spoiled her prettiness and made her "lose all her nice ways" (82); he thinks she is too proud of her strength. Ántonia, however, tells Jim: "Oh, better I like to work out-of-doors than in a house. . . . I not care that your grandmother say it makes me like man. I like to be like a man" (92).

29. Kate Douglas Wiggin, *Rebecca of Sunnybrook Farm* (New York: Grosset & Dunlap, 1903), p. 13. Further references are noted in parentheses within the text.

30. Female characters of all ages are frequently ill from no apparent physical cause; it will be recalled that Eliza Wharton went into a mysterious "decline" when she recognized the limited nature of the choices available to her. For a discussion of invalidism as a tool of protest in the nineteenth century, see Barbara Ehrenreich and Deirdre English, *Complaints and Disorders: The Sexual Politics of Sickness* (New York: Feminist Press, 1973), pp. 38–43. For a review of the literature, see Martha H. Verbrugge, "Women and Medicine in Nineteenth-Century America," *Signs*, 1 (Summer 1976), 957–72.

31. Mary Johnston, *Hagar* (Boston: Houghton Mifflin, 1913), p. 16. Further references are noted in parentheses within the text.

32. Zona Gale, *A Daughter of the Morning* (Indianapolis: Bobbs-Merrill, 1917), p. 30. Further references are noted in parentheses within the text.

33. Fiedler, *Love and Death*, pp. 67–68.

34. *Letters of Hawthorne to William D. Ticknor, 1851–1864* (Newark, N.J.: The Carteret Book Club, 1910), II, 50, I, 29–30.

The career of Kate Chopin illustrates the dangers of psychology and candor. The hostile reception of *The Awakening* (1899), which was called an "unutterable crime against polite society," put an end to her writing career. Chopin made the following statement about her passionate heroine: "Having a group of people at my disposal, I thought it might be entertaining to throw them together and see what would happen. I never dreamed of Mrs. Pontellier making such a mess of things and working out her own damnation as she did." Quoted in Edmund Wilson, *Patriotic Gore* (New York: Oxford University Press, 1966), p. 591. Although Chopin's comment is characteristically ironic, it is quite possible that, in setting out to portray candidly the psychology of a restless wife, she really did not anticipate what she was going to uncover.

35. Sarah Orne Jewett, *Betty Leicester* (Boston: Houghton Mifflin, 1889), p. 130.

36. Dorothy Canfield Fisher, *The Bent Twig* (New York: Henry Holt, 1917), p. 104.

37. Grace King, *Monsieur Motte* (Freeport, N.Y.: Books for Libraries Press, 1969), p. 186. Further references are noted in parentheses within the text.

38. Witham, p. 2.

39. Witham, p. 13; Johnson, "The Adolescent Hero: A Trend in Modern Fiction," p. 9.

Chapter III. On the Threshold: Edith Wharton's *Summer*

1. Edith Wharton, *Summer* (New York: D. Appleton & Co., 1917), p. 9. Further references are noted in parentheses within the text.
2. Alexander Cowie, *The Rise of the American Novel*, pp. 414–15.
3. Louisa May Alcott, *Little Women*, pp. 267–68.
4. Edith Wharton, *A Backward Glance* (New York: D. Appleton-Century Co., 1934), p. 356.
5. R. W. B. Lewis, *Edith Wharton* (New York: Harper & Row, 1975), p. 396.
6. Edith Wharton, *Ethan Frome* (New York: Charles Scribner's Sons, 1939), p. 14.
7. Wharton, *A Backward Glance*, pp. 294–95; Lewis, p. 398.
8. Wharton, *A Backward Glance*, pp. 126–27.
9. Susanna Rowson, *Charlotte Temple*, p. 152.
10. We do not know whether Wharton actually read *The Lamplighter*. Perhaps she did not, since as a girl she was forbidden popular novels and restricted to the "classics," which were mainly by men. She did read the Brontës, an abridged version of Richardson's *Clarissa Harlowe*, and *Little Women* and *Little Men*. Wharton discusses her early reading in *A Backward Glance*, p. 51 and pp. 65–69.
11. See, for instance, Louis Auchincloss, "Edith Wharton," in *Seven Modern American Novelists*, ed. William Van O'Connor (Minneapolis: University of Minnesota Press, 1959), p. 26.
12. Elizabeth Ammons, *Edith Wharton's Argument with America* (Athens: University of Georgia Press, 1980), pp. 133, 141. Also, in "The Desolation of Charity Royall: Imagery in Edith Wharton's *Summer*," *Colby Library Quarterly*, XVIII (Dec. 1982), 241–48, Linda Morante finds images of death and entrapment in *Summer*.
13. G. Stanley Hall, *Adolescence*, I, pp. viii, xiii, *passim*.
14. Annis Pratt and Barbara A. White discuss the phenomenon of "growing down" in women's fiction in "The Novel of Development," in Pratt, *Archetypal Patterns in Women's Fiction*, pp. 29–37.
15. Ammons, pp. 136–37.
16. For Jungian interpretation of American sentimental fiction see Carl Bode, "The Scribbling Women: The Domestic Novel Rules the 'Fifties," in *The Anatomy of American Popular Culture, 1840–1861* (Berkeley: University of California Press, 1959), pp. 169–87. For discussion of the original Rochester as a representation of male sexuality see Richard Chase, "The Brontes, or Myth Domesticated," in *Jane Eyre*, ed. Richard Dunn (New York: Norton, 1971), pp. 462–71.
17. See Pratt and White, "The Novel of Development," pp. 16–24, for discussion of the young heroine and the "green world." Muddy boots are

a prominent part of the description of the Rochester-like St. Elmo in Augusta Evans Wilson's best-selling *St. Elmo*.

18. Cynthia Griffin Wolff, "Introduction" to *Summer* (New York: Perennial Library, 1980), p. xi.

19. Sandra M. Gilbert and Susan Gubar, *The Madwoman in the Attic* (New Haven, Conn.: Yale University Press, 1977), p. 292.

20. Wolff, p. xii.

21. Cynthia Griffin Wolff, *A Feast of Words: The Triumph of Edith Wharton* (New York: Oxford University Press, 1977), p. 292.

22. Marilyn French, "Introduction" to *Summer* (New York: Berkley Books, 1981), p. xlviii.

23. Augusta J. Evans [Wilson], *St. Elmo* (New York: Carleton, Publisher, 1867), pp. 568–69.

24. Nina Baym, *Woman's Fiction*, pp. 11–12.

25. Ruth Suckow, "Literary Soubrettes," pp. 517–19.

26. Maria S. Cummins, *The Lamplighter*, p. 134.

27. Frederick Hoffman, *Freudianism and the Literary Mind* (Baton Rouge: Louisiana State University Press, 1957), p. 43. One critic writing in the 1920's claims that the "newer psychology" provided the impetus for novelists to treat family relations in the first place; she argues that before the early 1920's "seldom do we find, as a theme for a novel, the relationship between parents and children." See Eva v. B. Hansl, "Parents in Modern Fiction," *Bookman*, LXII (Sept. 1925), 21–27.

Chapter IV. Nice Girls and Their Folks: The Adolescent and the Family in Ruth Suckow's Fiction

1. There are two books on Suckow's fiction: Leedice McAnelly Kissane's *Ruth Suckow* (New York: Twayne, 1969) and Margaret Stewart Omrcanin's *Ruth Suckow: A Critical Study of Her Fiction* (Philadelphia: Dorrance Co., 1972). Neither was able to benefit from the insights of feminist literary criticism, nor do they argue for reconsideration of Suckow's literary reputation. For the latter see Fritz Oehlschlaeger, "The Art of Ruth Suckow's 'A Start in Life,' " *Western American Literature*, 15 (Fall 1980), 177–86, and my "Ruth Suckow" in *Dictionary of Literary Biography: American Short Story Writers to World War II*, ed. William E. Grant, forthcoming.

2. Ruth Suckow, *The Odyssey of a Nice Girl* (New York: Alfred Knopf, 1925), p. 263. Further references are noted in parentheses within the text.

3. See H. L. Mencken, "The Library," *American Mercury*, 7 (Apr. 1926), 506–7. Suckow consistently objected to being classified as a "re-

gionalist." She once stated that if her works did not "cast a shadow beyond localism," she would not have taken the trouble to write them—Kissane, p. 153.

4. Quotations are from Suckow's first novel, *Country People* (New York: Alfred Knopf, 1924), p. 202. Mothers in the later generations have more latitude in their "sphere" of caring for the house and children, but the patriarchal structure of the family remains intact throughout Suckow's fiction. For an interesting and effective portrayal of a wife's loss of identity in marriage, see "The Resurrection" in Ruth Suckow, *Iowa Interiors* (New York: Alfred Knopf, 1926). In this short story a woman's family has never "thought of her as a person in herself. She had been Mother, and, then, Grandma" (197).

5. Ruth Suckow, *The Bonney Family* (New York: Alfred Knopf, 1928), p. 200. Further references are noted in parentheses within the text.

6. Ruth Suckow, *The Folks* (New York: Farrar & Rinehart, 1934), p. 199. Further references are noted in parentheses within the text.

7. Ruth Suckow, "The Best of the Lot," *Smart Set*, 69 (Nov. 1922), 30.

8. Ruth Suckow, *The Kramer Girls* (New York: Alfred Knopf, 1930), p. 120.

9. Kissane, p. 89.

10. Ruth Suckow, *Children and Older People* (New York: Alfred Knopf, 1931), p. 174. Further references are noted in parentheses within the text.

11. Suckow, *Iowa Interiors*, p. 11.

12. Simone de Beauvoir, *The Second Sex*, pp. 306-7.

13. C. John McCole, *Lucifer at Large* (New York: Books for Libraries Press, 1937), p. 304.

14. Ruth Suckow, *Cora* (New York: Alfred Knopf, 1929), p. 116. Further references are noted in parentheses within the text.

15. For a discussion of the problems involved in assessing direct influence, see Frederick Hoffman, *Freudianism and the Literary Mind* (Baton Rouge: Louisiana State University Press, 1957), pp. 87-115.

16. See especially *Some Others and Myself* (New York: Rinehart, 1952), pp. 92-96, 170-72. The Elsie Dinsmore essay is "Elsie Dinsmore: A Study in Perfection," *Bookman*, 66 (Oct. 1927), 126-33.

17. For discussion of the Oedipus complex, see Sigmund Freud, "Infantile Sexuality," in *Three Essays on the Theory of Sexuality*, ed. and trans. James Strachey (New York: Basic Books, 1962); "Family Romances," in *Collected Papers*, ed. James Strachey, V (London: Hogarth Press, 1950); "Development of the Libido and Sexual Organizations," in *A General Introduction to Psychoanalysis*, trans. G. Stanley Hall (New York: Boni & Liveright, 1920); "The Passing of the Oedipus Complex," in *Collected Papers*, ed. James Strachey, II (London: Hogarth Press,

1950); "Some Psychological Consequences of the Anatomical Distinction Between the Sexes," in *Collected Papers*, ed. James Strachey, V (London: Hogarth Press, 1950); and *An Outline of Psychoanalysis*, trans. James Strachey (New York: W. W. Norton, 1949), pp. 80–99. For further analysis of the recurrence of the Oedipal conflict at puberty, see Helene Deutsch, *The Psychology of Women*, I (New York: Bantam, 1944), p. 3, and Patrick Mullahy, *Oedipus Myth and Complex* (New York: Grove Press, 1948), p. 29.

18. Freud, "Some Psychological Consequences," p. 196.

19. Shulamith Firestone, *The Dialectic of Sex*, pp. 47–52. Erik Erikson's comments in *Childhood and Society* (New York: Norton, 1950) lend support to Firestone's view. Erikson contends that American men in psychoanalysis first appear to feel abandoned by their mothers. "But wherever our methods permit us to look deeper, we find at the bottom of it all the conviction, the mortal self-accusation, that it was *the child who abandoned the mother*, because he had been in such a hurry to become independent" (255).

20. Freud, "Some Psychological Consequences," p. 193.

21. The major points in Freud's theory of female development are presented in "Infantile Sexuality" (1905), "Family Romances" (1909), "Some Psychological Consequences of the Anatomical Distinction Between the Sexes" (1925), "Female Sexuality" (1931), and "Femininity" (1933).

Freud himself uses the term "female Oedipus complex" rather than "Electra complex"; he argues, somewhat illogically, that the term "Electra complex" is more likely to lead readers to the mistaken conclusion that the situation of the sexes is analogous. I am retaining the term "Electra complex" since it is better known.

Freud notes that an alternative to the Electra complex in some girls is a "masculinity complex," in which the girl "clings in obstinate assertion to her threatened masculinity" and identifies with her father ("Female Sexuality," in *Collected Papers*, ed. James Strachey, London: Hogarth Press, V, 257). However, Suckow does not give any of her adolescents this "complex"; they do not identify with their fathers, do not want to be like men (although they claim male privileges), and do not even go through a "tomboy" stage.

22. Even early psychoanalysts make this point. See Deutsch, pp. 239–44, and Karen Horney, *Feminine Psychology* (New York: Norton, 1967), pp. 57–58.

23. Kissane, p. 102.

24. Harlan Hatcher, *Creating the Modern American Novel* (New York: Russell & Russell, 1965), p. 105; Joseph Baker, "Regionalism in the Middle West," *American Review*, 4 (Nov. 1934–March 1935), 606. Suckow

has obviously made Margaret Ferguson a "dark lady"; in her essay "Literary Soubrettes," she notes that this type is often punished by male authors and condemned by literary critics.

25. Freud, "Female Sexuality," pp. 252–53.

26. Nancy Chodorow, *The Reproduction of Mothering: Psychoanalysis and the Sociology of Gender* (Berkeley: University of California Press, 1978), pp. 137–40. The strength of the mother-daughter attachment is represented in Greek mythology in the story of Demeter and Persephone. Persephone is stolen from Demeter by Hades and fated to spend half the year with him and half with her mother. Demeter's other daughter, Athena, asks to be reborn of man and, after she emerges full-grown from the head of Zeus, remains loyal to her "father" and champions men. In receiving a new existence through a man, Athena follows the pattern of the "Electra complex," whereas Persephone remains in conflict between justification through a man and adherence to her mother.

27. Kissane, p. 72.

28. Freud, "Female Sexuality," p. 257.

29. Nancy Chodorow, "Family Structure and Feminine Personality," in *Woman, Culture, and Society*, ed. Michelle Zimbalist Rosaldo and Louise Lamphere (Stanford, Calif.: Stanford University Press, 1974), p. 63.

30. *Ibid.*, p. 65.

31. Freud, "Female Sexuality," pp. 252–53.

32. Deutsch, p. 9.

33. Deutsch, p. xv.

34. Kissane, p. 62.

35. Edith Wharton, *Summer*, p. 274.

36. Joseph Kett, *Rites of Passage*, p. 265.

Chapter V. Loss of Self in Carson McCullers' *The Member of the Wedding*

1. Carson McCullers, *The Member of the Wedding*, in *The Ballad of the Sad Café: The Novels and Stories of Carson McCullers* (Boston: Houghton Mifflin Co., 1951), p. 617. Further references are noted in parentheses within the text.

2. Edmund Wilson, rev. of *The Member of the Wedding*, by Carson McCullers, *New Yorker*, March 30, 1946, p. 87. For McCullers' reaction to the review, see Virginia Spencer Carr, *The Lonely Hunter: A Biography of Carson McCullers* (Garden City, N.Y.: Doubleday & Co., 1975), pp. 266–67.

3. Francis Dedmond, "Doing Her Own Thing: Carson McCullers'

Notes

Dramatization of *The Member of the Wedding*," *South Atlantic Bulletin*, 40 (May 1975), 47. The play was published by New Directions in 1951.

4. Oliver Evans, *The Ballad of Carson McCullers* (New York: Coward-McCann, 1966), p. 102. This view of the novel is developed most fully in Evans, pp. 102–9, and in Chester Eisinger, *Fiction of the Forties* (Chicago: University of Chicago Press, 1963), pp. 243–56. See also Oliver Evans, "The Theme of Spiritual Isolation in Carson McCullers," in *South: Modern Southern Literature in Its Cultural Setting*, ed. Louis Rubin and Robert Jacobi (New York: Dolphin, 1961), pp. 333–40.

5. Reviews quoted in Evans, *The Ballad of Carson McCullers*, pp. 119–22. See also Irving Malin, *New American Gothic* (Carbondale: Southern Illinois University Press, 1962), p. 58.

6. Joseph Baker, "Regionalism in the Middle West," p. 609; Leedice McAnelly Kissane, *Ruth Suckow*, p. 63. For critical reaction to *Summer*, see Marlene Springer, *Edith Wharton and Kate Chopin: A Reference Guide* (Boston: G. K. Hall & Co., 1976). Some critics make it appear that Royall is the protagonist of *Summer*, e.g. "Lawyer Royall, in *Summer*, a man of Ethan Frome's dignified stature, is thwarted and humiliated by his passion for his self-centered ward Charity"—Blake Nevius, *Edith Wharton: A Study of Her Fiction* (Berkeley and Los Angeles: University of California Press, 1953), p. 108.

7. Eisinger, p. 258.

8. Leslie Fiedler, *No! in Thunder*, p. 286.

9. Eisinger, p. 250.

10. Carson McCullers, *The Heart Is a Lonely Hunter*, in *The Ballad of the Sad Café: The Novels and Stories of Carson McCullers* (Boston: Houghton Mifflin Co., 1951), p. 184. Further references are noted in parentheses within the text.

11. Evans, *The Ballad of Carson McCullers*, p. 111. See also Frank Baldanza, "Plato in Dixie," *Georgia Review*, 12 (Summer 1958), 151–67. Only Winifred Dusenbury, who views Frankie's problems as the direct result of her being motherless, sees Berenice as an inadequate substitute; see Dusenbury's *The Theme of Loneliness in Modern American Drama* (Gainesville, Fla.: University of Florida Press, 1960), p. 58.

12. Richard Wright, *Native Son* (New York: Harper and Row, 1940), pp. 21–23.

13. Evans, "The Theme of Spiritual Isolation," p. 340.

14. James Johnson, "The Adolescent Hero: A Trend in Modern Fiction," p. 6.

15. Robert Phillips, "The Gothic Architecture of *The Member of the Wedding*," *Renascence*, 16 (Winter 1964), 68.

16. Simone de Beauvoir, *The Second Sex*, p. 330.

17. *Ibid.*, p. 333.

18. Leslie Fiedler, *Love and Death*, p. 482.

19. *Ibid.*, p. 383.

20. Leslie Fiedler, *An End to Innocence* (New York: Stein and Day, 1972), p. 149.

21. Stuart Burns, "The Novel of Adolescence in America: 1940–1963," p. 127. Phillips, p. 70.

22. Ihab Hassan, "Carson McCullers: The Alchemy of Love and Aesthetics of Pain," *Modern Fiction Studies*, 5 (Winter 1959–60), 314. The incest theory is developed in Irving Buchen, "Carson McCullers: A Case of Convergence," *Bucknell Review*, 21 (Spring 1973), 15–28.

23. Phillips, pp. 64–65; Fiedler, *No! in Thunder*, p. 188.

24. A. S. Knowles, "Six Bronze Petals and Two Red: Carson McCullers in the Forties," in *The Forties*, ed. Warren French (Florida: Everett/Edwards, 1969), pp. 91, 98.

There is a metaphor for the state of McCullers criticism in her short story "A Tree. A Rock. A Cloud." In this story a stranger stops at a café and befriends a newsboy, explaining that he has learned to love humanity. When the stranger (McCullers) tells the boy he loves him, the obtuse café owner (Fiedler) and the rest of the men at the counter (subsequent critics) titter and warn the stranger that the boy is a minor. The only critic to recognize the significance of McCullers' "boy-girls" without reacting negatively is Louise Westling. Her "Carson McCullers's Tomboys" *Southern Humanities Review*, 14 (1980), 339–50, follows my discussion in "Growing Up Female: Adolescent Girlhood in American Literature" (Diss., University of Wisconsin, 1974), 88–134.

25. Hassan, p. 321.

26. Jack Moore discusses Mick's fear of sex in "Carson McCullers: The Heart Is a Timeless Hunter," *Twentieth Century Literature*, 2 (July 1965), 76–81. Eisinger, p. 250, notes that Mick's sexual experience is "more redolent of surrender than glory." Mick feels "like her head was broke off from her body and thrown away" (235).

27. Johnson, p. 7.

28. James Joyce, *A Portrait of the Artist as a Young Man* (London: Jonathan Cape, 1916), p. 104.

29. Carson McCullers, *The Mortgaged Heart*, ed. Margarita G. Smith (New York: Bantam, 1967), p. 77.

30. McCullers, *The Mortgaged Heart*, p. 81. It is interesting that although "Like That" was accepted by *Story* magazine in 1936, it was never published; perhaps its theme was considered inappropriate. The story was recently discovered among the magazine archives at Princeton University (4). In her autobiographical sketch "The Orphanage," also included in *The Mortgaged Heart*, McCullers gives another instance of the association of sex with loss of status. When McCullers was ten, her friend and "ini-

tiator," Hattie, explained "what made colored people colored. If a girl, said Hattie, kissed a boy she turned into a colored person, and when she was married her children were colored, too. Only brothers were excepted from this law" (54).
31. Dusenbury, p. 59; Malin, p. 58.
32. Alfred Kazin, *Bright Book of Life* (Boston: Little, Brown & Co., 1971), p. 53. Frederick Hoffman, *The Art of Southern Fiction* (Carbondale: Southern Illinois University Press), p. 71.
33. W. Tasker Witham, *The Adolescent in the American Novel, 1920–1960*, p. 169.
34. Louise Gossett, *Violence in Recent Southern Fiction* (Durham, N.C.: Duke University Press, 1965), pp. 164–66.
35. Burns, pp. 126–27; Evans, *Ballad*, p. 123; Hassan, p. 322; Phillips, p. 71.
36. This juxtaposition is discussed in Richard Cook, *Carson McCullers* (New York: Frederick Ungar Publishing Co., 1975), pp. 77–78.
37. Gossett, p. 166. Gossett's argument resembles the familiar one that Western cultures should provide for their youth clearcut "rites of passage" like those of so-called primitive societies. As we shall see in the next chapter, however, the main object of these primitive rites is to initiate boys and girls into fixed sex roles.
38. Walter Allen, *The Modern Novel in Britain and the United States* (New York: E. P. Dutton, 1964), p. 134. Emphasis mine. Lawrence Graver, in *Carson McCullers* (Minneapolis: University of Minnesota Press, 1969), p. 33, also claims that Frankie has gained "new wisdom about the limits of *human* life." Emphasis mine.
39. Johnson, p. 7.
40. Carson McCullers, [untitled manuscript], *The Mortgaged Heart*, p. 136.
41. Charlotte Goodman, "The Lost Brother, the Twin: Women Novelists and the Male-Female Double *Bildungsroman*," *Novel*, 17 (Fall 1983), 31.

Chapter VI. Initiation in Jean Stafford's *The Mountain Lion*

1. There are relatively few critical studies of Stafford's work, and in the many recent books and articles on female writers she is seldom mentioned. Narda Lacey Schwartz, in her *Articles on Women Writers 1960–1975* (Santa Barbara, Calif.: Clio Press, 1977), lists only six articles on Stafford. For comparable novelists, such as Caroline Gordon and Carson McCullers, there are from twenty-five to fifty entries.
2. Elements of this interpretation appear in contemporary reviews of *The Mountain Lion*. The interpretation is developed in the following

works: Stuart Burns, "The Novel of Adolescence in America: 1940–1963"; Stuart Burns, "Counterpoint in Jean Stafford's *The Mountain Lion*," *Critique*, 9 (June 1967), 20–32; Helen White Childers, "American Novels About Adolescence, 1917–1953"; Chester Eisinger, *Fiction of the Forties*; Ihab Hassan, "Jean Stafford: The Expense of Style and the Scope of Sensibility," *Western Review*, 19 (Spring 1955), 185–203; Ihab Hassan, *Radical Innocence*; and Olga Vickery, "The Novels of Jean Stafford," *Critique*, 5 (Spring-Summer 1962), 14–26. The only critics to show awareness of gender in *The Mountain Lion* are Blanche H. Gelfant and Charlotte Goodman. Gelfant's review in *The New Republic*, May 10, 1975, pp. 22–25, and her reading in "Revolutionary Turnings: *The Mountain Lion* Reread," *Massachusetts Review*, 20 (Spring 1979), 117–25, share some elements with my interpretation in "Growing Up Female: Adolescent Girlhood in American Literature" (Diss., University of Wisconsin, 1974), 135–185. Goodman's view in "The Lost Brother, the Twin: Women Novelists and the Male-Female Double *Bildungsroman*," *Novel*, 17 (Fall 1983), 28–43, is similar to mine in "Initiation, the West, and the Hunt in Jean Stafford's *The Mountain Lion*," *Essays in Literature*, 9 (Fall 1982), 194–210.

3. Jean Stafford, *The Mountain Lion* (New York: Harcourt, Brace & World, 1947), pp. 10–11. Further references are noted in parentheses within the text.

4. Childers, p. 237; Hassan, *Radical Innocence*, p. 71; Burns, "The Novel of Adolescence," p. 40.

5. Actually the Fawcett home is in California and the ranch in Colorado, but in the novel Colorado represents "the West." Grandfather Kenyon tells Ralph and Molly that California is not the West but "a separate thing like Florida and Washington, D.C." (8).

6. Leslie Fiedler, *Love and Death in the American Novel*, pp. 4, 445.

7. Leslie Fiedler, *No! in Thunder*, pp. 266–67.

8. In her introductory note to *Collected Stories* (New York: Farrar, Straus and Giroux, 1969), Stafford tells us that her father wrote Western stories under the pseudonym "Jack Wonder." Her own early attempts were also Western stories where "all the foremen of all the ranches had steely blue eyes to match the barrels of their Colt .45's." Later she recognized the mythical nature of both the "wicked West" and the "noble West."

9. Robert Bickham, "The Origins and Importance of the Initiation Story in 20th Century British and American Fiction," p. 42. It should be added that the boy's hostility may outwardly be converted into friendliness, but there is probably a residue of guilt.

10. Bickham, p. 43.

11. In *The Adolescent in the American Novel, 1920–1960*, p. 229, W.

Tasker Witham notes that girls are almost never involved with killing at all.

12. Eisinger, p. 26.

13. Burns, "The Novel of Adolescence," p. 178.

14. Stafford, *Collected Stories*, p. 457.

15. It is tempting to call intelligence one of Molly's few virtues. As Louis Auchincloss points out, one of Stafford's artistic accomplishments in *The Mountain Lion* is that she does not sentimentalize Molly "despite the fact that she must have strong feelings of identification with her," *Pioneers and Caretakers* (Minneapolis: University of Minnesota Press, 1961), p. 157. Stafford portrays Molly as often obnoxious and unpleasant. She avoids sentimentalizing Molly even in death by referring to the dead Molly as looking like a "tall, slim monkey" (230).

16. Burns, "Counterpoint in Jean Stafford's *The Mountain Lion*," p. 25.

17. Harvey Breit, *The Writer Observed* (New York: World Publishing Co., 1956), p. 224.

18. Burns, "Counterpoint in Jean Stafford's *The Mountain Lion*," p. 26.

19. Most critics seem to consider Molly "crazy," and readers may agree that some of her behavior, such as pouring acid on her hand, is "abnormal." We must still take note of Phyllis Chesler's point, in *Women & Madness* (New York: Avon, 1972), that to be female in this society is to be defined as "mad." According to Chesler, "madness" is defined as "either the acting out of the devalued female role or the total or partial rejection of one's sex-role stereotype" (75). If a woman exhibits female role characteristics, such as passivity, submissiveness, dependence, excitability, and subjectivity, she is "mad" or "crazy" because these qualities are considered immature and unhealthy; but any other characteristics are unacceptable in a woman—if she is aggressive, independent, etc., she is "mad" also (86).

20. See Mircea Eliade, *Birth and Rebirth* (London: Harvill Press, 1958), pp. 21–23.

21. Lucille H. Charles, "Growing Up through Drama," *Journal of American Folklore*, 59 (1946), 260. Emphasis mine.

22. Bickham, p. 13.

23. Bruno Bettelheim, *Symbolic Wounds* (Glencoe, Ill.: Free Press, 1954), p. 106. A. M. Hocart, in his discussion of initiation rites of primitive boys, contends that initiation "confers not manhood but manliness, if by manliness we understand success in all the pursuits of men, in achieving women, in rearing a family, in war, hunting or whatever may be considered man's work." *The Life-Giving Myth* (London: Methuen & Co., 1970), p. 162.

24. Blake Nevius, *Edith Wharton: A Study of Her Fiction*, p. 108;

Margaret B. McDowell, *Edith Wharton* (Boston: Twayne Publishers, 1976), p. 71; Harlan Hatcher, *Creating the Modern American Novel*, p. 105; Joseph Baker, "Regionalism in the Middle West," p. 606; Leedice McAnelly Kissane, *Ruth Suckow*, p. 64; Margaret Stewart Omrcanin, *Ruth Suckow: A Critical Study of Her Fiction*, p. 104; Oliver Evans, *The Ballad of Carson McCullers*, pp. 119–22; Vickery, "The Novels of Jean Stafford," p. 22.

Chapter VII. The Adolescent Heroine and "God's Plan for Girls"

1. I consistently put the word "tomboy" in quotation marks because the connotations of this frequently used term are problematical. Although "tomboy" no longer carries its original suggestion of sexual looseness, "tom" is still a "generic slight," as in "tom-fool"—J. S. Farmer and W. E. Henley, *Slang and Its Analogues* (New York: Arno Press, 1970), pp. 149–50. The implication is that boys are superior and some activities are "naturally" for them. At best a girl can only be an inferior boy, and if she plays baseball or wears comfortable clothing, she must be imitating boys. Interestingly, it is thought "normal" and "healthy" for a girl to be a "tomboy" (see Helene Deutsch, *The Psychology of Women*, I, 17–18); but a boy who insisted on wearing skirts and playing with dolls would be cause for alarm. The premise, again, is that men are superior; it is "normal" to envy and imitate superiority but not to actually wish to be inferior.

2. Peggy Goodin, *Clementine* (New York: E. P. Dutton & Co., 1946), p. 13. In this chapter, after a novel is first noted, page references will be given thereafter in parentheses within the text.

3. Agnes Smedley, *Daughter of Earth* (New York: Coward-McCann, 1929), p. 9.

4. Jane Mayhall, *Cousin to Human* (New York: Harcourt, Brace & World, 1960), p. 165.

5. Frances Frost, *Innocent Summer* (New York: Farrar & Rinehart, 1936), p. 39.

6. Louise Meriwether, *Daddy Was a Number Runner* (New York: Pyramid Books, 1971), p. 77.

7. Elizabeth Pollet, *A Family Romance* (New York: New Directions, 1950), p. 70.

8. Pamela Moore, *Chocolates for Breakfast* (New York: Rinehart & Co., 1956), p. 15.

9. Winifred Van Etten, *I Am the Fox* (New York: Popular Library, 1936), p. 22.

10. [Ruth Seid] Jo Sinclair, *The Changelings* (New York: McGraw-Hill Book Co., 1955), pp. 16–17.

11. Katherine Anne Porter, *Old Mortality*, in *The Old Order* (New York: Harcourt, Brace & World, 1958), p. 119.

12. Katherine Anne Porter, "The Old Order," in *The Old Order* (New York: Harcourt, Brace & World, 1958), pp. 28, 23, 26.

13. Sylvia Plath, *The Bell Jar* (New York: Bantam Books, 1972), p. 68.

14. Helen Hull, *Quest* (New York: Macmillan Co., 1922), p. 159.

15. Katherine Dunn, *Truck* (New York: Harper & Row, 1971), p. 138.

16. Dorothy Myra Page, *Gathering Storm* (New York: International Publishers, 1932), p. 101.

17. Shirley Jackson, *Hangsaman* (New York: Ace, 1951), p. 33.

18. Dorothy Canfield Fisher, *The Deepening Stream* (New York: Modern Library, 1930), p. 61.

19. Laura Beheler, *The Paper Dolls* (Boston: Houghton Mifflin Co., 1956), p. 48.

20. Dorothy James Roberts, *A Durable Fire* (New York: Macmillan Co. 1945), p. 268.

21. Dana Faralla, *The Madstone* (Philadelphia: J. B. Lippincott Co. 1958), p. 136.

22. Gladys Schmitt, *Alexandra* (New York: Dial Press, 1947), p. 32.

23. Mary Ellen Chase, *Mary Peters* (New York: Macmillan Co., 1934), p. 75.

24. Elizabeth Madox Roberts, *The Time of Man* (New York: Viking Press, 1926), p. 33.

25. When she is in a semi-hallucinatory state, Esther mistakes a patient in the mental hospital for Mrs. Tomolillo, the woman she observed in childbirth. Plath connects each of Esther's experiences with the general oppression of women and with her later breakdown. It is symbolic that Esther and several other girls are poisoned at a luncheon given by *Ladies' Day* magazine.

26. Hope Field, *Stormy Present* (New York: E. P. Dutton & Co., 1942), p. 65.

27. Toni Morrison, *The Bluest Eye* (New York: Holt, Rinehart, and Winston, 1970), p. 44.

28. Mildred Gilman, *Fig Leaves* (New York: Siebel Co., 1925), pp. 79–81.

29. Rosemary Wells, *The Fog Comes on Little Pig Feet* (New York: Avon Books, 1972), p. 9.

30. Dorothy Day, *The Eleventh Virgin* (New York: Boni, 1924), p. 19.

31. It is interesting that some of the books in my survey have been proscribed reading for adolescents. I can remember teachers in my high school confiscating copies of *Chocolates for Breakfast* and *Peyton Place*. Caroline Slade's *The Sterile Sun* (New York: Vanguard Press, 1936), a

novel about adolescent prostitutes, has an amusing introductory note by a minister. He warns that the novel is "for professionals only and should not be placed on the shelves of a public library for young people with a pornographic urge to read [sic!]."

32. Deutsch, p. 12.

33. This is not the case with college novels having male protagonists. See John Lyons, *The College Novel in America*.

34. Margery Latimer, *This Is My Body* (New York: Jonathan Cape, 1930), p. 15.

35. In both novels it is significant that the helpful psychiatrist is a woman. Green's Deborah Blau cannot be reached by a male psychiatrist because she objects to the "austerity of his manner" and his "icy logic"; she sees him as "intruding" into her mind (New York: Signet, 1964), p. 160. Esther Greenwood dislikes her first psychiatrist as soon as she sees a conventional family photograph on his desk. "I thought, how could this Doctor Gordon help me anyway, with a beautiful wife and beautiful children and a beautiful dog haloing him like the angels on a Christmas card?" (106). When Dr. Gordon gives her electric shock treatment, Esther sees him as a punitive figure, a representative of the oppressive society that electrocuted the Rosenbergs. Esther and Deborah are surprised when they are eventually given female psychiatrists—Esther did not know they existed, and Deborah first mistakes her psychiatrist for the housekeeper, but both are pleased.

36. Harriette Simpson Arnow, *The Weedkiller's Daughter* (New York: Alfred A. Knopf, 1970), p. 366.

37. Nora Johnson, *The World of Henry Orient* (Boston: Little, Brown and Co., 1958), p. 205.

38. See W. Tasker Witham, *The Adolescent in the American Novel, 1920–1960*, pp. 65–67.

39. Kathleen Millay, *Against the Wall* (New York: Macaulay Co., 1929), pp. 411–12.

40. In *Growing Up Absurd* (New York: Random House, 1955), Paul Goodman states outright that "our 'youth troubles' are boys' troubles— female delinquency is sexual: 'incorrigibility' and unmarried pregnancy." Goodman equates women with their sex organs to such an extent that it never occurs to him that girls might have problems of personal identity. While he sees the rebellion of "angry young men" as justified because society does not provide them with worthwhile goals, he claims that the question of "how to be useful and make something of oneself" does not apply to girls. "A girl does not *have* to, she is not expected to, 'make something' of herself. Her career does not have to be self-justifying, for she will have children, which is absolutely self-justifying, like any other natural or creative act" (13).

41. Instead of dreading or resenting menarche, like many protagonists, Rachel looks forward to it as a sign of being "normal." Clem Kelley reacts positively to her first menstruation for the same reason.

42. Anne Nall Stallworth, *This Time Next Year* (New York: Vanguard Press, 1971), p. 95.

43. Anzia Yezierska, *Bread Givers* (Garden City, N.Y.: Doubleday, Page & Co., 1925), p. 130.

44. Mildred Walker, *Winter Wheat* (New York: Harcourt, Brace & World, 1944), p. 10.

45. Alix Kates Shulman, *Memoirs of an Ex-Prom Queen* (New York: Alfred A. Knopf, 1972), p. 69.

46. Anne Tyler, *A Slipping-Down Life* (New York: Alfred A. Knopf, 1970), p. 87.

47. Daphne Athas, *The Weather of the Heart* (New York: Appleton-Century-Crofts, 1947), p. 52.

48. Jessamyn West, *Cress Delahanty* (New York: Harcourt, Brace & World, 1948), p. 12.

49. Shirley Ann Grau, *The House on Coliseum Street* (New York: Alfred A. Knopf, 1961), p. 138.

50. Helen Woodbury, *The Misty Flats* (Boston: Little, Brown and Co., 1925), p. 26.

51. Josephine Johnson, *Now in November* (New York: Simon & Schuster 1935), p. 23; Katherine Dunn, *Truck*, p. 12.

52. Olive Higgins Prouty, *Conflict* (Boston: Houghton Mifflin Co., 1927), p. 10.

53. The bell jar image also occurs in Josephine Johnson's *Wildwood* (New York: Harper & Row, 1946), where the protagonist feels "surrounded by a glass wall" (44). In *The Member of the Wedding* Frankie Addams perceives her environment as "like a green sick dream, or like a silent crazy jungle under glass" (1).

54. Critics sometimes resemble the oppressive adult characters in adolescent novels who equate non-conformity with "madness." Often the purpose of the critic in labelling an adolescent heroine "mad" is to deny the social implications of her experience Thus, Alfred Kazin ignores Sylvia Plath's insistence that all girls are under bell jars of some sort and contends that "there is no connection between the girl's world and the surrender of herself to the bell jar"—*Bright Book of Life*, p. 185. To Frederic Carpenter, McCullers' Mick Kelly is "disturbed," but Cress Delahanty, who adjusts to womanhood, is a "typical adolescent American girl"— "The Adolescent in American Fiction," pp. 316–18.

55. This is also the view of Toni Morrison in *The Bluest Eye*. Morrison's perception of the value of being a "nice girl" is different from her characters'. She includes, in her own voice, a five-page criticism of Black "nice

girls," who have carefully developed "thrift, patience, high morals, and good manners." According to Morrison, they sing second soprano in the choir, "do not drink, smoke, or swear, and . . . still call sex 'nookey' " (64).

56. Zora Neale Hurston, *Their Eyes Were Watching God* (Philadelphia: J. B. Lippincott Co., 1937), p. 37. At age seventeen Janie leaves her first husband to marry another respectable and comparatively wealthy man. She discovers that "he wanted her submission and he'd keep on fighting until he felt he had it. So gradually, she pressed her teeth together and learned to hush" (111). She feels "beaten down" (118) until the second half of the novel when, in her forties, she decides to stop being "nice."

57. Paule Marshall, *Brown Girl, Brownstones* (New York: Random House, 1959), p. 196.

58. Jessie Redmon Fauset, *Plum Bun* (New York: Frederick A. Stokes Co., 1929), pp. 87–88.

59. James Baldwin, "Foreword" to Louise Meriwether, *Daddy Was a Number Runner* (New York: Pyramid Books, 1971), pp. 7–8.

60. Baldwin, p. 8. Although Baldwin interprets Francie's experience in terms of the problems of black men, he was unusual in 1971 for recognizing, even momentarily, that Francie faces a "terrifying womanhood." Black criticism has paralleled the white in emphasizing male protagonists. For instance, in Catherine Juanita Starke's *Black Portraiture in American Fiction* (1971), there is a section called "Youthful Males in Search of Self" but no mention of youthful females. The classic essay on the emerging Black feminist criticism is Barbara Smith, "Toward a Black Feminist Criticism," *Conditions: Two*, 1 (Oct. 1977), 25–44. A slightly revised version appears in *But Some of Us Are Brave: Black Women's Studies*, ed. Gloria T. Hull, Patricia Bell Scott, and Barbara Smith (Old Westbury, N.Y.: Feminist Press, 1982), pp. 157–75. This anthology also includes critical and bibliographic essays on black women writers.

61. The white author of *The Changelings* shows a black girl uniting with Judy Vincent on the common ground of gender. The girls become friends after Clara witnesses Vincent's humiliation before her gang. Clara is furious at the boys' treatment of Vincent. She says, "I hate guys like that. They think a girl is a punk," and lends Vincent a knife for her protection (22–23).

Chapter VIII. The New Girls

1. Rita Mae Brown, *Rubyfruit Jungle* (Plainfield, Vt.: Daughters, 1973), p. 78. In this chapter, after a novel is first noted, page references will be given thereafter in parentheses within the text.

2. Pat Burch, *Early Losses* (Plainfield, Vt.: Daughters, 1973), p. 11.

3. Blance M. Boyd, *Nerves* (Plainfield, Vt.: Daughters, 1973), pp. 118, 129.

4. Ruth Doan MacDougall, *The Cheerleader* (New York: G. P. Putnam's Sons, 1973), p. 205.

5. Hilma Wolitzer, *Hearts* (New York: Pocket Books, 1982), p. 23. As in earlier novels of adolescence, protagonists may dislike sex but want to lose their virginity as a badge of adulthood. In Elana Nachman's *Riverfinger Women* (Plainfield, Vt.: Daughters, 1974), the heroine explains that loss of virginity has nothing to do with girls' attitude toward men or sex. "It is a ritual, and it is performed for our own benefit"; it is "a way of saying 'I want to be, I want to be admitted to the world' " (27). In Natalie Petesch's *The Odyssey of Katinou Kalokovich* (Pittsburgh: Motheroot Publications, 1974) the protagonist considers virginity "a handicap which falsely differentiated her from men: by limiting her experience it limited her humanity" (15).

6. Joyce Maynard, *Baby Love* (New York: Alfred A. Knopf, 1981), p. 10.

7. Sonia Pilcer, *Teen Angel* (New York: Coward, McCann & Geoghegan, 1978), pp. 175, 158.

8. Louise Blecher Rose, *The Launching of Barbara Fabrikant* (New York: David McKay Co., 1974), p. 129.

9. John Lyons, "The College Novel in America: 1962–1974," *Critique*, 16 (1974), 125.

10. Sharon Isabell, *Yesterday's Lessons* (Oakland, Calif.: Women's Press Collective, 1974), p. 29.

11. Linsey Abrams, *Charting by the Stars* (New York: Harmony Books, 1979), p. 106.

12. Abrams, p. 83.

13. Jill Robinson, *Perdido* (New York: Alfred A. Knopf, 1978), p. 160.

14. Susan Ries Lukas, *Fat Emily* (New York: Stein and Day, 1974), p. 111.

15. Petesch, p. 19.

16. Alice Hoffman, *White Horses* (New York: G. P. Putnam's Sons, 1982), p. 196.

17. Marianne Hauser, *The Talking Room* (New York: Fiction Collective 1976), p. 35. Jean Stafford describes this condition, without the modern terminology, in her short story "The Echo and the Nemesis." Stafford, who was always interested in the relation of eating disorders and female identity, traces her adolescent heroine's uncontrollable eating to her fear of approaching womanhood.

18. Beth Gutcheon, *The New Girls* (New York: G. P. Putnam's Sons, 1979), p. 122.

19. In *Early Losses* Freda's odd eating habits are related to her am-

bivalence about leaving home. She diets when she decides to escape her
mother's control and eats her mother's fudge when fear of the outside
world takes over.

20. Marge Piercy, *Braided Lives* (New York: Ballantine Books, 1982),
p. 25.

21. Ann Bannon, *Odd Girl Out* (Tallahassee, Fla.: Naiad Press, 1983)
pp. 189–90.

22. Barbra Ward, *The Short Year* (New York: G. P. Putnam's Sons,
1967), p. 242.

23. Sarah Aldridge, *All True Lovers* (Tallahassee, Fla.: Naiad Press,
1982), p. 225.

24. Bonnie Zimmerman, "Exiting from Patriarchy: The Lesbian Novel
of Development," in *The Voyage In: Fictions of Female Development*,
ed. Elizabeth Abel, Marianne Hirsch, and Elizabeth Langland (Hanover,
N.H.: University Press of New England, 1983), p. 244.

25. Nachman, p. 13.

26. Maureen Brady, *Give Me Your Good Ear* (Argyle, N.Y.: Spinsters,
Ink, 1979), pp. 9–10.

27. Kate Stimpson, *Class Notes* (New York: Avon Books, 1980), pp.
211, 251.

28. Ella Leffland, *Rumors of Peace* (New York: Fawcett Popular Library, 1979), p. 271.

29. See Shirley Frank, "Feminist Presses," in *Women in Print II*, ed.
Joan E. Hartman and Ellen Messer-Davidow (New York: Modern Language Association, 1982), pp. 89–115.

30. Jane Rule, *Lesbian Images* (Garden City, N.Y.: Doubleday & Co.,
1975), pp. 194–95.

31. Carol Burr Megibow, "The Use of Story in Women's Novels of the
Seventies," in *Women's Culture: The Women's Renaissance of the Seventies*, ed. Gayle Kimball (Metuchen, N.J.: Scarecrow Press, 1981), p.
200. Similar criticisms have been made of Alice Walker's *The Color Purple* (1982), a novel that also presents very positive images of women; see,
for instance, Robert Towers' review in *New York Review of Books*, August
12, 1982, p. 35.

32. Ellen Morgan, "Humanbecoming: Form & Focus in the Neo-Feminist Novel," pp. 185, 204.

33. Ellen Morgan, "The Feminist Novel of Androgynous Fantasy,"
Frontiers, II (Fall 1977), 40. Further references are noted in parentheses
within the text.

34. " 'Dear FRONTIERS': Letters from Women Fantasy and Science
Fiction Writers," *Frontiers*, II (Fall 1977), 62.

35. Joanna Russ, *The Two of Them* (New York: Berkley Publishing
Co., 1978), pp. 36, 73.

36. Marge Piercy, *Dance the Eagle to Sleep* (Garden City, N.Y.: Doubleday & Co., 1970), p. 5.

37. Carolyn G. Heilbrun, *Reinventing Womanhood* (New York: W. W. Norton & Co., 1979), p. 82. Further references are noted in parentheses within the text.

38. Patricia Meyer Spacks, *The Adolescent Idea: Myths of Youth and the Adult Imagination* (New York: Basic Books, 1981), p. 13. Further references are noted in parentheses within the text.

39. Barton Friedberg, "The Cult of Adolescence in American Fiction," p. 26.

40. Friedberg, p. 27.

41. Ihab Hassan, "The Idea of Adolescence in American Fiction," pp. 314–15.

42. Ihab Hassan, *Radical Innocence*, p. 41. Further references are noted in parentheses within the text. I retain Hassan's use of the pronoun "he" because he appears to be discussing male protagonists. Almost all the novels Hassan refers to in his comments on existentialist heroes are by and about men. The only time he mentions women is to remark that "we" naturally regret the "growing lack of differentiation between the role [sic] men and women play in society. . . . We shake our heads in silence when someone mentions the increasing wealth, longevity, and political power of women in America" (75).

43. Spacks tries to do the same for gender when she notes that the adolescent girl "provides a metaphor" for the "twentieth-century phenomena of alienation and experienced powerlessness for all ages, all conditions" (52).

For an interesting comparison of the reviews of *Invisible Man* and the reviews of Gwendolyn Brooks's novel *Maud Martha* (1953), see Mary Helen Washington, "Plain, Black, and Decently Wild: The Heroic Possibilities of Maud Martha," in *The Voyage In: Fictions of Female Development*, ed. Elizabeth Abel, Marianne Hirsch, and Elizabeth Langland (Hanover, N.H.: University Press of New England, 1983), pp. 270–86. Washington shows that Brooks's novel was not considered universal and "placed in a tradition" like Ellison's, "suggesting that the real 'invisible man' of the 1950's was the black woman" (272).

44. Alfred Kazin, *Bright Book of Life*, pp. 173–74. Kazin thus criticizes Shirley Jackson because she writes many novels "where a woman as victim is the main figure and where her defenselessness is the story" (174); on the other hand, Joyce Carol Oates receives his approbation because he thinks "she is not concerned with demonstrating power relationships" (199).

45. Jacqueline St. Joan, "Afterword" to Maureen Brady, *Give Me Your Good Ear* (Argyle, N.Y.: Spinsters, Ink, 1979), p. 138. Further references are noted in parentheses within the text.

46. Elaine Showalter, "Women Writers and the Double Standard," in *Woman in Sexist Society*, ed. Vivian Gornick and Barbara K. Moran (New York: Basic Books, 1971), p. 474.

47. Nina Baym, "Melodramas of Beset Manhood: How Theories of American Fiction Exclude Women Authors," *American Quarterly*, 33 (Summer 1981), 123.

48. Cheri Register, "American Feminist Literary Criticism: A Bibliographical Introduction," in *Feminist Literary Criticism: Explorations in Theory*, ed. Josephine Donovan (Lexington: University Press of Kentucky, 1975), p. 2.

49. Nancy Jo Hoffman, "Reading Women's Poetry: The Meaning and Our Lives," *College English*, 34 (Oct. 1972), 52.

50. Roslyn Belkin, "Changing Conventions in Fiction Written by Women," *Canadian Newsletter of Research on Women*, 7 (July 1978), 19. Register, above, also argues that "a literary work should provide *role-models*, instill a positive sense of feminine identity by portraying women who are 'self-actualizing, whose identities are not dependent on men' " (20).

51. Bonnie Hoover Braendlin, "Alther, Atwood, Ballantyne, and Gray: Secular Salvation in the Contemporary Feminist Bildungsroman," *Frontiers*, IV (Spring 1979), 18. This is also the age range emphasized in the critical articles in *The Voyage In: Fictions of Female Development* (1983); there are very few adolescent heroines discussed.

52. Annis Pratt, *Archetypal Patterns in Women's Fiction*, p. 135. Further references are noted in parentheses within the text.

53. Sheila Ballantyne, *Imaginary Crimes* (New York: Viking Press, 1982), p. 61.

BIBLIOGRAPHY

A. Novels of Female Adolescence, 1920–1982

This is a list of approximately 275 novels by American women with female adolescent protagonists. I follow W. Tasker Witham's *The Adolescent in the American Novel, 1920–1960* (1964) in omitting novels with settings outside the United States and historical novels that take place before 1870. I also exclude murder mysteries and detective fiction. Nearly all the works on this list are novels, i.e. extended pieces of prose fiction; however, I do include collections of short stories when the stories are arranged to show the continuous development of an adolescent character—for example, Katherine Anne Porter's Miranda stories and Ann Petry's *Miss Muriel and Other Stories* (1971).

I omit novels intended for children and adolescents. In placing works in this category I have relied on Witham's excellent appendix, publishers' designations, and Library of Congress classification. There are some cases in which an author has stated that she intended her novel for adults, although publishers and librarians decided to market it otherwise; Ann Head's *Mr. and Mrs. Bo Jo Jones* (1967) is an example. When I have this information, I include the novel.

The age range for the female adolescents in the fiction on my list is twelve to nineteen; the characters may be introduced at an earlier age and/or taken beyond their teens, but this period is usually emphasized. Adolescence has to be a major concern in the novel. My rule of thumb has been that over half the novel must treat the character's adolescence.

My criteria, Witham's and Jane S. Bakerman and Mary Jean DeMarr's in their *Adolescent Female Portraits in the American Novel 1961–1981: An Annotated Bibliography* (New York: Garland Publishing, 1983) all differ in some respects. Witham includes male authors and protagonists and

Bakerman and DeMarr male authors, mysteries, and juveniles; since the
latter are interested in any portraits which "reveal important attitudes
toward women," they also include works containing brief images of female
adolescence or depicting girls in subplots or as "adjuncts (often motivation
for the behavior) of male protagonists" (x). If one wanted to compile a
comprehensive list of novels of adolescence from 1920 to 1982, one would
have to consult Witham, Bakerman and DeMarr, and my bibliography
plus, for male protagonists after 1960, Stuart Burns's "The Novel of Adolescence in America: 1940–1963" (1964) and Thomas Gregory's *Adolescence in Literature* (1978).

I have read almost all the novels on the list that follows. There are
about 35 that I could not obtain but that seem from reviews and/or descriptions in Witham or Bakerman and DeMarr to fit my criteria; these
entries are followed by an asterisk (*) and reference to my source.

When the original publication date of a novel differs from the date of
the cited edition, the original date appears in parentheses at the end of
the entry.

Abaunza, Virginia. *Sundays from Two to Six*. Indianapolis: Bobbs-Merrill
      Co., 1957. *Listed in Witham.
Abel, Hilde. *The Guests of Summer*. Indianapolis: Bobbs-Merrill Co.,
      1951.
Abrams, Linsey. *Charting by the Stars*. New York: Harmony Books, 1979.
Albert, Mimi. *The Second Story Man*. New York: Fiction Collective, 1975.
Aldis, Dorothy. *All the Year Round*. Boston: Houghton Mifflin Co., 1938.
———. *Poor Susan*. New York: G. P. Putnam's Sons, 1942. *Listed in
      Witham.
Aldridge, Sarah. *All True Lovers*. Tallahassee, Fla.: Naiad Press, 1982
      (1978).
Anderson, Barbara. *The Days Grow Cold*. New York: Macmillan Co.,
      1941.
———. *Southbound*. New York: Farrar, Straus and Co., 1949.
Ansell, Helen. *Lucy*. New York: Harper & Row, 1969. *Reviewed in
      Publishers' Weekly, Feb. 24, 1969, p. 63.
Applewhite, Cynthia. *Sundays*. New York: Avon Books, 1979. *Listed
      in Bakerman and DeMarr.
Arnow, Harriette Simpson. *The Weedkiller's Daughter*. New York: Alfred
      A. Knopf, 1970.
Athas, Daphne. *Entering Ephesus*. New York: Viking Press, 1971.
———. *The Fourth World*. New York: G. P. Putnam's Sons, 1956.
———. *The Weather of the Heart*. New York: Appleton-Century-Crofts,
      1947.

Aydelotte, Dora. *Long Furrows*. New York: D. Appleton-Century Co.,
    1935.
Ballantyne, Sheila. *Imaginary Crimes*. New York: Viking Press, 1982.
Bannon, Ann. *Odd Girl Out*. Tallahassee, Fla.: Naiad Press, 1983 (1957).
Barber, Elsie Oakes. *The Trembling Years*. New York: Macmillan Co.,
    1949.
Barnes, Carman. *Schoolgirl*. London: T. Werner Laurie, 1930.
Barrett, B. L. *Love in Atlantis*. Boston: Houghton Mifflin Co., 1969.
Barton, Betsey. *Shadow of the Bridge*. New York: Duell, Sloan and Pearce,
    1950.
Beheler, Laura. *The Paper Dolls*. Boston: Houghton Mifflin Co., 1956.
Benson, Sally. *Junior Miss*. New York: Random House, 1941.
Bentham, Josephine. *Janie*. New York: Dial Press, 1940. *Listed in
    Witham.
Berkley, Sandra. *Coming Attractions*. New York: E. P. Dutton & Co.,
    1971. *Listed in Bakerman and DeMarr.
Betts, Doris. *The Scarlet Thread*. New York: Harper & Row, 1964.
Blake, Katherine. *My Sister, My Friend*. New York: Reynal & Co.,
    1965. *Listed in Bakerman and DeMarr.
[Blake, Sally Mirliss] Sara. *When Mist Clothes Dream and Song Runs
    Naked*. New York: McGraw-Hill Book Co., 1965.
Blanton, Margaret Gray. *The White Unicorn*. New York: Rudo S. Globus,
    Publisher, 1961.
Boyd, Blanche M. *Nerves*. Plainfield, Vt.: Daughters, 1973.
Boyd, Shylah. *American Made*. New York: Farrar, Straus & Giroux, 1975.
Boylen, Margaret. *The Marble Orchard*. New York: Random House,
    1956. *Listed in Witham.
Brady, Maureen. *Give Me Your Good Ear*. Argyle, N.Y.: Spinsters, Ink,
    1979.
Bro, Margueritte Harmon. *Sarah*. Garden City, N.Y.: Doubleday & Co.,
    1949.
Brown, Rita Mae. *Rubyfruit Jungle*. Plainfield, Vt.: Daughters, 1973.
Buchan, Perdita. *Girl with a Zebra*. New York: Charles Scribner's Sons,
    1966.
Burch, Pat. *Early Losses*. Plainfield, Vt.: Daughters, 1973.
Burt, Katharine Newlin. *Escape from Paradise*. New York: Charles Scrib-
    ner's Sons, 1952. *Listed in Witham.
Cahill, Susan. *Earth Angels*. New York: Harper & Row, 1976.
Calisher, Hortense. *Queenie*. New York: Arbor House, 1971.
Carlisle, Helen Grace. *The Merry, Merry Maidens*. New York: Harcourt,
    Brace and Co., 1937.
Carrighar, Sally. *The Glass Dove*. Garden City, N.Y.: Doubleday & Co.,
    1962.

Carson, Josephine. *Drives My Green Age*. New York: Harper & Row, 1957.

———. *Where You Goin, Girlie?* New York: Dial Press, 1975.

Carson, Katherine. *Mrs. Pennington*. New York: G. P. Putnam's Sons, 1939. *Listed in Witham.

Chamberlain, Anne. *The Tall, Dark Man*. Indianapolis: Bobbs-Merrill Co., 1955.

Chase, Mary Ellen. *Mary Peters*. New York: Macmillan Co., 1934.

Chidester, Ann. *Young Pandora*. New York: Charles Scribner's Sons, 1942.

Chute, B. J. *Katie*. New York: E. P. Dutton & Co., 1978.

Coffey, Marilyn. *Marcella*. New York: Charterhouse, 1973. *Listed in Bakerman and DeMarr.

Colebrook, Joan. *The Cross of Lassitude*. New York: Alfred A. Knopf, 1967.

Coursen, Dorothy. *Beauty? I Wonder*. New York: Elliot Holt, 1929.

———. *Fire of Spring*. New York: Henry Holt and Co., 1928.

Crawford, Joanne. *Birch Interval*. Boston: Houghton Mifflin Co., 1964.

Daly, Maureen. *Seventeenth Summer*. New York: Dodd, Mead and Co., 1942.

Daniels, Sally. *The Inconstant Season*. New York: Atheneum, 1962.

Day, Dorothy. *The Eleventh Virgin*. New York: Boni, 1924.

Day, Lillian. *The Youngest Profession*. New York: Doubleday, Doran & Co., 1940.

Deal, Babs H. *The Reason for Roses*. Garden City, N.Y.: Doubleday & Co., 1974.

Deutsch, Babette. *A Brittle Heaven*. New York: Greenberg, Publisher, 1926.

Dornfield, Iris. *Jeeney Ray*. New York: Viking Press, 1962.

Drexler, Roslyn. *I Am the Beautiful Stranger*. New York: Grossman Publishers, 1965.

Duncan, Julia Coley. *Halfway Home*. New York: St. Martin's Press, 1979.

Dunn, Katherine. *Truck*. New York: Harper & Row, 1971.

Dutton, Louise. *Going Together*. Indianapolis: Bobbs-Merrill Co., 1923.

Eliot, Ethel Cook. *Angels' Mirth*. New York: Sheed and Ward, 1936. *Listed in Witham.

Faralla, Dana. *The Madstone*. Philadelphia: J. B. Lippincott Co., 1958.

Farnham, Mateel Howe. *Rebellion*. New York: Dodd, Mead and Co., 1927.

Fauset, Jessie Redmon. *Plum Bun*. New York: Frederick A. Stokes Co., 1929.

Fenwick, Elizabeth. *Days of Plenty*. New York: Harcourt, Brace, 1956. *Listed in Witham.

Ferber, Edna. *Ice Palace*. Garden City, N.Y.: Doubleday & Co., 1958.

Field, Hope. *Stormy Present*. New York: E. P. Dutton & Co., 1942.

Fisher, Dorothy Canfield. *The Deepening Stream*. New York: Modern Library, 1930.

Flagg, Fannie. *Coming Attractions*. New York: William Morrow and Co., 1981.

Freely, Maureen. *Mother's Helper*. New York: Delacorte Press/Seymour Lawrence, 1979.

Frost, Frances. *Innocent Summer*. New York: Farrar & Rinehart, 1936.

Gilbert, Julie Goldsmith. *Umbrella Steps*. New York: Random House, 1972. *Listed in Bakerman and DeMarr.

Gilman, Mildred. *Fig Leaves*. New York: Siebel Co., 1925.

Glasgow, Ellen. *The Sheltered Life*. Garden City, N.Y.: Doubleday & Co., 1932.

Goodin, Peggy. *Clementine*. New York: E. P. Dutton & Co., 1946.

———. *Take Care of My Little Girl*. New York: E. P. Dutton & Co., 1950.

Grace, Carol. *The Secret in the Daisy*. New York: Random House, 1955. *Listed in Witham.

Grant, Dorothy. *Devil's Food*. New York: Longmans, Green & Co., 1949.

Grau, Shirley Ann. *The Hard Blue Sky*. Greenwich, Conn.: Fawcett Pub., (1955) 1972.

———. *The House on Coliseum Street*. New York: Alfred A. Knopf, 1961.

[Greenberg, Joanna] Hannah Green. *The Dead of the House*. Garden City, N.Y.: Doubleday & Co., 1972.

———. *I Never Promised You a Rose Garden*. New York: Signet, 1964.

[Guest, Mary Lapsley Caughey] Mary Lapsley. *The Parable of the Virgins*. New York: Richard R. Smith, 1931.

Gutcheon, Beth. *The New Girls*. New York: G. P. Putnam's Sons, 1979.

Hahn, Harriet. *The Plantain Season*. New York: W. W. Norton & Co., 1976.

Hale, Nancy. *Secrets*. New York: Coward, McCann & Geoghegan, 1971.

Halequa, Lillian. *The Pearl Bastard*. London: Women's Press, 1978 (1961).

Harnden, Ruth. *I, A Stranger*. New York: McGraw-Hill Book Co., 1950.

Harris, Marilyn. *Hatter Fox*. New York: Random House, 1973.

Harris, Sara. *The Wayward Ones*. New York: Crown, Publishers, 1952.

Hauser, Marianne. *The Talking Room*. New York: Fiction Collective, 1976.

Head, Ann. *Mr. and Mrs. Bo Jo Jones*. New York: G. P. Putnam's Sons, 1967.

Hitchens, Dolores. *Fool's Gold*. Garden City, N.Y.: Doubleday & Co., 1958. *Listed in Witham.

Hoff, Marilyn. *Dink's Blues*. New York: Harcourt, Brace & World, 1966.
Hoffman, Alice. *The Drowning Season*. New York: E. P. Dutton & Co.,
      1979.
————. *Property Of*. New York: Farrar, Straus & Giroux, 1977. *Listed
      in Bakerman and DeMarr.
————. *White Horses*. New York: G. P. Putnam's Sons, 1982.
Hormel, Olive Deane. *Co-Ed*. New York: Charles Scribner's, 1926. *Listed
      in Witham.
Howe, Fanny. *First Marriage*. New York: Avon Books, 1974.
Hull, Helen. *Candle Indoors*. New York: Coward-McCann, 1936.
————. *Quest*. New York: Macmillan Co., 1922.
Hutchins, Maude. *A Diary of Love*. New York: New Directions, 1950.
————. *Victorine*. Denver: A. Swallow, 1959.
Isabell, Sharon. *Yesterday's Lessons*. Oakland, Calif.: Women's Press
      Collective, 1974.
Jackson, Shirley. *Hangsaman*. New York: Ace, 1951.
————. *We Have Always Lived in the Castle*. New York: Viking Press,
      1962.
Johnson, Josephine. *Now in November*. New York: Simon & Schuster,
      1935.
————. *Wildwood*. New York: Harper & Row, 1946.
Johnson, Nora. *A Step Beyond Innocence*. Boston: Little, Brown and Co.,
      1961.
————. *The World of Henry Orient*. Boston: Little, Brown and Co., 1958.
Jordan, Elizabeth. *Daddy and I*. New York: D. Appleton-Century Co.,
      1935.
Kelley, Ethel M. *Beauty and Mary Blair*. Boston: Houghton Mifflin Co.,
      1921.
Keogh, Theodora. *Meg*. New York: Creative Age Press, 1950.
————. *The Tattooed Heart*. New York: Farrar, Straus & Young, 1953.
Kilbourne, Fanny. *A Corner in William*. New York: Dodd, Mead, 1922.
King, Mary. *Quincie Bolliver*. Boston: Houghton Mifflin Co., 1941.
Klein, Norma. *Domestic Arrangements*. New York: M. Evans and Co.,
      1981.
Kline, Nancy E. *The Faithful*. New York: William Morrow & Co., 1968.
Kumin, Maxine. *Through Dooms of Love*. New York: Harper & Row,
      1965.
Lane, Rose Wilder. *Old Home Town*. New York: Longmans, Green and
      Co., 1935.
Larrimore, Lida. *No Lovelier Spring*. Philadelphia: Macrae-Smith-Co.,
      1935.
Latimer, Margery. *This Is My Body*. New York: Jonathan Cape, 1930.
Leavitt, Caroline. *Meeting Rozzy Halfway*. New York: Seaview Books,
      1980.

Lee, Marjorie. *The Eye of Summer*. New York: Simon and Schuster, 1961. *Listed in Bakerman and DeMarr.

Leffland, Ella. *Rumors of Peace*. New York: Fawcett Popular Library, 1980 (1979).

L'Engle, Madeleine. *Camilla Dickinson*. New York: Simon and Schuster, 1951.

———. *The Small Rain*. New York: Vanguard Press, 1945.

Lincoln, Victoria. *Celia Amberley*. New York: Rinehart & Co., 1947.

———. *February Hill*. New York: Farrar & Rinehart, 1934.

———. *Out from Eden*. New York: Rinehart & Co., 1951.

Lindau, Joan. *Mrs. Cooper's Boardinghouse*. New York: McGraw-Hill Book Co., 1980.

Lockwood, Mary. *Child of Light*. New York: William Morrow and Co., 1967.

Logan, Jane. *The Very Nearest Room*. New York: Charles Scribner's Sons, 1973.

Loveland, Constance. *Veronica*. New York: Vanguard Press, 1958.

Lowry, Beverly. *Come Back, Lolly Ray*. Garden City, N.Y.: Doubleday & Co., 1977.

———. *Emma Blue*. Garden City, N.Y.: Doubleday & Co., 1978.

Lukas, Susan Ries. *Fat Emily*. New York: Stein and Day, 1974.

Lynn, Elizabeth A. *The Northern Girl*. New York: Berkley Publishing Co., 1980.

McCullers, Carson. *The Heart Is a Lonely Hunter. The Novels and Stories of Carson McCullers*. Boston: Houghton Mifflin Co., 1951 (1940).

———. *The Member of the Wedding. The Novels and Stories of Carson McCullers*. Boston: Houghton Mifflin Co., 1951 (1946).

MacDougall, Ruth Doan. *The Cheerleader*. New York: G. P. Putnam's Sons, 1973.

[McLean, Kathryn] Kathryn Forbes. *Transfer Point*. New York: Harcourt, Brace and Co., 1947.

Marshall, Catherine. *Christy*. New York: McGraw-Hill Book Co., 1967.

Marshall, Kathryn. *My Sister Gone*. New York: Harper & Row, 1975.

Marshall, Paule. *Brown Girl, Brownstones*. New York: Random House, 1959.

Martin, Helen R. *Emmy Untamed*. New York: Appleton-Century, 1937.

Mather, Melissa. *One Summer in Between*. New York: Harper & Row, 1967.

[Mayer, Jayne, and Speigel, Clara] Clare Jaynes. *Early Frost*. New York: Random House, 1952.

Mayhall, Jane. *Cousin to Human*. New York: Harcourt, Brace & World, 1960.

Maynard, Joyce. *Baby Love*. New York: Avon Books, 1982 (1981).

Means, Florence Crannell. *Shuttered Windows*. Boston: Houghton Mifflin
    Co., 1938.
Meriwether, Louise. *Daddy Was a Number Runner*. New York: Pyramid
    Books, 1971 (1970).
Metalious, Grace. *Peyton Place*. New York: Julian Messner, 1956.
Millay, Kathleen. *Against the Wall*. New York: Macaulay Co., 1929.
Miller, Heather Ross. *The Edge of the Woods*. New York: Atheneum,
    1964.
Mojtabai, A. G. *The 400 Eels of Sigmund Freud*. New York: Simon &
    Schuster, 1976.
Moore, Pamela. *Chocolates for Breakfast*. New York: Rinehart & Co.,
    1956.
Moore, Ruth. *The Fire Balloon*. New York: William Morrow & Co.,
    1948.
Moore, Susanna. *My Old Sweetheart*. Boston: Houghton Mifflin Co.,
    1982.
Morrison, Toni. *The Bluest Eye*. New York: Holt, Rinehart, and Winston,
    1970.
Nachman, Elana. *Riverfinger Women*. Plainfield, Vt.: Daughters, 1974.
Nelson, Shirley. *The Last Year of the War*. New York: Harper & Row,
    1978.
Newman, Frances. *The Hard-Boiled Virgin*. New York: Boni & Liveright,
    1926.
Oakey, Virginia. *Thirteenth Summer*. New York: A. A. Wyn, 1955. *Listed
    in Witham.
Oates, Joyce Carol. *Angel of Light*. New York: E. P. Dutton & Co.,
    1981.
————. *With Shuddering Fall*. New York: Vanguard Press, 1964.
Osborn, Mary Elizabeth. *Days Beyond Recall*. New York: Coward-
    McCann, 1942.
Page, Dorothy Myra. *Gathering Storm*. New York: International Pub-
    lishers, 1932.
Parmenter, Christine Whiting. *As the Seed Is Sown*. New York: Crowell
    1940.
Perrin, Ursula. *Ghosts*. New York: Alfred A. Knopf, 1967.
Perutz, Kathrin. *The Garden*. New York: Atheneum, 1962.
Peterkin, Julia. *Scarlet Sister Mary*. Indianapolis: Bobbs-Merrill Co., 1928.
Petesch, Natalie. *The Odyssey of Katinou Kalokovich*. Pittsburgh: Moth-
    eroot Publications, 1974.
Petry, Ann. *Miss Muriel and Other Stories*. Boston: Houghton Mifflin
    Co., 1971.
Piercy, Marge. *Braided Lives*. New York: Ballantine Books, 1983 (1982).
————. *Dance the Eagle to Sleep*. Garden City, N.Y.: Doubleday & Co.,
    1970.

Pilcer, Sonia. *Maiden Rites*. New York: Viking Press, 1982.
———. *Teen Angel*. New York: Coward, McCann & Geoghegan, 1978.
Plath, Sylvia. *The Bell Jar*. New York: Bantam Books, 1972 (1963).
Pollet, Elizabeth. *A Family Romance*. New York: New Directions, 1950.
Porter, Katherine Anne. *The Old Order*. New York: Harcourt, Brace & World, 1958 (1934–41).
[Profitt, Josephine] Sylvia Dee. *And Never Been Kissed*. New York: Macmillan Co., 1949. *Listed in Witham.
Prouty, Olive Higgins. *Conflict*. Boston: Houghton Mifflin Co., 1927.
———. *Stella Dallas*. New York: Grosset & Dunlap, 1923.
Raphaelson, Dorshka. *Morning Song*. New York: Random House, 1948.
Reed, Kit. *The Better Part*. New York: Farrar, Straus & Giroux, 1967. *Listed in Bakerman and DeMarr.
Rehder, Jessie C. *Remembrance Way*. New York: G. P. Putnam's Sons, 1956. *Listed in Witham.
Rios, Isabella. *Victuum*. Ventura, Calif.: Diana Etna, 1974.
Ritner, Ann. *The Green Bough*. Philadelphia: J. B. Lippincott Co., 1950.
Roberts, Dorothy James. *A Durable Fire*. New York: Macmillan Co., 1945.
———. *With Night We Banish Sorrow*. Boston: Little, Brown and Co., 1960.
Roberts, Elizabeth Madox. *The Time of Man*. New York: Viking Press, 1926.
Robinson, Alice M. *The Unbelonging*. New York: Macmillan Co., 1958.
Robinson, Jill. *Perdido*. New York: Alfred A. Knopf, 1978.
Robinson, Marilynne. *Housekeeping*. New York: Farrar, Straus & Giroux, 1980.
Roe, Judy. *The Same Old Grind*. Milbrae, Calif.: Les Femmes Publishing, 1975. *Listed in Bakerman and DeMarr.
Rose, Louise Blecher. *The Launching of Barbara Fabrikant*. New York: David McKay Co., 1974.
Rosenberg, Jessie. *Sudina*. New York: E. P. Dutton and Co., 1967. *Listed in Witham.
Rushing, Jane Gilmore. *Tamzen*. Garden City, N.Y.: Doubleday & Co., 1972.
Russ, Joanna. *The Two of Them*. New York: Berkley Publishing Co., 1978.
Sandburg, Helga. *The Owl's Roost*. New York: Dial Press, 1962.
———. *The Wheel of Earth*. New York: McDowell, Obolensky, 1958.
———. *The Wizard's Child*. New York: Dial Press, 1967. *Listed in Bakerman and DeMarr.
Sanguinetti, Elise. *The Last of the Whitfields*. New York: McGraw-Hill Book Co., 1962.

―――. *The New Girl*. New York: McGraw-Hill Book Co., 1964.

Savage, Elizabeth. *The Girls from the Five Great Valleys*. Boston: Little, Brown and Co., 1977.

Schmitt, Gladys. *Alexandra*. New York: Dial Press, 1947.

Schoonover, Shirley. *Mountain of Winter*. New York: Coward-McCann, 1965.

Schwartz, Lynne Sharon. *Balancing Acts*. New York: Harper & Row, 1981.

Scott, Jessie. *The Charity Ball*. New York: Macmillan Co., 1946.

[Seid, Ruth] Jo Sinclair. *The Changelings*. New York: McGraw-Hill Book Co., 1955.

Seton, Cynthia Propper. *The Half-sisters*. New York: W. W. Norton and Co., 1974.

Sherman, Susan. *Give Me Myself*. Cleveland: World Publishing Co., 1961.

Shulman, Alix Kates. *Memoirs of an Ex-Prom Queen*. New York: Alfred A. Knopf, 1972.

Simmons, Helen. *Lark*. New York: Smith and Durrell, 1942. *Listed in Witham.

Slade, Caroline. *Margaret*. New York: Vanguard Press, 1946.

―――. *The Sterile Sun*. New York: Vanguard Press, 1936.

Smedley, Agnes. *Daughter of Earth*. New York: Coward-McCann, 1929.

Smith, Betty. *Joy in the Morning*. New York: Harper & Row, 1963.

―――. *A Tree Grows in Brooklyn*. New York: Harper & Row, 1947.

Snyder, Anne. *Goodbye, Paper Doll*. New York: New American Library, 1980.

Soloman, Barbara Probst. *The Beat of Life*. Philadelphia: J. B. Lippincott Co., 1960.

Soman, Florence Jane. *A Break in the Weather*. New York: G. P. Putnam's Sons, 1959. *Listed in Witham.

Stafford, Jean. *Boston Adventure*. New York: Harcourt, Brace & World, 1944.

―――. *The Mountain Lion*. New York: Harcourt, Brace & World, 1947.

Stallworth, Anne Nall. *This Time Next Year*. New York: Vanguard Press, 1971.

Stern, Elizabeth. *A Marriage Was Made*. New York: J. H. Sears & Co., 1928.

Stimpson, Kate. *Class Notes*. New York: Avon Books, 1980 (1979).

Suckow, Ruth. *The Bonney Family*. New York: Alfred A. Knopf, 1928.

―――. *Cora*. New York: Alfred A. Knopf, 1929.

―――. *The Folks*. New York: Farrar & Rinehart, 1934.

―――. *The Kramer Girls*. New York: Alfred A. Knopf, 1930.

―――. *The Odyssey of a Nice Girl*. New York: Alfred A. Knopf, 1926.

Sumner, Cid Ricketts. *Tammy Out of Time*. Indianapolis: Bobbs-Merrill Co., 1948. *Listed in Witham.

————. *Tammy Tell Me True*. Indianapolis: Bobbs-Merrill Co., 1959.
Sykes, Hope Williams. *Second Hoeing*. New York: G. P. Putnam's Sons, 1935.
Tanner, Louise. *Miss Bannister's Girls*. New York: Farrar, Straus and Co., 1963.
Topkins, Katherine. *Kotch*. New York: McGraw-Hill Book Co., 1965. *Listed in Bakerman and DeMarr.
Tyler, Anne. *A Slipping-down Life*. New York: Alfred A. Knopf, 1970.
Van der Veer, Judy. *November Grass*. New York: Longmans, Green and Co., 1940. *Listed in Witham.
Van Etten, Winifred. *I Am the Fox*. New York: Popular Library, 1936.
Walker, Mildred. *Winter Wheat*. New York: Harcourt, Brace & World, 1944.
Ward, Barbra. *The Short Year*. New York: G. P. Putnam's Sons, 1967.
Welles, Patricia. *Babyhip*. New York: E. P. Dutton & Co., 1967. *Listed in Bakerman and DeMarr.
Wells, Rosemary. *The Fog Comes on Little Pig Feet*. New York: Avon Books, 1972.
Welty, Eudora. *Delta Wedding*. New York: Harcourt, Brace & World, 1946.
West, Jessamyn. *Cress Delahanty*. New York: Harcourt, Brace & World, 1948.
————. *The Witch Diggers*. New York: Harcourt, Brace and Co. 1951.
Wilkinson, Sylvia. *A Killing Frost*. Boston: Houghton Mifflin Co., 1967.
————. *Moss on the North Side*. Boston: Houghton Mifflin, 1966.
Williams, Vinnie. *Walk Egypt*. New York: Viking Press, 1960.
Winnek, Marian. *Juniper Hill*. Indianapolis: Bobbs-Merrill Co., 1932.
Winslow, Anne Goodwin. *The Springs*. New York: Alfred A. Knopf, 1949.
Winsor, Kathleen. *America with Love*. New York: G. P. Putnam's Sons, 1957. *Listed in Witham.
Winter, Alice. *The Velvet Bubble*. New York: William Morrow & Co., 1965. *Listed in Bakerman and DeMarr.
Witherspoon, Mary-Elizabeth. *Somebody Speak for Katy*. New York: Dodd, Mead, 1950. *Listed in Witham.
Wolff, Ruth. *A Crack in the Sidewalk*. New York: John Day Co., 1965.
————. *I, Keturah*. New York: John Day Co., 1963.
Wolitzer, Hilma. *Hearts*. New York: Pocket Books, 1982 (1980).
Woodbury, Helen. *The Misty Flats*. Boston: Little, Brown and Co., 1925.
Yezierska, Anzia. *Arrogant Beggar*. Garden City, N.Y.: Doubleday, Page & Co., 1927.
————. *Bread Givers*. New York: George Braziller, 1925.

B. Secondary Sources

This is a list of secondary sources referred to in the text or notes. The original publication date appears in parentheses at the end of the entry when it differs from the date of the cited edition.

Abel, Elizabeth; Hirsch, Marianne; and Langland, Elizabeth, eds. *The Voyage In: Fictions of Female Development.* Hanover, N.H.: University Press of New England, 1983.

Agee, William. "The Initiation Theme in Selected Modern American Novels of Adolescence." Diss. Florida State University, 1966.

Allen, Walter. *The Modern Novel in Britain and the United States.* New York: E. P. Dutton, 1964.

Ammons, Elizabeth. *Edith Wharton's Argument with America.* Athens: University of Georgia Press, 1980.

Ariès, Philippe. *Centuries of Childhood.* Trans. Robert Baldick. New York: Vintage, 1962 (1960).

Auchincloss, Louis. "Edith Wharton." *Seven Modern American Novelists.* Ed. William Van O'Connor. Minneapolis: University of Minnesota Press, 1959. Pp. 11–45.

———. *Pioneers and Caretakers.* Minneapolis: University of Minnesota Press, 1961.

Baker, Joseph. "Regionalism in the Middle West." *American Review*, 4 (Nov. 1934–March 1935), 603–14.

Bakerman, Jane S., and DeMarr, Mary Jean. *Adolescent Female Portraits in the American Novel 1961–1981: An Annotated Bibliography.* New York: Garland Publishing, 1983.

Baldanza, Frank. "Plato in Dixie." *Georgia Review*, 12 (Summer 1958), 151–67.

Baldwin, James. Foreword to Louise Meriwether, *Daddy Was a Number Runner.* New York: Pyramid Books, 1971. pp. 7–9 (1970).

Baym, Nina. "Melodramas of Beset Manhood: How Theories of American Fiction Exclude Women Authors." *American Quarterly*, 33 (Summer 1981), 123–39.

———. *Woman's Fiction: A Guide to Novels by and about Women in America, 1820–1870.* Ithaca, N.Y.: Cornell University Press, 1978.

Beales, Ross. "In Search of the Historical Child: Miniature Adulthood and Youth in Colonial New England." *American Quarterly*, 27 (Oct. 1975), 379–98.

Beauvoir, de, Simone. *The Second Sex.* Trans. H. M. Parshley. New York: Bantam Books, 1968 (1949).

Belkin, Roslyn. "Changing Conventions in Fiction Written by Women." *Canadian Newsletter of Research on Women*, 7 (July 1978), 18–19.

Bettelheim, Bruno. *Symbolic Wounds.* Glencoe, Ill.: Free Press, 1954.

Bickham, Robert. "The Origins and Importance of the Initiation Story in Twentieth Century British and American Fiction." Diss. University of New Mexico, 1961.

Bode, Carl. "The Scribbling Women: The Domestic Novel Rules the 'Fifties." *The Anatomy of American Popular Culture, 1840–1861.* Berkeley: University of California Press, 1959. Pp. 169–87.

Braendlin, Bonnie Hoover. "Alther, Atwood, Ballantyne, and Gray: Secular Salvation in the Contemporary Feminist Bildungsroman." *Frontiers,* IV (Spring 1979), 18–22.

———. "*Bildung* in Ethnic Women Writers." *Denver Quarterly,* 17 (Winter 1983), 75–87.

———. "New Directions in the Contemporary Bildungsroman: Lisa Alther's *Kinflicks.*" *Gender and Literary Voice.* Ed. Janet Todd. New York: Holmes & Meier Publishers, 1980. pp. 160–71.

Breit, Harvey. *The Writer Observed.* New York: World Publishing Co., 1956.

Brown, Herbert. *The Sentimental Novel in America, 1789–1860.* Durham, N.C.: Duke University Press, 1940.

Buchen, Irving. "Carson McCullers, A Case of Convergence." *Bucknell Review,* 21 (Spring 1973), 15–28.

Buckley, Jerome. *Season of Youth: The Bildungsroman from Dickens to Golding.* Cambridge, Mass.: Harvard University Press, 1974.

Burns, Stuart. "Counterpoint in Jean Stafford's *The Mountain Lion.*" *Critique,* 9 (June 1967), 20–32.

———. "The Novel of Adolescence in America: 1940–1963." Diss. University of Wisconsin, 1964.

Carpenter, Frederic. "The Adolescent in American Fiction." *English Journal,* 46 (Sept. 1957), 313–19.

Carr, Virginia Spencer. *The Lonely Hunter: A Biography of Carson McCullers.* Garden City, N.Y.: Doubleday & Co., 1975.

Chadwick, Mary. *Adolescent Girlhood.* New York: John Day Co., 1933.

Charles, Lucille H. "Growing Up through Drama." *Journal of American Folklore,* 59 (1946), 247–52.

Chase, Richard. "The Brontës, or Myth Domesticated." *Jane Eyre.* Ed. Richard Dunn. New York: Norton, 1971. Pp. 462–71.

Cheney, Ednah, ed. *Louisa May Alcott: Her Life, Letters, and Journals.* Boston: Little, Brown, and Co., 1910.

Chesler, Phyllis. *Women & Madness.* New York: Avon Books, 1973 (1972).

Childers, Helen White. "American Novels about Adolescence, 1917–1953." Diss. George Peabody College, 1958.

Chodorow, Nancy. "Family Structure and Feminine Personality." *Woman, Culture, and Society.* Ed. Michelle Zimbalist Rosaldo and Louise

Lamphere. Stanford, Calif.: Stanford University Press, 1974. Pp. 43–66.

———. *The Reproduction of Mothering: Psychoanalysis and the Sociology of Gender.* Berkeley: University of California Press, 1978.

Cook, Richard. *Carson McCullers.* New York: Frederick Ungar Publishing Co., 1975.

Cowie, Alexander. *The Rise of the American Novel.* New York: American Book Co., 1948.

Coyle, William, ed. *The Young Man in American Literature.* New York: Odyssey Press, 1969.

Davis, Clyde, ed. *Eyes of Boyhood.* Philadelphia: J. B. Lippincott, 1953.

" 'Dear FRONTIERS': Letters from Women Fantasy and Science Fiction Writers." *Frontiers,* II (Fall 1977), 62–78.

Dedmond, Francis. "Doing Her Own Thing: Carson McCullers' Dramatization of *The Member of the Wedding.*" *South Atlantic Bulletin,* 40 (May 1975), 47–52.

De Jovine, F. Anthony, ed. *The Young Hero in American Fiction: A Motif for Teaching Literature.* New York: Appleton-Century-Crofts, 1971.

Demos, John, and Demos, Virginia. "Adolescence in Historical Perspective." *Journal of Marriage and the Family,* 31 (Nov. 1969), 632–38.

Deutsch, Helene. *The Psychology of Women.* 2 vols. New York: Bantam Books, 1973 (1944).

Dusenbury, Winifred L. *The Theme of Loneliness in Modern American Drama.* Gainesville: University of Florida Press, 1960.

Ehrenreich, Barbara, and English, Deirdre. *Complaints and Disorders: The Sexual Politics of Sickness.* Glass Mountain Pamphlet, No. 2. New York: Feminist Press, 1973.

Eisinger, Chester. *Fiction of the Forties.* Chicago: University of Chicago Press, 1963.

Eliade, Mircea. *Birth and Rebirth.* London: Harvill Press, 1958.

Erikson, Erik. *Childhood and Society.* New York: Norton, 1950.

Evans, Oliver. *The Ballad of Carson McCullers.* New York: Coward-McCann, 1966.

———. "The Theme of Spiritual Isolation in Carson McCullers." *South: Modern Southern Literature and Its Cultural Setting.* Ed. Louis Rubin and Robert Jacobs. New York: Dolphin, 1961. Pp. 333–40.

Fiedler, Leslie. *An End to Innocence.* 2nd ed. New York: Stein and Day, 1972.

———. *Love and Death in the American Novel.* 2nd ed. New York: Dell Publishing, 1969 (1966).

———. *No! in Thunder.* 2nd ed. New York: Stein and Day, 1972.

Firestone, Shulamith. *The Dialectic of Sex.* New York: Bantam Books, 1971 (1970).

Frank, Shirley. "Feminist Presses." *Women in Print II*. Ed. Joan E. Hartman and Ellen Messer-Davidow. New York: Modern Language Association, 1982. Pp. 89–115.

French, Marilyn. "Introduction" to *Summer*, by Edith Wharton. New York: Berkley Books, 1981. Pp. vi-xlviii.

Freud, Sigmund. *Collected Papers*. Ed. James Strachey. Vols. II and V. London: Hogarth Press, 1950. Includes "Family Romances" (1909), "The Passing of the Oedipus Complex" (1925), "Some Psychological Consequences of the Anatomical Distinction between the Sexes" (1925), and "Female Sexuality" (1931).

———. *A General Introduction to Psycho-Analysis*. Trans. G. Stanley Hall. New York: Boni & Liveright, 1920. Includes "Development of the Libido and Sexual Organizations."

———. *New Introductory Lectures on Psychoanalysis*. Trans. James Strachey. New York: W. W. Norton & Co., 1964. Includes "Femininity" (1933).

———. *An Outline of Psychoanalysis*. Trans. James Strachey. New York: W. W. Norton & Co., 1949 (1940).

———. *Three Essays on the Theory of Sexuality*. Ed. and trans. James Strachey. New York: Basic Books, 1962. Includes "Infantile Sexuality" (1905).

Friedberg, Barton. "The Cult of Adolescence in American Fiction." *Nassau Review*, 1 (Spring 1964), 26–35.

Friedenberg, Edgar. *The Vanishing Adolescent*. New York: Dell Publishing 1963 (1959).

Gelfant, Blanche H. Review of *The Mountain Lion*, by Jean Stafford. *New Republic*, 10 May 1975, pp. 22–25.

———. "Revolutionary Turnings: *The Mountain Lion* Reread." *Massachusetts Review*, 20 (Spring 1979), 117–25. Reprinted in *The Voyage In: Fictions of Female Development*. Ed. Elizabeth Abel, Marianne Hirsch, and Elizabeth Langland. Hanover, N.H.: University Press of New England, 1983. Pp. 149–60.

Gilbert, Sandra M., and Gubar, Susan. *The Madwoman in the Attic: The Woman Writer and the Nineteenth-Century Literary Imagination*. New Haven, Conn.: Yale University Press, 1979.

Ginsberg, Elaine. "The Female Initiation Theme in American Fiction." *Studies in American Fiction*, 3 (Spring 1975), 27–38.

Goodman, Charlotte. "The Lost Brother, the Twin: Women Novelists and the Male-Female Double *Bildungsroman*." *Novel*, 17 (Fall 1983), 28–43.

Goodman, Paul. *Growing Up Absurd*. New York: Random House, 1956.

Gossett, Louise. *Violence in Recent Southern Fiction*. Durham, N.C.: Duke University Press, 1965.

Graver, Lawrence. *Carson McCullers*. Minneapolis: University of Minnesota Press, 1969.

Gregory, Thomas, ed. *Adolescence in Literature*. New York: Longman, 1978.

Griffin, Mary Nell. "Coming to Manhood in America—A Study of Significant Initiation Novels, 1797–1970." Diss. Vanderbilt University, 1971.

Guillory, Daniel. "The Mystique of Childhood in American Literature." *Tulane Studies in English*, 23 (1978), 229–47.

Hall, G. Stanley. *Adolescence*. 2 vols. New York: D. Appleton and Co. 1924 (1904).

Hansl, Eva v. B. "Parents in Modern Fiction." *Bookman*, LXII (Sept. 1925), 21–27.

Hassan, Ihab. "Carson McCullers: The Alchemy of Love and Aesthetics of Pain." *Modern Fiction Studies*, 5 (Winter 1959–60), 311–26.

———. "The Idea of Adolescence in American Fiction." *American Quarterly*, 10 (Fall 1958), 312–24.

———. "Jean Stafford: The Expense of Style and the Scope of Sensibility." *Western Review*, 19 (Spring 1955), 185–203.

———. *Radical Innocence*. Princeton, N.J.: Princeton University Press, 1961.

Hatcher, Harlan. *Creating the Modern American Novel*. New York: Russell & Russell, 1965.

Heilbrun, Carolyn G. *Reinventing Womanhood*. New York: W. W. Norton & Co., 1979.

Hirsch, Marianne. "The Novel of Formation as Genre: Between Great Expectations and Lost Illusions." *Genre*, XII (Fall 1979), 293–311.

Hocart, A. M. *The Life-Giving Myth*. London: Methuen & Co., 1970 (1952).

Hoffman, Frederick. *The Art of Southern Fiction*. Carbondale: Southern Illinois University Press, 1967.

———. *Freudianism and the Literary Mind*. Baton Rouge: Louisiana State University Press, 1957.

Hoffman, Nancy Jo. "Reading Women's Poetry: The Meaning and Our Lives." *College English*, 34 (Oct. 1972), 48–62.

Horney, Karen. *Feminine Psychology*. New York: W. W. Norton & Co., 1973 (1967).

Howe, Susanne. *Wilhelm Meister and His English Kinsmen*. New York: AMS Press, 1966 (1930).

Hull, Gloria T.; Scott, Patricia Bell; and Smith, Barbara, eds. *But Some of Us Are Brave: Black Women's Studies*. Old Westbury, N.Y.: Feminist Press, 1982.

Hunt, Morton. *Her Infinite Variety*. New York: Harper & Row, 1962.

Johnson, James. "The Adolescent Hero: A Trend in Modern Fiction."
  Twentieth Century Literature, 5 (April 1959), 3–11.
Kalish, Richard. "The Old and the New as Generation Gap Allies."
  Readings in Human Socialization. Ed. Elton McNeil. Belmont,
  Calif.: Brooks/Cole Co., 1971. Pp. 250–57.
Kazin, Alfred. *Bright Book of Life*. Boston: Little, Brown & Co., 1971.
Kelley, Mary. "The Sentimentalists: Promise and Betrayal in the Home."
  Signs, 4 (Spring 1979), 434–46.
Keniston, Kenneth. "Youth: A 'New' Stage of Life." *American Scholar*,
  XXXIX (1970), 631–54.
Kett, Joseph. "Adolescence and Youth in Nineteenth-Century America."
  The Family in History: Interdisciplinary Essays. Ed. Theodore Rabb
  and Robert Rotberg. New York: Harper & Row, 1973. pp. 95–
  110.
————. *Rites of Passage: Adolescence in America 1790 to the Present*. New
  York: Basic Books, 1977.
Kiell, Norman. *The Adolescent through Fiction: A Psychological Ap-
  proach*. New York: International Universities Press, 1959.
Kissane, Leedice McAnelly. *Ruth Suckow*. New York: Twayne, 1969.
Knowles, A. S. "Six Bronze Petals and Two Red: Carson McCullers in
  the Forties." *The Forties*. Ed. Warren French. Florida: Everett/
  Edwards, 1969. Pp. 89–98.
Larcom, Lucy. *A New England Girlhood*. Boston: Houghton Mifflin Co.,
  1889.
Lenz, Millicent, and Mahood, Ramona, eds. *Young Adult Literature:
  Background and Criticism*. Chicago: American Library Associa-
  tion, 1980.
Lewis, R. W. B. *Edith Wharton*. New York: Harper & Row, 1975.
Loshe, Lillie Deming. *The Early American Novel*. New York: Columbia
  University Press, 1907.
Lyons, John. *The College Novel in America*. Carbondale: Southern Illinois
  University Press, 1962.
————. "The College Novel in America: 1962–1974." *Critique*, 16 (1974),
  121–28.
McCole, C. John. *Lucifer at Large*. New York: Books for Libraries Press,
  1937.
McDowell, Margaret B. *Edith Wharton*. Boston: Twayne, 1976.
McNall, Sally Allen. *Who Is in the House? A Psychological Study of Two
  Centuries of Women's Fiction in America, 1795 to the Present*. New
  York: Elsevier, 1981.
Malin, Irving. *New American Gothic*. Carbondale: Southern Illinois Uni-
  versity Press, 1962.
Marcus, Mordecai. "What Is an Initiation Story?" *Journal of Aesthetic
  and Art Criticism*, 19 (Winter 1960), 221–24.

Mead, Margaret. "Adolescence in Primitive and Modern Society." *The New Generation*. Ed. V. F. Calverton and Samuel Schmalhausen. New York: Macaulay Co., 1930. Pp. 169–88.

Megibow, Carol Burr. "The Use of Story in Women's Novels of the Seventies." *Women's Culture: The Women's Renaissance of the Seventies*. Ed. Gayle Kimball. Metuchen, N.J.: Scarecrow Press, 1981.

Melito, Ignatius. "Themes of Adolescence: Studies in American Fiction of Adolescence." Diss. University of Denver, 1965.

Mencken, H. L. "The Library." *American Mercury*, 7 (April 1926), 506–07.

Miller, Nathan. *The Child in Primitive Society*. New York: Brentano's, 1926.

Moore, Jack. "Carson McCullers: The Heart Is a Timeless Hunter." *Twentieth Century Literature*, 2 (July 1965), 76–81.

Morante, Linda. "The Desolation of Charity Royall: Imagery in Edith Wharton's *Summer*." *Colby Library Quarterly*, XVIII (Dec. 1982), 241–48.

Morgan, Ellen. "The Feminist Novel of Androgynous Fantasy." *Frontiers*, II (Fall 1977), 40–49.

———. "Humanbecoming: Form & Focus in the Neo-Feminist Novel." *Images of Women in Fiction: Feminist Perspectives*. Ed. Susan Koppelman Cornillon. Bowling Green, Ohio: Bowling Green University, University Popular Press, 1972. Pp. 183–205.

Mullahy, Patrick. *Oedipus Myth and Complex*. New York: Grove Press, 1948.

Nevius, Blake. *Edith Wharton: A Study of Her Fiction*. Berkeley and Los Angeles: University of California Press, 1953.

O'Brien, Sharon. "Tomboyism and Adolescent Conflict: Three Nineteenth-Century Case Studies." *Woman's Being, Woman's Place: Female Identity and Vocation in American History*. Ed. Mary Kelley. Boston: G. K. Hall Co., 1979. Pp. 351–72.

Oehlschlaeger, Fritz. "The Art of Ruth Suckow's 'A Start in Life.' " *Western American Literature*, 15 (Fall 1980), 177–86.

Omrcanin, Margaret Stewart. *Ruth Suckow: A Critical Study of Her Fiction*. Philadelphia: Dorrance, 1972.

Papashvily, Helen Waite. *All the Happy Endings*. New York: Harper, 1956.

Pascal, Roy. *The German Novel*. Manchester, Eng.: Manchester University Press, 1956.

Petter, Henri. *The Early American Novel*. Columbus: Ohio State University Press, 1971.

Phillips, Robert. "The Gothic Architecture of *The Member of the Wedding*." *Renascence*, 16 (Winter 1964), 59–72.

Pratt, Annis. *Archetypal Patterns in Women's Fiction*. Bloomington: Indiana University Press, 1981.

Register, Cheri. "American Feminist Literary Criticism: A Bibliographical Introduction." *Feminist Literary Criticism: Explorations in Theory*. Ed. Josephine Donovan. Lexington: University Press of Kentucky, 1975. Pp. 1–28.

Rule, Jane. *Lesbian Images*. Garden City, N.Y.: Doubleday & Co., 1975.

St. Joan, Jacqueline. "Afterword" to Maureen Brady, *Give Me Your Good Ear*. Argyle, N.Y.: Spinsters, Ink, 1979. Pp. 135–41.

Schlissel, Lillian. "Contemplating 'The American Eve.' " *American Women and American Studies*. Ed. Betty E. Chmaj. Pittsburgh: KNOW, 1971. P. 258.

Schwartz, Narda Lacey. *Articles on Women Writers 1960–1975*. Santa Barbara, Calif.: Clio Press, 1977.

Scudder, Horace. *Childhood in Literature and Art*. Boston and New York: Houghton Mifflin Co., 1894.

Sequeira, Isaac. "The Theme of Initiation in Modern American Fiction." Diss. University of Utah, 1970.

Sherman, Bernard. "The Fictive Jew, Jewish-American Education Novels: 1916–1964." Diss. Northwestern University, 1966.

Showalter, Elaine. "Women Writers and the Double Standard." *Woman in Sexist Society*. Ed. Vivian Gornich and Barbara K. Moran. New York: Basic Books, 1971. Pp. 452–79.

Smith, Barbara. "Toward a Black Feminist Criticism." *Conditions: Two*, 1 (Oct. 1977), 25–44. Revised version in *But Some of Us Are Brave*: *Black Women's Studies*. Ed. Gloria T. Hull, Patricia Bell Scott, and Barbara Smith. Old Westbury, N.Y.: Feminist Press, 1982. Pp. 157–75.

Smith-Rosenberg, Carroll. "The Hysterical Woman: Sex Roles and Role Conflict in Nineteenth-Century America." *Social Research*, 39 (1972), 652–78.

―――. "Puberty to Menopause: The Cycle of Femininity in Nineteenth-Century America." *Clio's Consciousness Raised*. Ed. Mary S. Hartman and Lois Banner. New York: Octagon Books, 1976. Pp. 23–29.

Spacks, Patricia Meyer. *The Adolescent Idea: Myths of Youth and the Adult Imagination*. New York: Basic Books, 1981.

Springer, Marlene. *Edith Wharton and Kate Chopin: A Reference Guide*. Boston: G. K. Hall & Co., 1976.

Stansell, Christine. "Elizabeth Stuart Phelps: A Study in Female Rebellion." *Woman: An Issue*. Ed. Lee R. Edwards, Mary Heath, and Lisa Baskin. Boston: Little, Brown and Co., 1972. Pp. 239–56.

Starke, Catherine Juanita. *Black Portraiture in American Fiction*. New York: Basic Books, 1971.

Stewart, Philip. "The Child Comes of Age." *Yale French Studies*, No. 40 (1968), 134–41.

Suckow, Ruth. "Elsie Dinsmore: A Study in Perfection." *Bookman,* 69 (Oct. 1927), 126–33.

———. "Literary Soubrettes." *Bookman*, 63 (July 1926), 517–19.

Tennyson, G. B. "The *Bildungsroman* in Nineteenth-Century English Literature." *Medieval Epic to the "Epic Theater" of Brecht.* Ed. Rosario Armato and John Spalek. 2 vols. Los Angeles: University of Southern California Press, 1968. Pp. 135–46.

Thrall, William; Hibbard, Addison; and Holman, C. Hugh. *A Handbook to Literature.* Revised ed. New York: Odyssey Press, 1960.

Tocqueville, de, Alexis. *Democracy in America.* New York: Alfred A. Knopf, 1945 (1840).

Tompkins, Jane P. "Sentimental Power: *Uncle Tom's Cabin* and the Politics of Literary History." *Glyph*, 8 (1981), 79–102.

Towers, Robert. Review of *The Color Purple*, by Alice Walker. *New York Review of Books*, 12 August 1982, p. 35.

Verbrugge, Martha H. "Women and Medicine in Nineteenth-Century America." *Signs*, 1 (Summer 1976), 957–72.

Vickery, Olga. "The Novels of Jean Stafford." *Critique*, 5 (Spring-Summer 1962), 14–26.

Washington, Mary Helen. "Plain, Black, and Decently Wild: The Heroic Possibilities of Maud Martha." *The Voyage In: Fictions of Female Development.* Ed. Elizabeth Abel, Marianne Hirsch, and Elizabeth Langland. Hanover, N.H.: University Press of New England, 1983. Pp. 270–86.

Westling, Louise. "Carson McCullers's Tomboys." *Southern Humanities Review*, 14 (1980), 339–50.

White, Barbara A. "Growing Up Female: Adolescent Girlhood in American Literature." Diss. University of Wisconsin, 1974.

———. "Initiation, the West, and the Hunt in Jean Stafford's *The Mountain Lion.*" *Essays in Literature*, 9 (Fall 1982) 194–210.

———. "Ruth Suckow." *Dictionary of Literary Biography: American Short Story Writers to World War II.* Ed. William Grant. Forthcoming.

Wilson, Edmund. *Patriotic Gore.* New York: Oxford University Press, 1966 (1962).

———. Review of *The Member of the Wedding*, by Carson McCullers. *New Yorker*, 30 March 1946, p. 87.

Witham, W. Tasker. *The Adolescent in the American Novel, 1920–1960.* New York: Frederick Ungar Publishing Co., 1964.

Wolff, Cynthia Griffin. *A Feast of Words: The Triumph of Edith Wharton.* New York: Oxford University Press, 1977.

————. "Introduction" to *Summer*, by Edith Wharton. New York: Perennial Library, 1980. Pp. v-xxviii.

Zimmerman, Bonnie. "Exiting from Patriarchy: The Lesbian Novel of Development." *The Voyage In: Fictions of Female Development.* Ed. Elizabeth Abel, Marianne Hirsch, and Elizabeth Langland. Hanover, N.H.: University Press of New England, 1983. Pp. 244–57.

INDEX

About the Author

BARBARA A. WHITE is Associate Professor and Curator of Rare Books at the University of New Hampshire. She is co-editor of the recently published *Hidden Hands: An Anthology of American Women Writers, 1790–1870*. She is also the author of *American Women Writers: An Annotated Bibliography of Criticism* and has contributed several bibliographic and critical articles to professional journals.